CONTEMPORARY EUROPEAN PHILOSOPHY

φιλόσοφος ἱερεύς τις καὶ ὑπουργὸς θεῶν.

MARCUS AURELIUS

Contemporary European Philosophy

BY I. M. BOCHEŃSKI

Translated from the German by
Donald Nicholl and Karl Aschenbrenner

GREENWOOD PRESS, PUBLISHERS
WESTPORT, CONNECTICUT

Library of Congress Cataloging in Publication Data

Bocheński, Innocentius M., 1902–
    Contemporary European philosophy.

    Translation of: Europäische Philosophie der Gegenwart.
    Reprint. Originally published: Berkeley : University
of California Press, 1957.
    Bibliography: p.
    Includes index.
    1. Philosophy, Modern––20th century. I. Title.
B804.B563 1982   190'.9'04   82-2987
ISBN 0-313-23490-6 (lib. bdg.)   AACR2

Europäische Philosophie der Gegenwart, first published in Berne
by A. Francke A.G. Verlag, 1947; 2d ed., 1951

Translated from the second, revised German edition.

Reprinted with the permission of the University of
California Press.

Reprinted in 1982 by Greenwood Press,
A division of Congressional Information Service, Inc.
88 Post Road West, Westport, Connecticut 06881

Printed in the United States of America

10 9 8 7 6 5 4 3 2 1

Preface

This book hopes to achieve a double purpose. First, it aims at providing a general guide in the domain of contemporary philosophy for the reader who is without any specialist training in the subject; second, it is hoped that those who have completed this general survey will find suggestions here for more systematic studies of their own. These considerations taken together formed an urgent motive for this undertaking, because apart from the work of M. F. Sciacca (in Italian) we have no recent introductory survey which gives an account of either the growing penetration, or the newly won regions of contemporary thought. I feel that this introduction is all the more justified in that Sciacca's otherwise excellent book does not fulfil my second purpose.

The present undertaking was a thankless task for three reasons. In the first place, its completion meant that for a long time I had to abandon those more detailed investigations which alone retain a real hold upon philosophers and historians of philosophy. On the other hand, as I know only too well, such a work can never prove satisfactory. This limitation was expressed by one of the most distinguished philosophers of our time, Bertrand Russell, when he dealt with it as far as he himself was concerned, in his *History of Western Philosophy*, and what he says there (page x) applies far more to this present work. The knowledge that a whole lifetime of study is necessary for a deep understanding of even a single philosopher is not altogether an encouragement to writing such books as this. Finally, one is forced to schematize and make painful amputations in any such work; and yet there is no other course available when the number of pages for each author is so limited. It is easy to imagine what one makes of the philosophy of a

Whitehead, a Bergson, or a Husserl under such circumstances. The author begs indulgence from such thinkers!

Although the main purpose of the book is to provide information, it has a definite orientation, which must be stated from the beginning.

I have not thought it possible to avoid summary appreciations of the various systems presented. There is a widely held opinion that the historian of thought should maintain a neutral position in regard to the thinkers whom he is discussing—but this is only a half-truth. So far as it demands the utmost objectivity in selecting and interpreting systems the thesis is valid and represents the attitude which I have done my best to adopt, but it is untrue if it is taken to mean that philosophical systems should be dealt with as though they were all equally tenable, irrespective of their truth value. If we make such an assumption we are denying to philosophers the respect which is due them; because if systems contradict each other—as they do—but all have the same value, then all of them are false, and can only claim to be appreciated as works of art. This would constitute the greatest perversion of the thought of philosophers worthy of the name, for they are all servants of the one truth and should be treated as such. And so, if alongside my expositions of the various thinkers, the evaluation of their main tenets, and an appreciation of their positive and lasting contributions, I have also indicated where they are, in my judgment, inadequate and one-sided, I have done so purely out of respect. Whatever criticism there is—and it is only marginal—has been made from the standpoint of a realist and spiritual metaphysic.

But this question of standpoint is secondary to two convictions of which I had to be certain before I could ever attempt such a work, and which in fact form its foundation.

The first concerns the problem of correctly evaluating the role of philosophical effort in the development of history, because this part is so often underestimated. It is said that philosophy is nothing but purely abstract speculation of no importance for life, and that it is sufficient to study the practical sciences such as sociology, economics, and politics which are essential for every branch of technical progress (including education and the care of souls). Since *primum vivere, deinde philosophari*, "philosophari" adds nothing of value to life. This opinion, so widely current nowadays, I regard as false and as a disastrous spiritual abberration. For if science and wisdom are limited to their technical and practical aspects one need only know *how* to do this or that. But the question *why* comes before the question how, and the answer to it is ultimately to be found either in religion or in philosophy. Nor is it enough to reply that man's common sense suffices, because history has often shown so-called common sense to be nothing more than the residue of previous philosophical speculation. As a rational animal man has no choice about using his reason, so that if he does not use it consciously and philosophically he will use it unconsciously and superficially. This applies without exception even to those who consider themselves emancipated from philosophy; they are merely dilettante philosophers setting up their own useless and superfluous systems out of contempt for the intellectual achievement of men who are immeasurably superior to them in mental power. As far as religion is concerned, despite its independence of philosophy we have to recognize that it must be interpreted and clarified in accordance with man's rational nature. Here, as in other fields, the fact is that unless one carries out such essential clarification by philosophizing rationally one becomes a slave to prejudice.

Nor could anything be more misguided than to deny that philosophy is important for life. A philosopher, it is true, does not always exert great influence upon the issues of the day, and it is his fate usually to be understood only after his death. Of

Preface

course, some philosophers have enjoyed fame even in their own lifetimes—one thinks of Plotinus, Thomas Aquinas, Hegel, and Bergson—but what all of these enjoyed was a fashionable vogue rather than genuine comprehension of their thought. A philosopher does not reckon upon the needs of the hour or the demands of his day. Should he be blamed for this? Does not man, if he is really man, transcend what is purely of the moment? Do we not incur the risk of reducing man to the level of a beast when we take the affairs of the moment to be the object of knowledge? Whoever lives the life of reason, whatever may be his philosophical convictions, knows from the mere fact that philosophy transcends the *hic et nunc* and does not provide a plan of immediate action, that it is a most powerful factor in enabling us to retain our humanity, to become more and more human, and not to relapse into barbarism.

But even that is not the whole story, for despite its apparent unimportance, philosophy is even a powerful force in history. Whitehead was right when, in comparing the achievements of an Alexander, a Caesar, and a Napoleon with the apparently insignificant results of philosophy, he commented that it is thought which changes the outlook of humanity. Yet it is not necessary to go as far back as the Pythagoreans, as Whitehead does, for an instance of this; one has only to remember the amazing paths of destiny opened up by Hegel, a thinker who is difficult to understand and does not fit easily into our own time. Fascists, National Socialists, and Communists, all alike regard him as their forerunner; he is one of the forces that are changing the world. The people make a laughing stock of the philosopher as a person harmlessly absorbed in his ideas, though really he is a terrifying force and his thought has the effect of dynamite. He sticks to his own course, conquers inch by inch, asserts his grip upon the masses, until eventually the day dawns when he triumphantly overcomes all obstacles and is free to determine the destiny of mankind—or spread a shroud over its remains. Therefore those who wish to know in what direction they are going would do well to give their attention not to the politicians but to the philosophers, for what they propound today will be the faith of tomorrow.

In addition to this primary conviction about the importance of philosophy a second thesis at the basis of this book seems equally significant to me.

It is a widespread opinion that there is a basic contemporary philosophy. According to this simple-minded and unfortunate concept, there is one single philosophy which has gained the day and is now established as *the* philosophy of our time and that supersedes all other schools. Positivism, materialism, idealism, and existentialism have all been chosen for this role at one and the same time. Nothing could be more mistaken. The richness of contemporary philosophical thought cannot be confined within such narrow categories. Today, as always, a violent struggle is raging between antagonistic views of the world, and it is possibly more violent in our own time than it was during the past century. Rarely has it been of such intensity, with such a wealth of opposing viewpoints or expressed in such elaborate and refined conceptual frameworks. There is indeed a contemporary philosophy in the sense that all thinkers have to face definite problems of the moment and all must take account of certain novel positions; but that is a far cry from the notion that there is a single school or a single tendency. Present-day philosophy is astonishingly rich and variegated.

Finally a remark about the way to use this book. It has been said that every book on the history of philosophy is like a guide book, and that such a history can no more excuse one from studying the original texts themselves than a guide book can absolve one from traveling. To facilitate this study of the

Preface

texts I have added a copious bibliography. If my presentation succeeds in stirring in the reader an interest in the detailed study of contemporary philosophy and in showing the way, its aim will be accomplished.

This book is the result of lectures given to American military students during the winter term 1945-46. This may explain certain shortcomings, especially imperfections of form and expression.

PRINCIPLES OF SELECTION AND EXPOSITION

The selection from the extensive material of present-day philosophy was based upon the following principles:

Only English, French, and German philosophers were discussed; exceptions were made only in a limited number of especially outstanding cases (dialectical materialism, Croce, James, Dewey).

Even within these limits no attempt could be made to give a comprehensive picture of the philosophies of each country. I had to be content with mentioning just those schools and philosophers whom I considered particularly representative. Nor could I try to make a complete survey of every philosophical current—still less every philosopher—of our day; I could only sketch the main lines of contemporary thought.

The expression 'contemporary' admits of no easy definition. It denotes those thinkers who have published important works since the First World War, thus including Bergson and Scheler, for instance, and excluding Bradley. Even so, the limits have not always been respected, especially for philosophers whose effect at present is particularly striking. There is some doubt whether Kierkegaard belongs to this class; but at least short accounts of both James and Dilthey were inevitable.

Lastly there could be no hope of describing philosophical systems in their entirety, but only their fundamental parts and those which are of first-rate importance for contemporary philosophy. I discussed primarily the problems of ontology, anthropology, ethics, and fundamental method; therefore specialized questions, such as scientific method, sociology, the philosophy of history, aesthetics, and the philosophy of religion, have had to be almost completely ignored. Instead, the basic concepts and certain leading problems of mathematical logic, which in spite of its much debated philosophic character exerts great influence on the thought of many contemporary philosophers, have been discussed in an appended section.

The exposition seeks as far as possible to bring out the unity in the different parts of each author's work, and I took special care to reproduce the author's method, his mode of expression and his development, as well as his actual teaching. Faithfulness to the language of each work was a prime consideration; it demanded a different terminology for each chapter. Thus it seemed neither possible nor consistent to cut out the rich imagery of Bergson and Marcel while having to reproduce Heidegger's dry style in all its painful precision. Consequently there is a quite different degree of difficulty attached to each of the chapters. The beginner is advised at first reading to pass over the chapters on Neo-Kantianism, Husserl, Heidegger, and Whitehead, which are difficult, and to content himself for a start with reading introductory and concluding passages.

A bibliography has been added with a view to the most judicious possible use of the book; it contains a fairly complete list of the work of each author who has been made the subject of an individual chapter, along with a selection of the relevant literature. On this account the text itself largely avoids footnotes. Instead, reference is to be made to the works themselves. It is there that one should look for guidance to avoid the danger of false and unfounded interpretations.

I. M. B.

Preface

Preface to the Second German Edition

In this second edition two new sections are appended, a review of mathematical logic and a short survey of international philosophical organizations. The chapter on Sartre has been considerably enlarged and chapters 2, 4, 7, 13, 16, 19, 21, 22, and 23 as well as many sections of the remaining chapters have been reworked. The bibliography has been enlarged and the whole text has been reconsidered in respect to both content and manner of expression. In order to compensate for these extensions of the second edition some curtailment of presentation was unfortunately necessary. On the whole I think that what was essential in the first edition has been preserved in the new edition but improved and rounded out by many additions.

I find an agreeable confirmation of the opinion I expressed in chapter 4 regarding the frankness and mutual helpfulness of philosophers in the fact that I have received valuable information, advice and constructive criticism from adherents of many different schools of thought. I wish here to express my sincere thanks to all of them, in particular to Professors Raymond Bayer of the Sorbonne, E. W. Beth of Amsterdam, H. Gauss of Bern, P. Wyser of Fribourg, and to Dr. Yehoshuah Bar-Hillel of Jerusalem, Dr. M. I. Delfgaauw of Amsterdam, Dr. I. Thomas of Hawkesyard, and Dr. E. J. Walter of Zurich, from all of whom I have learned a great deal. I wish to thank also my former student, Dr. H. Kruse of Hamburg who revised one chapter for me.

Unfortunately not all critical suggestions could be incorporated; the first edition was sold out sooner than had been anticipated and there was time pressure for a new edition, because even now no similar vademecum has appeared. I therefore could not persuade myself to include in the work consideration of representatives of so-called minor-language areas.

In my remarks on the work of Professor Roman Ingarden I have expressed my attitude toward this problem.

I shall be indebted to scholars for still further constructive criticism.

I.M.B.

Publisher's Note

The first German edition of I. M. Bocheński's *Europäische Philosophie der Gegenwart* was published by A. Francke A. G. Verlag in Berne, Switzerland, in 1947. The present work is a translation of the second, revised, German edition, which appeared in 1951. Professor Donald Nicholl of the University College of North Staffordshire, Keele, England, translated the first edition; Professor Karl Aschenbrenner of the University of California, Berkeley, translated the additions and revisions the author made for the second edition. In this first English translation the work appears unchanged from the second German edition, except for the dates of persons who died since 1951. It is important to note, therefore, that the bibliography, while extensive, does not include works published after 1950.

Contents

Contents

Contents

Der "moderne Mensch," d. h. der
Mensch seit der Renaissance, ist
fertig zum Begraben werden.

GRAF PAUL YORCK VON WARTENBURG

I

Origin of Contemporary Philosophy

---

1. THE NINETEENTH CENTURY

A. THE NATURE AND GROWTH OF MODERN PHILOSOPHY

Modern philosophy, that is to say, philosophical thought of the period 1600-1900, is now no more than history. However, the philosophy of our times arises in its essential parts through differentiating itself from it and also through developing and attempting to transcend it; therefore an understanding of present thought presupposes a knowledge of the past, and we must attempt to retrace in broad outlines the basis and development of this modern philosophy.

It came into being with the decline of scholastic philosophy. Characteristic of scholasticism is its pluralism (assuming the plurality of really different beings and levels of being), its personalism (acknowledging the preëminent value of the human person), its organic conception of reality, as well as its theocentric attitude—God the Creator at its center of vision. Detailed logical analysis of individual problems is characteristic of scholastic method. Modern philosophy opposes every one of these tenets. Its fundamental principles are *mechanism*, which eliminates the conception of being as integral and hierarchical, and *subjectivism*, which diverts man from his previous concentration upon God and substitutes the subject as the center. In point of method modern philosophy turned its back on formal logic. With some notable exceptions, it was characterized by the development of great systems and by the neglect of analysis.

It is René Descartes (1596-1650) who brings to perfect expression this signal change. Descartes is above all a mechanist. Although he recognizes two levels of being, mind and matter, the whole of nonmental reality can be reduced, he thinks, to purely mechanical concepts (position, motion, impulse), and every occurrence can be explained by calculable, mechanical laws. At the same time he is a subjectivist—to him thought is the prime datum and the inevitable starting point of philosophy. Furthermore he is a nominalist—there is only sense perception of individual things, intellectual intuition being impossible. Finally, Descartes is an avowed opponent of formal logic. Actually he recognizes no specifically philosophical method whatever. He would like to apply to all situations the (philosophically unanalyzed) procedure of the mathematical natural sciences.

Once these principles are accepted, insoluble problems crop up. If the world structure is simply an aggregation of bodies comparable to a machine, how can its intellectual content be accounted for? On the other hand, how does one arrive at the reality of this world while setting out from thought as the sole immediate datum? Above all, the question remains as to how knowledge is possible if only individual things can be grasped, especially since this very knowledge continually makes use of general concepts and universal laws?

Descartes himself attempted to solve these problems by assuming that we have innate ideas, and that the laws of thought and of being run completely parallel. His famous "cogito" guaranteed him access to reality. Mind was thought to exert a causal influence upon matter. A group of thinkers, misnamed *rationalists*, adopted his theory of innate ideas, among them Baruch Spinoza (1632-1677), Gottfried Wilhelm Leibniz (1646-1716), and Christian Wolff (1679-1754). Another group, the British *empiricists*, proceeded more logically by acknowledging the full consequences of mechanism, extending its application to mind itself, and combining it with subjectivism and radical nominalism. This position could already be traced in the essays of Sir Francis Bacon (1561-1621) but received its systematic articulation from John Locke (1632-1704), George Berkeley (1685-1753), and, above all, David Hume (1711-1776). The latter regarded the soul as nothing but a bundle of images, so-called 'ideas' ("the mind is a bundle of ideas"). Ideas alone are directly knowable; universal laws are merely the result of repeated association, so that they cannot claim any objective validity, and even the existence of an external world is reduced to a matter of faith. Hume was saved from complete scepticism only by virtue of his fideism, his reliance on faith, without which everything would have been in doubt—mind, reality, and, especially, knowledge.

The natural sciences were making great strides at the same period and fostered an increasingly *materialistic outlook*, particularly so because there was no genuine philosophy in the arena to challenge it. The materialism initiated by Thomas Hobbes (1588-1679) was developed further by such philoso-

3

phers as Etienne Bonnet (1720-1793), Julien Offray La Mettrie (1709-1751), Paul Heinrich Dietrich von Holbach (1723-1789), Denis Diderot (1713-1784), and Claude Adrian Helvetius (1715-1771).

B. KANT

Immanuel Kant (1724-1804) found himself confronted with this truly desperate situation, this catastrophe for thought. He undertook the task of preserving mind, knowledge, morality, and religion without abandoning a single axiom of modern thought. Thus he unquestioningly adopted the whole of mechanism, which he recognized as valid for the entire empirical world, not excluding the world of subjective thought. But for him even this world was the result of a synthesis which the transcendental subject constructed out of the formless stuff of experience. It follows that the laws of logic, mathematics, and the natural sciences are valid for this world because it is thought which puts them there and provides their very foundations. But the "pure subject" does not come under these laws because it does not spring from the phenomenal world; on the contrary, it establishes this world and determines its laws. So knowledge and mind are both rescued at one sweep. But in this way it is impossible to know the thing-in-itself (the self-subsistent reality behind phenomena); knowledge is confined within the scope of sensible perception, and apart from experience "the categories are empty." It follows that no mode of knowledge is adequate for solving the deep problems of existence and of man's life—metaphysics is impossible. It is true that Kant does face up to the problem of God's existence, of immortality, and of freedom—for him they are the three ultimate philosophical problems—but he resolves them in a non-rational manner through postulates of the will.

Thus Kantian philosophy is a synthesis of modern philosophy's constituent elements, mechanism and subjectivism. Essentially it is derived from radical *conceptualism*—the transcendental subject is a formative principle shaping the intelligible content of the world, which content moreover can be reduced to simple relationships. So reality is split into two worlds, the one empirical and phenomenal which is invariably subject to the laws of mechanics, and the other a world of things-in-themselves, of "noumena" to which reason cannot attain. Kant gave modern philosophy its most plausible form and its most perfect expression; but he also initiated its fatal decline.

The effect of Kantianism upon the subsequent course of philosophy cannot easily be overestimated; he dominated the nineteenth century and has retained a considerable number of philosophical disciples until our own day, despite the reaction from him at the turn of the century; he is the source for the main currents of thought in the nineteenth century. Kant had contested the possibility of any rational metaphysics whatsoever and would allow only two means of knowing; first, reality might be explored by scientific method, in which case philosophy would be a synthesis of the results of the special sciences; second, one might study the processes by which reality is formed by the mind, in which case philosophy would be an analysis of the generation of ideas. Actually the two main branches of nineteenth-century philosophy are developments of both these possibilities. The positivists and the materialists gave philosophy the limited task of unifying the sciences whereas the idealists worked out systems in which they attempted to describe reality as the product of intellectual operations.

C. ROMANTICISM

Yet another factor at work in the early nineteenth century, and playing a considerable role later, was romanticism. It was

5

a many-sided movement and is difficult to define, but one can say without gross oversimplification that its essential features represent an upsurge of spiritual life brought about through the reaction and opposition to mechanism. Kant's attempt to eliminate the consequences of mechanism had been made in the name of reason but there remained another way—to reject reason. The harshness of the scientific world picture had repelled the poets and other gifted people, as one can imagine, and they now joined in the protest by setting up emotion, life, and religion as the answer to scientific rationalism, asserting that there were other approaches to reality besides that of science.

Still, romanticism was not necessarily irrationalistic, and it was occasionally found in the guise of reason's most enthusiastic champion. It always placed the greatest emphasis, however, upon movement, life, and growth. Seventeenth- and eighteenth-century philosophies had all stood for a static conception of the world because for the mechanists the world was a machine that had been set up once and for all, a huge structure which lost nothing and yet produced nothing new. Romanticism directed the whole weight of its attack upon this outlook and thereby ensured a great influence for itself during the course of the nineteenth century.

D. MAIN CURRENTS

An uncommonly strong tendency toward system-building characterized the nineteenth century. Synthesis overshadowed analysis. At the beginning of the century this tendency was especially striking in German idealism. The creative function of mind had been stressed by Kant, and this conception was now extended to support the romantic notion of becoming. Hence the idealistic systems of Johann Gottlieb Fichte (1762-1814), Friedrich Wilhelm Joseph Schelling (1775-1854), and, most outstanding, Georg Wilhelm Friedrich Hegel (1770-1831). The latter conceived of reality as the dialectical unfolding of absolute reason which passes through thesis and antithesis toward a new synthesis. The Hegelian philosophy is a radical rationalism, yet its dynamic and evolutionary character makes it romantic through and through.

This idealism soon gave way before a series of systems originating in the special sciences. Here mention must first be made of the *materialism* of Germans such as Ludwig Feuerbach (1804-1872), Jakob Moleschott (1822-1893), Ludwig Büchner (1824-1899), and Karl Vogt (1817-1895). These representatives of radical determinism denied the very existence of mind. Reference should also be made to *positivism*, started in France by Auguste Comte (1798-1857), finding an English disciple in John Stuart Mill (1806-1873) and German followers in Ernst Laas (1837-1885) and Friedrich Jodl (1848-1914). For all of these philosophy was simply unified science—science being taken in a mechanistic sense. The teaching of Charles Darwin (1809-1882), whose famous work *On the Origin of Species Through Natural Selection* (1859) described the evolution of species in purely mechanistic terms, gave a powerful impetus to both these tendencies. The romantic and Hegelian conception of evolution hereby received a scientific foundation which it managed to preserve, but with a mechanistic twist to it. It came to be the predominant teaching and led on to the monistic *evolutionism* whose outstanding and most typical representatives were Thomas Henry Huxley (1825-1895) and Herbert Spencer (1820-1903); Ernst Haeckel (1834-1919) also played a part as its most widely known popularizer.

In the period 1850-1870 it appeared as though the lead in Europe would remain with mechanistic evolutionism in what was usually a frankly materialistic form. Soon after 1870, however, a *return to idealism* took place, first in England, with

7

Thomas Hill Green (1836-1882) and Edward Caird (1835-1908), who gathered a considerable school around them; then in Germany an organized teaching center of Neo-Kantianism was established in the schools of Marburg and Baden associated with Otto Liebmann (1840-1912) and Johannes Volkelt (1848-1930). In France neocriticism was expounded by Charles Renouvier (1815-1903), and another important French idealist was Octave Hamelin (1856-1907). But this movement was unable to win a complete monopoly so that the turn of the century saw powerful mechanistic and evolutionistic tendencies still surviving.

It is clear, then, that the development of European thought in the course of the nineteenth century proceeded according to three dialectical stages—idealism, scientific evolutionism, and a simultaneous operation of both tendencies. Despite their antagonism both tendencies had certain essential features in common: the tendency toward system; a markedly rationalistic attitude toward the world of experience; a disinclination to penetrate into the area of reality behind appearances—or even to admit its existence; and, lastly, the monistic tendency which allows human personality to be merged into the Absolute or into the evolution of the universe. Rationalism, phenomenalism, evolutionism, monistic antipersonalism, and the development of great systems largely determined the pattern of the nineteenth century.

E. SUBSIDIARY CURRENTS

But idealism and positivistic evolutionism had not gained exclusive mastery over the thought of this age. Alongside them, of weaker growth and of little influence for the moment, there developed two highly significant movements—irrationalism and metaphysics.

The *irrationalism* propagated by the romantics sounded the

8

first challenge to Hegelian rationalism. Its spokesman was Arthur Schopenhauer (1788-1860) for whom the Absolute is not reason, but the blind irrational will. Following him the Danish religious thinker, Søren Kierkegaard (1813-1855), pushed the attack upon rationalism even further. Similar voluntaristic and irrational tendencies, if somewhat less marked, had previously found a French representative in François Pierre Maine de Biran (1766-1824).

Irrationalism later directed itself against the rationalism derived from the special sciences, yet at this time it still based itself upon the Darwinian theory of evolution. Its major prophet was Friedrich Nietzsche (1844-1900) who taught that vital instinct is superior to the reason, demanded a transvaluation of all values, and advocated the cult of superman. Evolutionism also provided the philosophy of Wilhelm Dilthey (1833-1912) with its starting point; he attributed supreme value to history and taught philosophical relativism. An original form of relativism was worked out by Georg Simmel (1858-1918).

Metaphysics provided nineteenth-century philosophical thought with its other subsidiary current. The metaphysicians claimed to have entry into a world behind phenomena and frequently showed tendencies toward metaphysical pluralism, along with a far-reaching insight into the concrete problems of human existence. They remained isolated thinkers who never formed themselves into larger and more organized schools. The Germans concerned were Johann Friedrich Herbart (1776-1841), Gustav Theodor Fechner (1801-1887), Rudolf Hermann Lotze (1817-1881), and Eduard von Hartmann (1842-1906), followed with variations by Wilhelm Wundt (1832-1920), Rudolf Eucken (1846-1926), and Friedrich Paulsen (1846-1908).

In France the representatives of metaphysics were Victor

9

Cousin (1792-1867) and his pupils, such as Paul Janet (1823-1899), while it took still firmer shape in the systems of Felix Ravaisson-Molien (1813-1900) and Jules Lachelier (1832-1918)—to name only the chief ones. On the other hand, no important tendencies of this type showed up in England.

Nevertheless, both the irrationalists and the metaphysicians of this period had to work upon the problems posed by Kant just as much as the others whom we discussed previously. Kant's teaching that metaphysical problems are not accessible to reason directly inspired one aspect of irrationalism, while his own rationalism was responsible for its other aspect by the opposition which it provoked. Nor did mechanistic empiricism of the Darwinian pattern fail to have its effect, especially upon Nietzsche. Despite appearances to the contrary the same is true of the metaphysicians of this age; they all fell in with dualism through severing the phenomenal world from things-in-themselves, and most of them joined company with the mechanists. All the same, it must be repeated that the importance of both tendencies was only relative, and cannot compare with that of idealism and empiricism, which were easily the weightiest factors in nineteenth-century European philosophy.

2. THE CRISIS

A. THE CHANGING SITUATION

There was evidence of a profound philosophical crisis at the turn of the century; its symptoms were to be seen in the rise of countermovements to the two strongest forces in modern philosophy, materialistic mechanism and subjectivism. The revolt extended far beyond the field of philosophy and may be compared with the general crisis which gave birth to modern culture at the time of the Renaissance. It is extraordinarily difficult to give a complete picture of it with its many contributory causes, and yet the facts themselves stand out clearly enough. Europe, at that time, was undergoing a notable change of direction in its social thought and suffering violent economic disturbances; there were remarkable alterations in religious opinion and drastic innovations in art. It is generally agreed that the beginning of the twentieth century should be regarded not so much as the end of a short period, but much more as the final curtain upon a great epoch drawing to its close, so that our own times can no longer be counted in the "modern" age. There is much to be said for the opinion that this later revolution is more drastic than what occurred at the Renaissance. In any case basic conceptions in all spheres of life have been shaken, and contemporary wars have helped to hasten the painful process of dissolution.

Of course such a radical change in intellectual life is intimately connected with changes in social relationships, is in fact at least partly conditioned by them. But in the present state of science this connection cannot as yet be traced in detail. We shall therefore confine ourselves to the establishment of the immediate intellectual causes and determinants of the change.

They can be divided into three groups. The first is the crisis in physics and mathematics which resulted on the one hand in a high development of analytic thought, and on the other in a collapse of certain intellectual attitudes typical of the nineteenth century. The second consists in two methods which begin to develop at this time, the mathematical and the phenomenological. The third, finally, comprises certain world views, notably irrationalism and the new realist metaphysics. These various intellectual movements are interrelated in numerous ways. So, for example, mathematical logic is intimately connected with the crisis in mathematics, while the crisis in physics lends aid to irrationalism; and very often it is the same thinkers

Origin of Contemporary Philosophy

who turn out to be the founders of the phenomenological method and of the new realism. There are mutual influences between the pioneers of phenomenology and those of mathematical logic.

In spite of these interrelationships, it would be difficult to cite a parallel for the simultaneous appearance of movements so utterly different both in their historical sources and in their aims. These movements contribute in fact to a total transformation of philosophy.

B. THE CRISIS IN NEWTONIAN PHYSICS

Most nineteenth-century philosophers regarded Newtonian physics as an absolutely true picture of nature. They saw in it a clear description of reality in which everything could be reduced to the position and impulse of material atoms (mechanism). Given the present position and the forces acting on material particles, the whole subsequent future development of the world was believed to be precisely calculable by mechanical laws (Laplacean determinism). The principles, and in fact the theories, of physics, were taken to be absolutely true (absolutism). Matter appeared as the simple given and everything was to be logically reduced to this simple given (materialism). Physics moreover was the oldest of natural sciences and had proved its value in technology. Other branches of knowledge which were destined to flourish later in the nineteenth century, above all, history, had not yet achieved prominence.

But at the turn of the century this physical picture of nature led to widespread doubt. Of course it is not true, as is so often supposed, that the new physics does not accept matter, that it wholly rejects determinism, or that it does not accept some propositions as certain. Yet much that has counted as absolutely certain heretofore now seems questionable. It is now beyond doubt that matter is not anything simple but highly complex and that there are still great obstacles to its scientific formulation. It has besides proved to be impossible to try to calculate the position and force of a material particle. In any case Laplacean determinism has become untenable. For most distinguished physicists it is still a moot question whether determinism as such has thereby become unacceptable or whether it can still be regarded as valid in some other form. The most outstanding astrophysicist, Eddington, has said that he is an indeterminist in the same way that he is an anti-the-moon-is-made-of-green-cheeseist; there is no evidence for either hypothesis. At the very least mechanism has assumed a new form. Whitehead, a most reliable judge of the situation, aptly remarks that the old physics thought of the world as a meadow full of freely galloping horses whereas the new physics sees it as a region criss-crossed by railway tracks on which trams run their preordained course. Thus the new "mechanism" comes very close to an organic formulation. Finally, the theory of relativity, the quantum theory, and other discoveries in physics have rendered doubtful much else that was once regarded as quite valid.

These reversals of thought in the domain of physics have exerted an influence on philosophy in two directions. Physicists themselves are no longer agreed whether and in what degree mechanism and determinism can still be maintained. Further, they all show concern as to how one can scientifically formulate matter, which now seems to be so much more complex, and they are forced to acknowledge the relativistic character of their theories. These facts make it impossible to ground mechanism and determinism upon the authority of physics and indeed demonstrate how highly questionable is any effort to explain being in terms of matter.[1]

_____
[1] Some leading exponents of natural science have drawn more far-reaching conclusions from all these facts, thinking that they can establish immaterial-

Origin of Contemporary Philosophy

Meanwhile another and even more momentous result of the crisis in physics has emerged clearly, namely that physical concepts and propositions cannot be taken over from philosophy without analysis, and the method of reaching conclusions about physical nature from the standpoint of philosophy cannot be regarded as valid a priori. Obviously Descartes and Kant in this connection committed an altogether naïve fallacy. But from all this we see that the crisis of physics in another way awakened the so-called analytical mode of thought which was destined to be typical of the philosophy of the twentieth century.

C. THE CRITIQUE OF SCIENCE

The situation just described is not the result of purely technical scientific developments. Thinkers in various other fields also contributed to it who analyzed and sometimes questioned the procedures of natural science long before the crisis broke out. The leaders in this so-called critique of science were French philosophers, notably Émile Boutroux (1845-1921, *De la contingence des lois de la nature*, 1874; *De l'idée de loi naturelle*, 1894), Pierre Duhem (1861-1916, first notable work: *Le Mixte et la combinaison chimique*, 1902) and Henri Poincaré (1853-1912, *La Science et l'hypothèse*, 1902).

This school ran parallel in time with the efforts of *empirio-*

---

ism, idealism, or even theism upon the basis of recent biological and physical discoveries. One need only mention the wellknown names of Sir Arthur Stanley Eddington (1882-1944), Sir James Hopwood Jeans (1877-1946), Max Planck (1858-1947) among the physicists and astronomers, Sir Arthur Thomson (1861-1933) and John Scott Haldane (1860-1936) among the biologists. However, even if their teachings contain much that is true and interesting, especially when they are criticizing materialism, their constructive thinking is usually so plainly amateurish that little attention is paid to them by philosophical specialists. Yet these philosophizing natural scientists are exercising a very strong influence upon the great mass of the people. With the latter the only thing which counts philosophically is the fact that it is really possible for such men to hold such opinions, for this in itself shows that we are a long way removed from the nineteenth-century mentality.

criticism, which came to even more radical conclusions from a positivistic standpoint. Richard Avenarius (1843-1896) published his *Kritik der reinen Erfahrung,* between 1888 and 1890, and Ernst Mach (1838-1916) brought out his major work in 1900, the latter representing a doctrine which furnished an extraordinarily incisive criticism of the theory that science has an absolute value.

The critique of science was applied as much to the value of concepts as it was to scientific systems. Penetrating analyses and historical investigations proved that both are largely subjective by nature because the man of science does not only make an arbitrary dissection of reality, but also continually employs concepts which originate in his own mind. And as to great theories, they are in the last analysis only convenient instruments for tidying up experience—"neither true, nor false but useful" (Poincaré). It is worth noticing that none of these French critics were conventionalists, not even Poincaré. They were attempting to point out that science was a long way removed from the ideal of infallibility so commonly attributed to it in the nineteenth century. The German empiriocritics went further than this and subscribed to a relativism which was close to scepticism.

The general effect was that science lost much of its authority in philosophers' minds, thus aggravating still more what the crisis within physics had set in motion. Henceforward one could not uphold a Newtonian view of nature such as one finds at the roots of Kantianism and of all previous European thought.

D. THE CRISIS OF MATHEMATICS: MATHEMATICAL LOGIC

Toward the end of the nineteenth century the evolution of mathematics led to another crisis no less profound and fraught with consequence than the crisis of physics. Of the many new

15

discoveries in the mathematical field, non-Euclidean geometry and set theory were especially influential upon philosophy. Both of these showed that many things once taken without question as simple presuppositions of mathematics were in fact not certain at all. They directed attention to the exact analysis of apparently simple concepts and to the axiomatic construction of systems. In the field of set theory, right at the end of the century, so-called paradoxes were discovered, that is, contradictions derived by correct methods of inference from apparently simple and obvious assumptions. With this the very foundations of mathematics seemed to totter.

In close conjunction with this development stands the renascence of formal logic, particularly in the form of so-called logistic—symbolic or mathematical logic. As already noted, modern philosophy had in this period allowed logic to fall into neglect and indeed into a state of "barbarous" decline. Of the leading philosophers Leibniz alone was an eminent logician. The others—Kant and Descartes are notable examples— scarcely knew the elements of formal logic. But in 1847 there appeared quite independently of one another the works of two English mathematicians, Augustus De Morgan (1806-1878) and George Boole (1815-1864), and these count as the first publications of modern mathematical logic. Their work was carried forward by Ernst Schröder (1841-1902), Giuseppe Peano (1858-1932), and above all Gottlob Frege (1848-1925), an outstanding thinker and logician. Yet mathematical logic remained largely unknown to philosophers until the beginning of the twentieth century. It was only when Bertrand Russell came in contact with Peano in 1900 and published his *Principles of Mathematics* in 1903 that philosophers, at least those in English-speaking countries, took note of these investigations. The development of the new discipline was markedly advanced by the publication in 1910-1913 of *Principia Mathe-*

matica by Whitehead and Russell, a work of supreme importance.

Mathematical logic has influenced philosophy in two ways. First, it has proved to be a most precise instrument for the analysis of concepts and proofs and to be applicable, its partisans believe, especially in those fields which cannot be mathematized—applicable because so-called "mathematical" logic is mathematical only "in origin" but in practice operates not with mathematical but with very ordinary concepts. Second, through these mathematical-logical investigations many old problems of philosophy have become serious issues again, for example, the problem of excluded middle, of the truth of axioms, of philosophical grammar (now called "semiotic"), and above all the problem of universals.

E. THE PHENOMENOLOGICAL METHOD

Another movement, working with altogether different assumptions and with an entirely different goal, has contributed to the break with the nineteenth century and to the development of contemporary philosophy, namely, phenomenology. In the strict sense, this designation applies particularly to the method and doctrine of Edmund Husserl, but it is used also for a whole group of other thinkers who represent a similar point of view. The founder of this movement is Franz Brentano (1838-1917). A Dominican in early life, he left the order and later also the church. But in many ways he remained under the influence of Aristotelian-Thomistic thought, for example, in his objectivism, in the high value he set upon particularistic analysis, and in his logic. He had numerous pupils. Three in particular were influential, Kazimierz Twardowski, Alois Meinong, and Edmund Husserl. Twardowski (1866-1938), though himself not a logician, became the founder of the Polish school of logicians which was to play a prominent role in the

17

development of mathematical logic. Alois Meinong (1853-1921) developed the theory of so-called "objectives" and founded his own small but influential school. The most eminent of Brentano's pupils, Edmund Husserl (1859-1938), was the principal architect of the phenomenological method. This method which consists mainly in the analysis of the essence of the given, the phenomenon, became the most widespread method of philosophical analysis, along with the mathematical-logical method, particularly after the Second World War. The most important difference between phenomenology and mathematical logic lies in the fact that the former dispenses with deduction altogether, is very little concerned with language, despite Husserl's own example, and does not analyze empirical fact but essences. It is worth noting that Meinong's principal work *Über die Annahmen* appeared in 1902, and Husserl's *Logische Untersuchungen*, one of the most influential works of the first half-century, was published in 1900-1901.

What is called "analysis" by G. E. Moore (b. 1873) is rather closely related to the phenomenological method. With Bertrand Russell it becomes mathematical-logical analysis but in Moore himself it retains a somewhat different character. In his *Principia Ethica* of 1903 Moore is close to Meinong in method and seems even to have been influenced by him to a degree. Meinong may also have influenced Russell in some ways, while the later mathematical logic owes a good deal to Husserl.

F. VITALISTIC IRRATIONALISM

Above all, mathematical logic and phenomenology are methods, not doctrines. Both of them proceed from reflection upon the foundations of the sciences and try to provide them with a new foundation with the aid of a rational method. Again, both positions are pluralistic and are opposed to the tendency of system building. They have uncovered and destroyed many of the gross oversimplifications of the nineteenth century. Both positions moreover are realistic, at least at the outset. In both Moore and Husserl a certain sympathy for Platonism, in an altogether new form, comes to the surface. But we must repeat that neither mathematical logic nor phenomenology, at least in *Principia Mathematica* and in *Logische Untersuchungen*, actually constitute philosophies.

In contrast to these there emerge at the same time two philosophic movements which are new in respect to content: vitalistic irrationalism and the new realist metaphysics. One of the consequences of the intellectual crisis of this time is the prodigious extension of irrationalistic tendencies characteristic of the turn of the century. Although Kant had denied that the world behind phenomena was accessible to reason, he had still maintained that the empirical world was subject to rational laws which could be discovered. The critique of science and the crisis within physics seemed to show clearly that this was not so, thereby generalizing the Kantian doubt as to the value of reason. Now for the nineteenth century "reason" meant the mechanistic reason of the sciences; therefore the scientific crisis produced a crisis within rationalism.

But this was not the unique source of the new tendencies. Paradoxically enough empiricism played a predominant part in their progress due to the fact that its own mechanistic outlook on life was taken over and assumed the form of *Darwinism*. The beginning of the twentieth century witnessed the oddity that this doctrine, with its basic device of explaining the higher in terms of the lower, was transferred to the fields of psychology and sociology. Accordingly all conscious life, including the reasoning faculties, had to be reduced to its lowest elements and subordinated to the instinctive laws of evolution; there was nothing permanent, nothing changeless, there were

Origin of Contemporary Philosophy

no eternal principles, only instinctive drives serving the evolution of life.

Finally, a part was played by the same causes that had called forth romanticism at the beginning of the nineteenth century, now fortified by the influence of tradition. The monistic and deterministic outlook propagated by science before 1900 had been so tyrannical as to provoke protests from a number of thinkers who felt called upon to preserve the rights of life, of the human person, and of spiritual values.

This power suddenly came to the fore in the persons of two philosophers, James and Bergson, who set themselves at the head of this philosophical movement. Spencer, the most typical representative of mechanistic empiricism, was still alive when there appeared almost simultaneously *Les Données immédiates de la conscience* (1889) and the *Principles of Psychology* (1890), shortly followed by *Matière et Mémoire* (1896) and *The Will to Believe* (1897). Both these philosophers are still exercising such an influence upon our immediate environment that they have to be discussed more fully (see sections 11 and 12). It is sufficient for the moment to point out that both are professedly irrationalist and make the concept of life the key notion of their philosophical thought. Owing to them irrationalism has achieved a leading position in thought after being only a minor current in the nineteenth century.

G. THE RENAISSANCE OF REALIST METAPHYSICS

At the same time another and far deeper tendency was crystallizing; realism and metaphysics returned and burst asunder for the first time that framework of Kantian principles which had enveloped the whole of philosophy for such a long time. It is difficult to lay bare their roots and their deepest causes, since their contributions toward original metaphysics are numerous and come from such different angles. In general, one may say, the resources of Kantianism began to be exhausted sometime about 1900; they were no longer sufficient, they no longer satisfied, and thought turned toward other solutions. The first noticeable tendency was toward a new *"critical" realism* which still maintained the Kantian framework. Alois Riehl (1844-1924) was one of its representatives. The Würzburg school worked upon the same lines but with greater drive and energy; its founder was Oswald Külpe (1862-1915) and his disciples include a number of brilliant names. But the actual revitalization of realism derives, like the phenomenological method, from Brentano and his pupils, especially from Meinong and Husserl. It is true that Husserl did not quite reach realism, still less the philosophy of being, but his drawing of attention away from fruitless epistemological problems to the analysis of the given was of the utmost importance for modern realism and metaphysics. Meinong's influence in this direction was likewise evident.

Besides this movement *realist metaphysics* gained ground in many other places under the impulse of various intellectual factors. Thomism experienced a rebirth about 1880 (the encyclical *Aeterni patris* was issued in 1879) and organized a large school which was soon to become extremely powerful. Its Fribourg organ, *La Revue Thomiste*, was started in 1893 and *La Revue Néoscolastique de Philosophie* of Louvain in 1894. It represents direct realism and traditional metaphysics.

Thomism did not stand alone, however, for in England G. E. Moore produced his famous essay, *The Refutation of Idealism*, in 1903 and along with Bertrand Russell he put forward an almost Platonic philosophy. The French thinkers Boutroux and Bergson both subscribed to realism in their different ways, while in Germany the main instance was the teaching of Hans Driesch (1867-1941), which aroused interest on account of its Aristotelian character.

21

Origin of Contemporary Philosophy

This new realist movement did not achieve the popularity of irrationalism but it was equally effective. Metaphysics, which was only a secondary and weak movement in the nineteenth century, became a leading doctrine of the times.

H. RETURN TO SPECULATION; PLURALISM

Toward the end of the nineteenth century philosophy declined under the heavy hand of positivism. Most philosophers were frightened, perhaps, to expound their own thought, with the result that most universities were dominated by a certain historicism, confining themselves to the sheer cataloguing of past doctrines. One of the most striking features of the early twentieth century was the return to systematic speculation which penetrated to the irrationalist and to most metaphysical schools.

But the most significant and unmistakable symptom was undoubtedly the return to personalistic pluralism, for just as the nineteenth century had shown itself monistically inclined in all its aspects, the new countermovements at the turn of the century were all pluralistic. They brought out the differences in the various levels of being and emphasized the plurality of self-subsistent beings. James gave expression to the most extreme form of this pluralism by going so far as to acknowledge a sympathy for polytheism. It found almost universal favor in the eyes of phenomenologists, English neorealists, and Thomists. The human person was beginning to recover its ancient rights and was rapidly becoming the center of philosophical interest; henceforward thought really became inflamed with the deep concerns of the spirit. If the nineteenth century had been an outstandingly monistic and materialistic age, it was obvious from the crisis in 1900 that the new age would be given over to spiritual personalism on the broadest basis.

Of course these ideas were very far from being universal

assumptions about 1900; indeed the first quarter of the century provided the setting for a general return to the old themes. Still the new ideas were there, were working themselves out, and were favorably received by most European thinkers after the First World War.

3. THE BEGINNING OF THE TWENTIETH CENTURY

A. CHARACTERISTICS

The following features are characteristic of philosophy in the first quarter of the twentieth century. First, it is a time of most strenuous philosophical activity. Many eminent thinkers appear or become influential; in this respect we must count it among the most fruitful periods in recent history. Second, it is a transitional period in which movements of the older schools retain their status and continue to grow alongside more modern tendencies. Although the heroes of the nineteenth century do not retain their former standing, they are still very much alive and influential, exercising their sway in many lands until World War I, for example, in England and Italy. Meanwhile, illustrious thinkers have been propagating new ideas and have secured a large audience for them; several of these earn high esteem for themselves, particularly Bergson and, to a lesser degree, Husserl. The principal thinkers are empiricists and idealists as followers of nineteenth-century ideas; life-philosophers, phenomenologists, and neorealists as advocates of "modernity."

B. THE EMPIRICISTS

A large number of thinkers accept the guidance of positivism, or even of materialism, and for them the idea of mechanistic evolution still holds good. In general, however, they are already breaking out of the positivistic framework, by their

23

Origin of Contemporary Philosophy

attempt to use science as the basis for a sort of general reconstruction of reality which they occasionally call "metaphysics." They can be divided into several groups, each with different aims and of unequal significance.

There are, to begin with, several French representatives whose influence now begins to make itself felt for the first time although most of their written work belongs to the nineteenth century. All of them base their versions of metaphysics upon scientific assumptions. The outstanding ones are Alfred Fouillée (1838-1912), with his doctrine of "effective ideas" *(idées forces)*, André Lalande (b. 1867), critic of evolutionary optimism and exponent of the law of dissolution, and the radical materialist Felix le Dantec, (1869-1917), who wrote a number of works directed against immaterialism, vitalism, and ontological individualism.

In Germany empiricist tendencies find their principal representatives among the positivists, of whom Theodor Ziehen (1862-1950) is the most noteworthy. Ernst Mach (1838-1916) still has some effect, and several of his pupils propagate his empiriocriticism. In this context Wilhelm Ostwald (1853-1932) must be mentioned as an example of an original and independent thinker. Beginning as a chemist he moved on to philosophy, where he invoked natural science in order to justify his actualist teaching, according to which the whole of reality is nothing but energy.

Materialistic currents show up particularly strong in *psychology*, principally in the behaviorist doctrine originated by John B. Watson (b. 1878). The main point at issue is that of a scientific methodology which refuses to study mental phenomena as events within the soul. It abandons introspection, and will recognize nothing but external behavior as a valid object for psychology. One of the consequences is the utter denial of mind. The Russian Ivan Pavlov (1849-1936) arrived at similar conclusions through his reflexology, according to which the higher mental functions can be explained by conditioned or inhibited reflexes.

Meanwhile the psychoanalysis of Sigmund Freud (1856-1939) is the most important movement arising out of empiricism. He adopts the axiom of evolutionistic mechanism whereby the higher is explained in terms of the lower, and uses the argument that conscious life is nothing but the result of a purely mechanical play of elements in the "subconscious." These elements, each with its own peculiar dynamic, form "complexes," have a tendency to reappear in consciousness, and influence its operations. The decisive motive force in the life of the soul is its "libido," which is erotic in the broadest sense. In *The Interpretation of Dreams* (1900) Freud expounded these initial principles upon which he, after 1913 *(Totem and Taboo)*, built systems for explaining religion, art, etc. He regards the highest mental phenomena as mere "sublimations" of erotic desire.

A similar general application of a limited scientific theory was made by the French sociological school with Emil Durkheim (1858-1917) as its founder and Lucien Lévy-Bruhl (1857-1939) as its subsequent spokesman. These sociologists believe that although society is exemplified in individual men it has an objective reality; it is grasped scientifically through objective methods of comparison, which study efficient causes only and exclude any kind of finality. The employment of this method leads Durkheim and Lévy-Bruhl to the statements that ethical and logical laws are completely relative—nothing more than expressions of what society needs for self-development; and religion consists in the cult of this society. The system culminates in a kind of speculative psychology according to which religion, logic, and morality belong to the social sphere while the individual man's province is secular, alogical, and

25

egoistical. It would regard the body as a principle of individuation.

All these systems, psychoanalysis and sociology especially, have a great popular following, but are merely the last flickers from the nineteenth-century world of thought. They are to be distinguished from the older form of empiricism, however, by one feature—their relativism. Le Dantec, Pavlov, Ziehen, Ostwald, Freud, Durkheim, and some others are relativists who recognize neither absolute laws, nor objective logic, nor unchanging morality. So this aspect of empiricism itself is an approach toward that irrationalism which is so widespread in philosophy.

It remains to be added that none of these doctrines are of any consequence from a philosophical point of view. They are all narrowly sensualist and nominalist, incapable of reaching beyond the limits of *imaginative thought;* mechanistic materialism is still strongly at work in them. It is a curious paradox that a place can still be found in the province of psychology and sociology for doctrines which have been outmoded in physics, and even in biology.

C. IDEALISM

In the course of the first 25 years of the twentieth century idealism still exercised the greatest influence in the chief countries of Europe but ceased to do so in most of them by about 1925. This is particularly true of England, for it retained its force in Germany, France, and Italy until the Second World War. It will be discussed at considerable length later. As English idealism no longer forms part of contemporary philosophy only a short sketch of its main lines is included in the summary here.

English idealism is a more original form of Hegelianism; its spokesmen are Francis Herbert Bradley (1846-1924), Bernard Bosanquet (1848-1923), and John McTaggart Ellis McTaggart (1866-1925), and of these the first two are monists. Bradley is probably the most profound. He bases his philosophy upon the idea of internal relations. According to him relations are not additions to the essence of the already constituted thing, but themselves constitute this very essence. On the one hand this doctrine leads to monism (reality as an organic whole) but on the other hand, by stressing the act of knowing, it leads to objective idealism (there is no essential difference between object and subject because both are merely manifestations of the whole, of the single Absolute). Bradley supports his thesis with penetrating observations about the internal contradictions of every empirical reality; these prove to him that such a reality is purely appearance behind which is hidden the true reality, the Absolute. But even though Bradley is the prophet of monistic idealism, he is far from reducing reality to an abstraction. Like Hegel, he insists upon the primacy of the concrete; his universal is no abstraction but a "concrete universal," richer than the singular in its content and more real than the particular. These are only a few fundamental aspects of Bradley's rich and versatile thought which produced a lasting effect upon a number of leading thinkers—as it still does. James and Marcel, for example, are directly indebted to him while it is precisely against his basic conceptions that English neorealism has been directed.

Bosanquet develops Hegelian idealism along the same lines, with possibly even greater stress upon the concrete nature of reality. The third thinker mentioned, McTaggart, moved away from Bosanquet and Bradley by accepting pluralism—he regards the Absolute as a community of spirits standing in a changing relationship toward each other. His philosophy is deeply spiritual and personalistic. Thus he stands as a bridge between idealism and the newly developing philosophy.

27

Origin of Contemporary Philosophy

D. FRESH CURRENTS

Only brief reference can be made here to the new philosophical movements which appear during the period under consideration because they all continued beyond 1925 and therefore belong to the contemporary philosophy which is the subject matter of the main body of this book. There are three of them: phenomenology, neorealism, and vitalistic irrationalism.

Phenomenology in the meantime became a powerful factor. The *Jahrbuch für Philosophie und phänomenologische Forschung* began to appear in 1913. On it a number of most capable thinkers coöperated with Husserl, among them Alexander Pfänder, D. v. Hildebrand, Moritz Geiger, Roman Ingarden, and, above all, Max Scheler whose main work *(Der Formalismus in der Ethik und die materiale Wertethik)* appeared in the first two volumes (1913-1916). The influence of phenomenology was extraordinarily strong so that on the one hand it even affected Neo-Kantianism—for example, Emil Lask (1875-1915)—and on the other hand it affected psychology, a province where it possessed a notable advocate in Carl Stumpf (1848-1936). In Germany this school was influential enough to challenge the lead of Neo-Kantianism, though until the First World War Neo-Kantianism remained the strongest philosophical force in that country.

The *new realism* was equally lively, especially in the writings of a Moore or a Russell, but was unable to establish a great school. Whitehead had not yet entered upon his metaphysical period; Alexander did not publish his main work, *Space, Time and Deity* until 1920 (thus toward the end of the period under discussion), while the English universities were completely dominated by idealism, more so even than those of Germany. But in France the leading realistic movement of the period, *Thomism*, was already producing very important works. The year 1909 saw the appearance of R. Garrigou-Lagrange's *Sens commun*, and 1915 his *Dieu*. In 1913 came the first of Jacques Maritain's significant contributions, aimed against Bergson. The Thomist school was therefore organized, but although its interior resources were fully developed, that age did not yet accord it the recognition which it enjoys at present—even in France, as elsewhere, the older movements dominated.

Only one new school succeeded in asserting itself and capturing the attention not only of specialist philosophical circles, but also of a wider literary-minded public—*vitalistic irrationalism*. It had not yet done so in Germany, since Dilthey had scarcely been discovered and the first specifically philosophical work by Klages was only just appearing. But in the English-speaking countries James scored an unprecedented success with the aid of F. C. S. Schiller's brilliant campaigning; the latter's main work *Humanism* (1903), was followed by one book after another during the quarter century under discussion. In France the rising star was Bergson whose fundamental work, *Creative Evolution*, appeared in 1907 and became a real center of philosophic debate. As head of the school he was surrounded by first-rate intellects more or less under the sway of his genius. Among the most noteworthy are the modernists, Le Roy, Blondel, Pradines, and Baruzi. Bergson's magnetism was great, but even Bergsonism was unable to eliminate entirely the older doctrines, which continued to flourish.

4. Main Currents of Contemporary Philosophy

A. THE SCHOOLS

The period of contemporary philosophy which we are to deal with here, stretching from the First World War to the present, has witnessed the coming of age of two new schools. One of them, *neopositivism*, is an original extension of the positivist position, while the other, *existential philosophy*, is something completely new, although in point of time it has a place in the continuation of life-philosophy and contains both phenomenological and metaphysical elements. All schools which were now in existence had their outstanding thinkers who developed their basic theses in grand fashion. This was particularly true of *metaphysics*, which could boast the names of Alexander, Whitehead, Hartmann, and an increasing number of Thomists; it was no less true of *phenomenology*, which claimed Scheler, and of *life-philosophy*, which included Bergson's last phase and the whole thought of Klages, to name but two.

The most significant systems of our period can be divided in two ways, in respect to the content of doctrine and in respect to method. Respecting doctrine, they can be classified in six groups. We have first two positions which still carry on in the spirit of the eighteenth century: empiricism or the philosophy of matter as a continuation of positivism, and idealism both in its Kantian and Hegelian forms. Then come two positions which effect the breach with that century: life-philosophy and the philosophy of essence or phenomenology. Finally there are two groups which make the most unique contribution of our time: existentialist philosophy and the new metaphysics of being.

This classification is naturally somewhat arbitrary. The profound differences between philosophies paired together under one heading are not to be overlooked. Thus we have applied the common classification "philosophy of matter" to such extremely different teachings as those of Russell, the neopositivists, and even the Marxists. In the same way the chapter on life-philosophy has had to include thinkers so various as

Dewey and Klages. Finally it must be emphasized that individual thinkers remain outside these groups and overlap them—as, for example, the representatives of the Baden school, which has points of contact both with historicism, which is a life-philosophy, and with Scheler's phenomenology, the latter itself being akin to existentialism. Every classification in a history of philosophical thought is an unavoidable expedient for a better view of the whole. It should not try to conceal the deep differences within each group nor their overlapping. With this caution we may claim, however, that our division into six groups illustrates the six main positions of our day—empiricism, idealism, life-philosophy, phenomenology, existentialism, and metaphysics.

In and of itself the classification of schools according to *method* should not be very decisive. But it nevertheless appears to be so in rather remarkable fashion, as was clearly evident in the Tenth International Congress of Philosophy in 1948. The fact is that within one and the same philosophical school a schism often arises which derives from the application of different methods, such as mathematical-logical analysis on the one hand, and phenomenological procedure on the other. While there are many philosophers who do not commit themselves to either of these two methods nor to both of them, still many of them seem nowadays to be segregated along these lines. The phenomenological method, which has advanced and evolved in the course of time, is employed not only by phenomenologists but by nearly all existentialist philosophers and also by certain metaphysicians. Other metaphysicians have allied themselves with the protagonists of mathematical logic, notably Whitehead. It is indeed remarkable that mathematical logic has been able to bring together in mutual understanding proponents of the most varied and even incompatible schools—Platonists, Aristotelians, nominal-

31

ists, and even Kantians and a few pragmatists—while the cleavage between those who employ this method and those who work with the methods of phenomenology seems often so great that no common understanding is any longer possible.

B. INFLUENCES

The present period is still affected by the conditions responsible for the break with the last century's thought. Thus physics has maintained the same increasing alienation from its old mechanistic basis as before. The illusion of progress through technology (still dominant in America and Russia) has suffered new reversals in Europe. The masses as well as the philosophers appear now to be cured of it, at the price of great sacrifices. We know only too well the series of events which called forth these frightful sufferings, so well calculated to fix man's gaze upon the urgent problems of the human person, his purpose and destiny, his sorrow, his death, and his communion with his fellows. A religious revival seems to be in full swing. Finally, a sort of general uncertainty and restlessness is taking hold of men who sense deeply this crisis-ridden situation and turn more readily to philosophy in the hope that it will give them an answer to the heart-rending questions of their harrowed lives. All this explains why existentialism has gained ground so quickly, why metaphysics has become such a force. It explains also the high respect in which the philosophic life now stands.

Powerful influences on the part of ancient thinkers are at work within these philosophies. The influence of Thomas Aquinas is greater at present than either Kant's or Hegel's according to Bertrand Russell who has to be counted among the philosophers of matter, the continuators of the nineteenth century. This would probably be endorsed by all philosophers of our day. If philosophy ascends to higher levels it does so in spiral fashion. Nowadays it is closer to Greek and scholastic thought than to any thought of the past hundred years, so far as its fundamental questions are concerned. Plato has been reborn in Whitehead; Aristotle in Driesch, Hartmann, and the Thomists; Plotinus in certain existentialists; Thomas Aquinas in the school named after him; the later scholastics in phenomenology and neopositivism; Leibniz in Russell.

Nevertheless, when the question arises as to who is exercising the most powerful influence upon contemporary philosophy we must without hesitation name two who belong to our own age; they are, as we have said already, Bergson and Husserl. Of course they have no monopoly, yet life-philosophy and phenomenology are playing their decisive roles everywhere without having any particularly strong school to represent them.

Briefly, what an attentive observer might have already seen coming to pass in 1900 has now been fully realized; nineteenth-century philosophy has been superseded in favor of a new conception of reality which originates at the beginning of the century and which, without being reactionary, is much more like the thought of past ages.

C. THE RELATIVE IMPORTANCE OF THE SYSTEMS

When estimating the importance of schools and systems two completely different points of view have to be taken into consideration. Generally speaking those systems which influence the general public most strongly do not affect philosophers in the same degree, and this for two reasons. On the one hand the masses are slow to comprehend, so that it is fifty or even a hundred years after its maturity in specialist circles before a philosophy has much prospect of becoming popular, no matter what importance the philosophers themselves attach to it. On the other hand the public is far more subject than

33

philosophers to those twin seductions of simplicity and spec-
tacular progaganda. A philosophy has a much greater chance
of becoming widespread the more down to earth it is and the
more support it receives from movements which are equipped
with efficient propaganda machines, whereas philosophers are
generally less affected by such factors.

Our survey is only concerned with philosophy in the academic sense of the word, not with the popular beliefs of the
mass. But it is not without point to ask which present day
philosophy is most popular, a title to which two philosophies in
particular might lay claim. First, the *philosophy of matter*, the
simplest, is easily understood by the nonphilosopher; furthermore the Marxist version of it is being propagated with all the
power of the world-wide Communist party as well as through
the patronage of some intellectuals—philosophical dilettants
who have succumbed to the magic of a simplified doctrine just
as the masses have done. Second, the greatest popularity is enjoyed by *existentialism*, particularly in the Latin countries.
This seems odd at first sight because existentialism is a wholly
modern movement and, what is more, an extremely technical
and subtle philosophy. But the oddity is soon explained if one
notices the simplified and digestible form in which it is handed
out to the public—in belles-lettres, plays, and popular writings.
No philosophers except the existentialists have indulged in
this kind of propaganda. Again, it is normally the irrationalist
and radically subjectivist aspect of existentialism which fasci-
nates nonphilosophers. Now subjectivism has been a familiar
doctrine for centuries past, and irrationalism was disseminated
by certain nineteenth-century philosophical currents, which
flowed over into the first quarter of this century through the
channels of life-philosophy, as mentioned earlier. Thus one
might compare the success of existentialism with that of
Stoic teaching during the first centuries of our era. Stoic phi-

losophy also was avowedly specialist, but was able to prevail over large cultural areas by broadcasting certain simple ideas of morality for which history had long since prepared the ground.

Compared with these two movements the other schools number but few adherents among the general public. Metaphysics at most comes within range of them, particularly in its Thomist branch which has a powerful tradition behind it and has the Catholic Church as patron. Life-philosophy and phenomenology are less known, especially the latter. Idealism appears to have suffered a great defeat.

Among thinkers themselves the influences of the schools are arrayed in a different order. Even here idealism would undoubtedly occupy the bottom place whereas life-philosophy and phenomenology would be much nearer the top, though merely in an indirect way through radiating over a number of schools. On the other hand the first place among the two philosophical schools which have arisen within our own day appears to belong to metaphysics rather than to existentialism. Finally, the philosophy of matter is in a curious position for in some forms—for example, in Spencerism or in dialectical materialism—it is plainly nonexistent, or nearly so in the universities; but the labors of Russell and the neopositivists, combined with a reaction from the crisis in science, have earned it a momentary revival in certain intellectual circles. Between 1930 and 1939 it seemed that neopositivism would have the fortune of attaining the status of a leading school, though now it is overshadowed on the continent by the other movements and only in England has it retained its admittedly very powerful position. Even in England (as in North America) its influence in contemporary philosophy is slowly waning.

In summing up one may indicate the relative importance of the systems as follows: At the top are metaphysics and existentialism, followed by life-philosophy and phenomenology

35

(these indirectly through the movements just mentioned); far behind comes the philosophy of matter. Idealism stands at the bottom.[2]

D. GENERAL CHARACTERISTICS

It is impossible to suggest any one general characteristic which is equally present in all streams of contemporary thought. One reason for this is that some of them adopt the nineteenth-century or, shall we say, the "modern" (1600-1900) position, while the rest are struggling to establish something that is radically new in comparison with them. And yet one may discern common features in most philosophers, though not in all. Whitehead seems to be right, for instance, when he states that the "bifurcation" so typical of the modern age between the world machine and the thinking subject is now obsolete. As we saw, both subjectivism and mechanism have in consequence suffered heavy defeat. On the whole there is an obvious tendency toward a more organic and better differentiated conception of reality, together with frank recognition of its hierarchical construction and its different levels of being. Present-day thought has a number of other traits which, although they do not permeate it, help to sharpen its outlines. The following are some of them.

a) *The antipositivist position.*—This fundamental feature is visible in all except the philosophy of matter and the philosophies of some idealists. In this respect, however, the phenome-

---

[2] The auxiliary board of the International Federation of Philosophical Societies (founded 1948, see section 26) has thirty members of which twenty-four are elected from Europe. Among these there are five Thomists, four metaphysicians of another school, two dialecticians, one positivist, one idealist, one dialectical materialist (from Czechoslovakia), and one existentialist. Six of these philosophers are adherents of mathematical logic. The composition of this board does not reflect the relative strength of the schools, but is nonetheless noteworthy.

nologists, the life-philosophers, and the existentialists go further than the metaphysicians, the latter being content to accord natural science a subordinate place as a source of philosophic knowledge while the former generally deny that it has any such value.

b) *Analysis.*—In explicit opposition to the nineteenth century, philosophers of the present carry on analysis and often with new and very precise methods.

c) *Realism.*—The metaphysicians, most life-philosophers, the philosophers of matter, as well as some existentialists are realists, and it is only the idealists who stick to the opposite viewpoint. The most representative form is that of immediate realism; it attributes to man the capacity for grasping being directly. In general the Kantian distinction between things-in-themselves and appearances has been thrown back along the whole front.

d) *Pluralism.*—Contemporary philosophers are usually pluralists in revolt against the idealistic and materialistic monism of the nineteenth century. There are some exceptions even here, both Alexander among the metaphysicians and Croce among the idealists being monists, for example. But they are a minority whose influence is obviously diminishing.

e) *Actualism.*—Nearly all philosophers of the day are actualists. Their preoccupation centers upon becoming—a becoming which they increasingly identify with the course of history, just as history has become the guide of irrationalist movements instead of biology, which played this role at the beginning of the century. Present-day actualism in philosophy denies the existence of substances, only Thomists and certain English neorealists being exceptions to this rule. Some philosophers take their actualism so far as to abandon the assumption of changeless ideal forms. This is true of the philosophers of matter, the life-philosophers, many idealists, and all existen-

Origin of Contemporary Philosophy

tialists. But these latter tendencies are strenuously resisted by other schools, particularly by Neo-Kantians, phenomenologists, and metaphysicians.

f) *Personalism.*—In most schools interest is concentrated upon the human person. Apart from the philosophers of matter, all present-day thinkers more or less acknowledge the existence of spirit and underline the unique value of the human person. This personalism assumes a peculiarly dramatic guise in the existentialists but is equally forcefully represented in many of the metaphysicians and phenomenologists. For this very reason contemporary philosophy possesses one marked feature distinguishing it from that of the past—it is closer to every-day reality than any of its predecessors.

E. EXTERNAL FEATURES

Besides these essential features of doctrine, several external features of contemporary philosophy are noteworthy. It is emphatically specialist and unusually productive, and its individual schools are much more closely linked together than they were in previous times.

a) *Technique.*—No professional philosopher nowadays produces works comparable in simplicity with those of a Plato or a Descartes. All schools (except dialectical materialism and occasionally pragmatism) have at their disposal specialized instrumental concepts of richly abstract connotations which they manipulate in the course of complicated and subtle argumentation. This is most obvious with existentialists and neopositivists, and is therefore typical of the two most recent schools, but it is more or less the same with the idealists, the phenomenologists, and the metaphysicians. From the outside, then, certain philosophic techniques of our day are strongly reminiscent of technical works such as Aristotle's, and even of the skillful elaborateness to be found in fifteenth-century scholasticism.

b) *Productivity.*—The productivity of contemporary philosophers is unusually high. There are some thirty specifically philosophical periodicals in Italy alone, while one international school, Thomism in the strict sense, accounts for more than twenty. The bibliography of the International Institute for Philosophy lists thousands of titles every year. To this quantitative achievement we must add the wealth of problems now being brought up, as well as the real importance of many works that are appearing. It is certainly difficult to say anything about their lasting value, but, unless appearances are altogether deceiving, some philosophers of our period will assuredly leave a permanent mark upon the history of philosophical thought. With scarcely any exaggeration it may be said that this century will count among the most fruitful in history.

c) *Interdependence.*—One characteristic of present-day European philosophy is the depth of sympathy between philosophers of the most diverse and opposite movements, and the establishment of relations between different countries. The early twentieth century saw the initiation of a series of international philosophical congresses which have been bringing together an increasing number of philosophers. Besides these congresses there are the international meetings for the special purposes of some particular discipline, movement, or school. Furthermore, some international schools (e.g., idealists, Thomists, neopositivists) have founded periodicals, and some of these include articles in several languages. The result is that philosophical currents flow into one another more than they have done at almost any previous period.

This is certainly obvious in the process by which the present schools were set up. English neorealism, for instance, springs from the "theory of objectives" (which is a kind of phenomenology), from certain empiricist ideas, and from the study of metaphysics (Russell on Leibniz). Neopositivism is closely related to the critique of science, classical empiricism, and English neorealism, and is influenced at the same time by Husserl, the founder of phenomenology. The latter is powerfully at work in existentialism and in certain branches of metaphysics. Idealism is not independent of its traditional opponent, positivism. Most unique of all is the genesis of existentialism which combines within itself positivist, idealistic, and phenomenological influences, although it is derived mainly from life-philosophy and is not without metaphysical elements.

The Stars, she whispers, blindly run.

TENNYSON

II

Philosophy of Matter

Several different movements are included under this general heading—Russell's philosophy, neopositivism, and dialectical materialism. These systems may not be very significant from a strict philosophical point of view but they exert an influence over wider areas than do any of the other philosophical currents. The reason for their unusual effect is easily accounted for by the fact that they are resurrecting ideas which were genuinely significant in philosophy some hundred years ago, and the general public is always about a century behind the development of scientific philosophy.

All thinkers belonging to this group are naturalists, exponents of science, and pronounced rationalists, more or less inclined toward materialism. They are *naturalists* in that they regard man simply as an integral constituent of nature and deny that there is any essential difference between himself and all other natural beings. They are *exponents of science* because of their unconditional faith that natural science is the supreme authority. In their estimation it is only the methods of natural science which can grasp reality, and whatever is not amenable to these methods should be treated as a pseudoproblem, and ultimately meaningless; they deny that ethical, aesthetic, and religious experience provide further sources of knowledge. Thus a decidedly antireligious position is typical of Russell and the dialectical materialists. For them, philosophy's only task is either to analyze the concepts of natural science or to synthesize its results, apart from which it means nothing. Although most followers of these schools cannot bring themselves to complete materialism, yet definite materialist tendencies are present in them all. Even the neopositivists will only take material phenomena into consideration; to discuss mental events is nonsense according to them. Finally all these thinkers are obviously rationalists in the sense that they place their faith in rational, analytic methods.

In order to fit the philosophic doctrines of Russell and the neopositivists into their historical context they will be introduced by a short account of British neorealism. Properly speaking this should be treated later, perhaps in conjunction with phenomenology, because it is one of the pioneering movements of the new period which have led to the construction of present-day metaphysics and mathematical logic. Particularly noteworthy is the fact that although the neorealist movement is very closely attached to scientific naturalism yet it has a much more general significance, since it leads some thinkers (Whitehead) to an almost Platonic view of the world.

5. Bertrand Russell

A. English Neorealism

The second half of the nineteenth century in England witnessed the appearance of a realist movement. It was rather weak and did not manage to form a school, nor to challenge the current predominance of Bradley's and Bosanquet's idealism. Yet it could claim some important representatives: Robert Adamson (1852-1902), for instance, who remained a Kantian but went over to critical realism toward the end of his life; George Dawes Hicks (1862-1941), whose doctrine of intentionality brought him near to Meinong and Husserl and who took up a stand half-way between idealism and neorealism; the critical realist Thomas Case (1844-1925), who thought he could argue from images to things themselves; and several others.

George Edward Moore (b. 1873) initiated the neorealist movement, publishing his famous article, *The Refutation of Idealism*, in 1903. Moore's influence upon contemporary English philosophy is so extensive that no one but Bergson or James can compare with him.

C. Lloyd Morgan (1852-1936), Alfred North Whitehead (1861-1947), Sir T. Percy Nunn (1870-1944), Bertrand Russell (b. 1873), Samuel Alexander (1859-1938), Charlie Dunbar Broad (b. 1887), John Laird (1887-1945) of the first generation; C. E. M. Joad (1891-1953), H. H. Price (b. 1899), A. C. Ewing (b. 1899), and Gilbert Ryle (b. 1900) of the second generation, are all indebted to Moore. Since Morgan, Alexander, Whitehead, and Laird each expound a metaphysics they must be discussed in another context. Of the other philosophers Russell is so much the most important both in his influence and his productivity that most of this section will describe his teaching, after a glance at the characteristics of neorealism.

Philosophy of Matter

B. COMMON CHARACTERISTICS OF NEOREALISM

As their name indicates the English neorealists stand in opposition to the idealists through adherence to realism and, generally, to direct realism; they consistently maintain that it is possible to apprehend immediately not merely mental images, but transsubjective reality. They have still further features in common, especially their unhesitating *empiricism*. They do not question that all our knowledge springs from experience and most of them consider that experience derives exclusively from the senses. The adoption of this axiom is strikingly widespread throughout the British tradition, which goes back to Locke, Berkeley, and Hume, and above all, perhaps, to Reid. Also the neorealists persistently gravitate toward the natural sciences, whose methods they nearly all regard as the truly philosophical ones. Their chief interests are physics and mathematics, and questions of theory have usually been primary for them. It is true that Moore has published an important work on morals, and Whitehead, like Russell, has occasionally given his attention to ethical and religious matters, but on the whole neorealists are interested in the purely theoretical questions of logic, epistemology, physics, or biology.

The most striking feature of the neorealists, however, is the way they are absorbed in investigating questions of detail. Their stand is, above all, antisystematic, and they attack all previous philosophical efforts with fierce, and frequently ungrounded, criticism. Even though some of them have themselves risen to systematic speculation in their later years, they have usually remained true to the "microscopic" method—the preference for particularizing problems and analyzing them. C. D. Broad is typical in this respect, but they all favor a similar procedure and often apply it with amazing thoroughness. The neorealist school is *the* analytic school.

C. BERTRAND RUSSELL'S PERSONALITY AND DEVELOPMENT

Bertrand Russell, born of an aristocratic English family, is incontestably one of the most read and discussed philosophers of the period between the two world wars. He has displayed an extraordinarily fruitful literary activity. His first publication in 1896 was followed by one and often two works, every year until 1947, in addition to countless articles in different journals. This multitude of publications reflect the many-sidedness of Russell's interests; there is no region of philosophy where he has not ventured. He has frequently espoused other causes, such as pacifism, in defense of which he was imprisoned for a time during the First World War. His works have achieved unusual popularity. For example, while no German translation existed of either Whitehead, Alexander, or Broad up to the Second World War, seventeen volumes of Russell had already been translated before 1935. Extremely clear and "scientific," Russell has been, and still is, *the* philosopher for a large circle who remain true to the positivist ideals of the nineteenth century. With his political and antireligious radicalism, set out in lucid language, he seems to be a kind of modern Voltaire—of smaller stature obviously. For all this Russell is to be distinguished from other popular authors of the same genre, such as Haeckel or even Voltaire, because he has not only influenced the general public but European philosophy through his specifically philosophical achievements which are anything but mere popularization.

Russell's views fall into two distinct categories, one of them deriving from his logic and his philosophy of mathematics, the other from his remaining theories. From the technical point of view the first of these is much the more important of the two. In this regard Russell has maintained for the most part the position he enunciated in 1903. The substantially condensed treatment which by necessity is given here allows to consider only Russell's general philosophical position. This is followed by a brief discussion of his logical and mathematical theories.

Two stages in his evolution may likewise be distinguished. Russell first was occupied with the study of mathematics, which seemed to him the model for philosophy. He spoke about mathematics with the enthusiasm of a Platonist; altogether, in those days, he was in fact a convinced Platonist. He was certain that besides empirical realities there do exist universals which we perceive directly and which have an existence of their own, independent of either things or minds. Philosophy he regarded at that time as a deductive science partially independent of sense experience. Out of this period comes his *Principia Mathematica,* one of the most influential works of European thought in the twentieth century.

Later, however, Russell gradually shifts his position. While his co-author on the giant work of the *Principia,* Whitehead, is drawn still deeper into metaphysics, Russell for his part turns to the positivists. The problem of universals seems pointless to him, metaphysics of any kind is nonsense, and philosophy is no longer deductive but empirically determined, in accordance with the traditional British interpretation. Even in mathematics he no longer discerns Platonic beauty, but simply a plain, practical, scientific instrument. In this stage of his thought Russell is a representative of scientism. He declares that the methods of natural science are the only ones which can provide us with knowledge; he believes in the perfection of mankind through technics, and speaks enthusiastically about progress. His realism is akin to Hume's, and a profound scepticism pervades his every thought process.

It must be observed that, despite his numerous publications upon the most various subjects and despite his great intellect,

Russell has never been able to construct a system, nor even to avoid contradictions. His intellectual position remains shifting and in constant flux.

D. CONCEPT OF PHILOSOPHY

The conception of philosophy at present defended by Russell is symptomatic of the whole neorealist school. In this respect, moreover, Russell himself is indebted to Moore. According to him philosophy must be essentially scientific; the questions which it posits must arise from the natural sciences and not from either religious or ethical codes; its ideal must be a scientific one. Ultimately its province is solely made up of those questions which cannot as yet be scientifically treated, and so it merely prepares the way for science. It must utterly rid itself of any "romanticism" or any "mysticism." Nor should one look to philosophy for a "cure from intellectual suffering"; instead, working patiently and dispassionately, one should plunge deeper into minute investigations.

Russell from the beginning did not believe that philosophy could give many definite answers. Since it is restricted to the prescientific region by its very nature, it must raise far more questions than it solves. Its main task is a critical one. The philosopher has to clarify the concepts, the constructions, and the verificatory methods of natural science, and so subject them to a thorough logical analysis. Moreover this procedure will act as a stimulus and at the same time will be more useful than eternally dubious answers. Later Russell was to become an avowed agnostic, convinced that only natural science can give information about reality and that for its own part it can only attain to probability. On these lines Russell is simply continuing the empiricist and positivist tradition, of Hume and Mill especially.

47

E. PLURALISM AND REALISM

One of the cornerstones of Russell's philosophy, as well as Moore's and most English neorealists, is his criticism of Bradley's teaching on internal relations. For Russell there are *no internal relations*, all existing relations being external ones added to the essence of the already existing thing—therefore the essence of this thing does not depend upon them in the least. Thus Russell rejects the fundamental maxim of Bradley's doctrine. Similarly he rejects Bradley's two main conclusions by advocating pluralism and by distinguishing object from subject. Pluralism is a primary feature of this whole philosophical movement; by it the world is thought to consist of many, possibly numberless, separate atoms held together through external relationships. Later Russell developed his pluralism into *logical atomism*, the doctrine that the world consists of sense-data which are bound to each other by purely logical relations. Also Hegelian idealism is decisively repudiated in favor of direct realism. Russell was led on to this pluralism through his preoccupation with Leibniz and his mathematical studies.

The impact of pluralism on epistemology has led to important philosophical consequences. Having disposed of objective idealism by their theory of external relations, Moore and Russell fiercely attack the subjective idealism of Berkeley and his disciples. From this idealism it follows that we can only know the contents of consciousness, that is ideas; the trans-subjective world escapes our knowledge. The neorealists now reject this theory as a clumsy paralogism; Berkeley obviously interchanges two meanings of the word "idea," by which either the act of knowing, or the thing known, may be signified. The thing known may not always need to exist in consciousness, it may exist outside consciousness and be different from the subject. In this way *direct realism* is established.

Matter for Russell, however, is not directly accessible to knowledge in spite of being real; we know only sense-data (as Moore also teaches). So the color of the table, its hardness, and the noise it emits when we strike it with our fist, are certainly realities, but are in no wise qualities of the table. This may be proved from the fact that different people experience different sense-data. The location of these sense-data is different according to the sense which perceives them and, *a fortiori*, according to the person perceiving them. The assumption that sense-data have a thing underlying them is a result of pure induction, and no direct proof of it can be given. Originally Russell asserted that the existence of such a thing must be recognized as the simplest explanation of sense-data, but later he changed his opinion and went over to the "atomist" theory, for which the world consists of sense-data logically linked to each other. It must be emphasized that this theory cannot be equated with classical phenomenalism in that it treats sense-data as non-mental realities independent of any subject—even from a transcendental or absolute subject. For Russell they are components of the real world, though in no way substances. This corresponds to Hume's teaching.

In his first period Russell also asserted that, besides the sensible apprehension of sense-data, there exists further a direct knowledge of *universals*. For example, we are not only acquainted with London and Edinburgh but also the relation (external!) between these two cities. This relation meanwhile is neither subjectively mental (since it exists whether we know it or not), nor is it a physical fact (since physical reality is composed exclusively of sense-data)—it is much more a kind of Platonic idea existing in its own right.

Russell develops this theory still further by defending the classical Platonic standpoint. But later he assumes an agnostic viewpoint akin to positivism.

F. PSYCHOLOGY

From the very beginning Russell doubts whether there is an immediate knowledge of the self, and is inclined to adopt Hume's attitude, in which the human soul is regarded simply as an association of ideas. In *The Analysis of Mind* Russell expressly sets forth this attitude and develops it in an original fashion; it involves neutrality toward materialism and idealism and proceeds toward the doctrine that there is *neither matter nor spirit* but only *sense-data,* which are differently constituted and controlled by different laws. The sense-data of different objects (e.g., stars), looked at from a single viewpoint, constitute the mind; the sense-data of different observers (e.g., the various aspects of the same star) constitute so-called matter. On the other hand mental and physical laws differ. Mental events are determined by "mnemonic determinism," which is apparently derived from the determinism of the nervous system; subjectivity is also a characteristic of mind and is materially explained as a concentration of sense-data in one spot (the brain). The circumstance that mental facts exist in consciousness is not enough to identify them as mental, says Russell, because they do not *always* exist in consciousness; nor can they be qualified by concepts such as habit, memory, or thought, because these are elaborations of mnemonic determinism.

Russell confesses his inclination toward materialism but the present condition of science and his own doctrine prevent him from accepting the materialistic teaching in its entirety. Nevertheless he maintains firmly that mental phenomena are utterly dependent upon physiological phenomena, and so denies, of course, the existence of a substantial soul. Yet mental events are more real to him than matter because the latter is not immediately given and is established by deduction and construction.

Man is but an insignificant part of nature; his thoughts are the result of events in his brain and of natural laws. Natural science, the unique source of knowledge, gives no support whatever for the belief in God or immortality. The doctrine of immortality is nonsense, moreover, because to be immortal the soul would have to occupy the whole of space. Religion is based on fear and is therefore an evil; it is the enemy of all that is good and decent in the modern world and is the symptom of immature man.

Man may be only an insignificant bit of nature in the order of existence yet he enjoys a completely different status in the order of values, which far transcends that of existence. We are free to create our life ideals, and Russell proposes as one such ideal, that of "the good life," a life of tender love guided by the light of *knowledge*. This ethical axiom is all we need. All theoretical morality is superfluous. To appreciate this, one has only to set oneself in the place of a mother with her sick child; what she needs is not a moralist but a good doctor. Certainly practical ethical rules are necessary but, unfortunately, rules nowadays frequently rest upon superstitious notions, as does the entire code of sexual morality (including monogamy) and of the treatment of criminals. Equally false is the ideal of individual salvation, an aristocratic notion, as opposed to the democratic ideal of social salvation. Happiness is the goal of our aspirations and it can be reached by subduing fear, by character-strengthening in education, and by perfecting the whole of mankind. Immense progress can be achieved so long as man does not remain in the grip of superstitious reverence for nature, because all nature, including even man's, has to become an object of scientific treatment if we are to attain happiness.

Philosophy of Matter

6. NEOPOSITIVISM

A. ANCESTRY AND CHIEF REPRESENTATIVES

At present the only genuinely new achievement of empiricism is found in the neopositivist school, springing from the classical positivism of Comte and Mill and echoing the British empiricism of the eighteenth century. Still, its immediate predecessor is German empiriocriticism. Through Joseph Petzoldt (1862-1929), a pupil of Avenarius, it acquired the direction of the periodical *Annalen der Philosophie* which gave birth to *Erkenntnis*, the most important journal of the neopositivist school between 1930 and 1938. Apart from empiriocriticism the weightiest influences upon neopositivism have been the French critique of science, Russell's teaching, and the developments in mathematical logic and recent physics (Einstein).

The school arose from a seminar of Moritz Schlick (1882-1936). Under the name "Vienna Circle" it sprang immediately into prominence with the publication of a manifesto *Wissenschaftliche Weltauffassung—Der Wiener Kreis* (1929). The next year, 1930, the periodical *Erkenntnis* began to appear, to be replaced after the political crisis in 1939 by the *Journal of Unified Science*, published in Chicago. A noteworthy succession of congresses took place; 1929 in Prague, 1930 in Königsberg, 1934 in Prague again, 1935 in Paris, 1936 in Copenhagen, 1937 in Paris once more, 1938 in Cambridge. This alone shows the energy of the new school and its truly international character. The most outstanding neopositivists sought refuge from Nazism in England and the United States. In the latter country they started an ambitious undertaking, the *International Encyclopedia of Unified Science*, and today they have great influence both in England and the United States. *Analysis*, the organ of a group akin to the neopositivists, has been appearing in England since 1933. The neopositivist school proved to be one of the strongest in 1934 at the Prague International Philosophical Congress. Since that date it has experienced a certain reverse on the Continent, but remains of first-rate importance and is reckoned even today as one of the leading schools of contemporary philosophy.

Its chief representatives are almost all German. Rudolf Carnap (b. 1891) who taught philosophy at Vienna, Prague, and Chicago, and now teaches at Los Angeles, deserves first mention. He seems to be the logician and, in a sense, the leader of the school. After him comes Hans Reichenbach (1891-1953), a professor at Berlin, Istanbul, and, finally, Los Angeles, who took part in the founding of the Vienna Circle and coöperated in the editing of *Erkenntnis*, but then abandoned orthodox neopositivism. Further representatives of the Vienna Circle worth remembering, in addition to Moritz Schlick (who was especially known for his writings on morality and was brutally murdered by a student) are Otto Neurath (1882-1945), who elaborated the idea of unified science and Hans Hahn (1880-1934). Various logicians, such as Alfred Tarski and Karl Popper, were closely related to this school.

Outside Germany neopositivism achieved major influence only in Great Britain. There it is even now the principal school. With it a number of philosophers are more or less closely associated, for example, the group which founded the journal *Analysis* in 1933: A. E. Duncan-Jones, C. A. Mace, L. Susan Stebbing among others, also Alfred J. Ayer, the most radical of the neopositivists, and above all Gilbert Ryle, who is probably the most influential English philosopher of the present time. There are a considerable number of more or less convinced positivists, such as John Wisdom in England, whose connection with the neopositivist school is looser. France has scarcely any distinguished representatives of neopositivism, but such as it has would include Louis Rougier, General Charles

Ernest Vouillemin (who attempts to publicize the work of the Vienna Circle), and Maurice Boll.

B. CHARACTERISTICS AND EVOLUTION

The neopositivists form a school in the proper sense, having a certain fundamental outlook in common and using the same methods of approach to their common problems. From the very beginning they exhibited unusual fervor and were profoundly convinced that their views were absolutely correct. One of their former leaders, Reichenbach, correctly points out that the school adopts a specifically religious, and even sectarian, attitude. On the other hand it must be admitted that few of their philosophical opponents know how to judge the neopositivist teaching with objective impartiality because, apart from anything else, this teaching is so revolutionary that it demands either unconditional adherence or frank opposition. Besides, the Vienna Circle was originally animated by an eager (even aggressive and polemical) proselytizing spirit.

Combined with this sectarian character is a strongly rationalist, logical, and analytical tendency so that from a formal viewpoint neopositivist writings resemble a new sort of scholasticism; at any rate, not since the Middle Ages have we seen such a belief in, and reverence for, logic. Again the neopositivist school upholds extreme scientism, much more so than either the neorealist or the dialectical materialists; it considers that the sole task of philosophy is to analyze the language of the natural sciences, which strictly determine its methodology.

Nevertheless certain changes in neopositivism may be discerned. Originally its representatives believed that the new logic afforded them a decisive weapon against all other philosophies. Later they found themselves unable to deal with the traditional problems of theoretical knowledge while relying exclusively upon the new logic—which other schools were also beginning to use. Finally a third phase, manifested, for example, in Reichenbach's teaching, is characterized by much greater tolerance and much less dogmatism than was exhibited in the early days of the Viennese school.

C. LUDWIG WITTGENSTEIN

The main lines of neopositivism were already drawn in his work *Logisch-philosophische Abhandlung* (translated as *Tractatus Logico-Philosophicus*) (1921) by Ludwig Wittgenstein, Russell's pupil and friend, who also taught at Cambridge. In this very difficult work composed of numbered aphorisms, Wittgenstein sets out from Russell's logical atomism, according to which the world is made up of facts absolutely independent of each other. Our knowledge is a copy of these concrete facts. Without exception universal statements are "truth functions" of singular propositions; that is to say, they are constructed from the latter by means of logical relations. For example the statement, "Every man is mortal," has the same meaning as the proposition, "Peter is mortal and John is mortal, etc." Logic is of a purely tautological character, it affirms nothing; *logical propositions are empty* and provide us with no information about reality. Reality must be investigated by natural science; philosophy cannot be a doctrine but only an activity.

Wittgenstein has also a theory of language according to which one cannot speak meaningfully about language, and therefore a logical analysis of grammar becomes impossible. But because all philosophical questions are ultimately reducible to this analysis they posit insoluble pseudoproblems. Wittgenstein concludes his puzzling book with the statement that his own work has no sense, and, "Whereof one cannot speak, thereof one must be silent."

55

D. LOGIC AND EXPERIENCE

Proceeding on the basis of Wittgenstein's ideas the neopositivists developed a very technical theory whose main thesis can be summed up by saying that there is but one source of knowledge, namely sensation, which can only grasp singular and material events. This is clearly the classical empiricist position, but beyond this neopositivism departs widely from empiricism and classical positivism. The empiricists maintained that logic itself is *a posteriori*, and consists in generalizations from observed singular facts. Kant held the contrary opinion, that there are laws established *a priori* (independently of experience) and yet synthetic (not tautological). The neopositivists take an intermediate position. According to them the laws of logic are *a priori*, independent of experience, but at the same time they are purely *tautological*, expressing nothing. They afford nothing but grammatical rules calculated to render the data of sense experience more manageable. Thus logic is derived from *syntactical rules* by means of axioms which are established arbitrarily. Once the axioms and the laws of derivation are admitted, the consequences must obviously be conceded, but such logic is based upon pure supposition.

In contrast to Wittgenstein, Carnap supports the theory that one can discuss language but that one requires another language, a metalanguage, in order to do so. Philosophy consists of metalogical analysis. It works out a system of signs to signify the words of scientific language, and so it becomes capable of analyzing the expressions of natural science. *Philosophy is the study of the logical syntax* of scientific statements.

E. THE MEANING OF A STATEMENT

To this doctrine must be added another one which has made the school famous—the doctrine of verification. For the neopositivists, the meaning of a statement lies in the method of its verification, or, following a more moderate formula, "a statement has meaning if, and only if, it is verifiable."

In fact, say the neopositivists, one can only know the meaning of a statement if one knows under what conditions it is false or true; this means that the verificatory method must always be given along with the meaning, and vice versa; and so, by the Leibnizian axiom of the identity of indiscernibles, they come to the same thing.

This is already an overwhelmingly revolutionary position but becomes genuinely paradoxical through a further assertion which is essential for neopositivist doctrine; verification must always be *intersubjective*, that is, it must be susceptible to being carried out by at least two observers. If it is not, then the truth of a statement cannot be tested and the statement is not a scientific one. But since every intersubjective verification is made by the senses, no statements can be verified other than those relating to the body and its movements; all statements of introspective psychology and classical philosophy are unverifiable, therefore meaningless. It follows that the sole meaningful language is that of physics (*physicalism*), and that all science should be unified (unified language and unified science).

One condition remains to be fulfilled for a statement to have meaning: it must be built in accordance with the syntactical rules of language. It is meaningful to say, "the horse eats," but "the eats eats" has no meaning. Classical philosophy violates not only the fundamental axiom of intersubjectivity but often syntax itself. A host of words used by the existentialists thus appear meaningless. Heidegger's "Das Nichts nichtet" is a classical example of this. "Das Nichts" (nothing) has the form of a substantive, it is true, but is not a substantive in the logical sense—it is the sign of negation and cannot assume the function of a subject.

57

Starting from these axioms the neopositivists have eagerly delved into the pseudoproblems of philosophy. Carnap distinguished several functions of language; it can either make an assertion, or it can simply give expression to wishes and feelings. Classical philosophers have interchanged these two meanings of expression; their philosophical statements apparently give expression to feelings, but they assert nothing. Their problems, such as realism or God's existence, are pseudoproblems and trying to solve them is simply a waste of time. Philosophy must confine itself to analyzing scientific language by logical methods.

F. PROTOCOL SENTENCES

The neopositivists have attempted to discover the purely empirical foundations of science relieved of all logical constructions. They regard science as a structure of logically ordered sentences. It is necessary to start with certain fundamental sentences to which Carnap gives the name "protocol sentences" (*Protokollsätze*) because they are found in the protocol of the laboratory or observatory. In their pure form they would run, "X at a certain time T, observed the phenomenon P, at location L."

This doctrine, however, involves great difficulties of various kinds. On the one hand, it may be pointed out, one protocol-sentence can be called into question and tested by another protocol-sentence. For example, the sanity of the physicist can be called into question and examined by the psychiatrist—and so on, to infinity. Great dissension arose throughout the school on account of these difficulties, but without tangible results, as one may easily imagine, because the only logical result would have been radical scepticism.

On the other hand, it has been justifiably asked, what is the basis of the protocol-sentence itself? True to their empiriocritical lineage the neopositivists reply that the object of experience can only be sensations—we cannot jump out of our skins and grasp reality. Questions about reality are pseudoproblems, because we never encounter anything but sensations and we can never verify the existence of things that are other than our sensations.

G. HANS REICHENBACH

Hans Reichenbach denies these conclusions. According to him, Carnap and the other neopositivists have made the mistake of looking for absolute certainty where there can only be probability; and so the principle of verifiability has to be altered if we are to make probability fundamental. Reichenbach distinguishes four levels of verifiability, the *technical* (which is possible in the conditions of present-day technique), the *physical* (not contradicting the laws of nature), the *logical* (not self-contradictory) and, lastly, the *superempirical*. Which of these levels is chosen for the definition of verifiability is simply a question of convenience, and Reichenbach himself considers that an intermediate one between the physical and the logical is most useful for science. Therefore Reichenbach defines "meaning" by saying that a statement has a meaning if its degree of probability can be determined (its probability verified). He shows further that by this supposition the realistic hypothesis (that there are things and not merely sensations) is more than meaningful—it is both more probable and more useful than the hypothesis of the classical neopositivists.

Neopositivist tendencies have received their most noteworthy formulation in Reichenbach's work, but most neopositivists disapprove of it and in their turn find themselves violently attacked by Reichenbach. He has applied his doctrine to different provinces of philosophy in a most interesting fashion, but these analyses can not be pursued here.

59

H. ANALYTICAL PHILOSOPHY

Since the war the doctrines of this group of philosophers have developed still further in the direction pioneered by Reichenbach. Nowadays one speaks of "analytical philosophy," which has evolved from Moore and from neopositivism. Several positions within this general approach can be distinguished. (1) In line with the most recent phases of Rudolf Carnap's thought, his followers seek exact definitions of the fundamental concepts of the sciences within the framework of an ideal formalized language. (2) The school of G. E. Moore, on the other hand, takes "ordinary language" as its foundation and maintains that the first requirement of a scientifically correct analysis is its correspondence with common sense. (3) The therapeutic Wittgensteinians regard philosophy as a kind of logical cure for pseudoproblems which is to be conducted in rigorous neopositivist fashion. (4) The *dialecticians*. (See below, pp. 61 ff.) (5) In addition there must be numbered among analytical philosophers those who proceed in quite independent fashion or represent viewpoints quite different from positivism and who are occupied with exact and minute analysis of the concepts and procedures of science and philosophy especially with the help of mathematical logic. But the latter, and also the dialecticians, can no longer be regarded as representatives of the philosophy of matter. Only in the similarity of their methods can they be assimilated to the analytical philosophers.

Newer developments, almost wholly in the United States, have led to the weakening of the verifiability principle, of phenomenalism, of nominalism, and even of physicalism. The whole movement has come perceptibly closer to pragmatism.

7. DIALECTICAL MATERIALISM

A. CHARACTERISTICS

Dialectical materialism occupies a place all its own in European philosophy. First of all it has very few exponents in academic circles outside Russia and its satellites, where, by contrast, it is established as the official philosophy and consequently has privileges such as are enjoyed by no other contemporary school. Besides, it is unique as the philosophy of a political party—the Communists; on this account it is closely linked to the economic and political theories as well as to the practical activity of that party, for which it is the "general theory." In Russia where the Communist party is in control, no one is permitted to teach any other philosophy than dialectical materialism, and even the exposition of its own classical philosophical texts is strictly supervised. This supervision—in combination, it is true, with the Russian national character— explains some of the odd features of dialectical-materialist publications; the latter are strikingly different from all others through their complete uniformity. All of their authors say exactly the same thing and make innumerable quotations from the classical authors, who are made to yield arguments for current theses at every turn. Perhaps this supervision is to be blamed also for the mediocrity of the philosophers in this school; it is in any case responsible for the extreme dogmatism, chauvinism, and aggressiveness of dialectical materialists.

Even more significant, however, than these peculiarities, which could be accidental, is the reactionary character of dialectical materialism, for this philosophy leads straight back to the mid-nineteenth century and seeks to restore the intellectual situation of that time without the slightest alteration.

61

Philosophy of Matter

B. ORIGIN AND REPRESENTATIVES

The Russians regard as the founder of dialectical materialism Karl Marx (1818-1883), the famous economist, with whom Friedrich Engels (1820-1895) worked in close coöperation. Marx belonged to the Hegelian school, which had split into a "left" and a "right" by the time he was studying at the University of Berlin (1837-1841). A prominent representative of the "left" was Ludwig Feuerbach (1804-1872) who interpreted the Hegelian system in a materialist sense and treated world history as the unfolding of matter and not of spirit. Marx firmly supported Feuerbach but simultaneously came under the influence of the scientific materialism which was spreading at the time; this explains his enthusiasm for science, his profound and ingenuous belief in progress, and his prejudice in favor of Darwinian evolutionism. In founding dialectical materialism he linked the Hegelian dialectic to the materialism of his day. Marx himself was chiefly a political economist, sociologist, and social philosopher. He is the founder of *historical* materialism while the general philosophical foundation of the system, which is *dialectical* materialism, is essentially the work of Engels. Dialectical materialism constitutes a link between the Hegelian dialectic and nineteenth-century materialism.

Vladimir Ilich Ulyanov (Nikolai Lenin, 1870-1924) subsequently thought out the doctrines of Marx and Engels afresh, then expounded them and prescribed them for the Communist party. He departed little from Engels' doctrine but developed it further by anathematizing its mechanistic and empiriocritical interpretations. His coöperator and successor as party leader, Iosif Vissarionovich Dzhugashvili (Joseph Stalin, 1879-1953) systematized Marx's teaching along the lines developed by Lenin. And so a philosophy was built up named "Marxism-

Leninism-Stalinism"[3] which in Russia is regarded as an indivisible whole. It is publicized in the form of encyclopedias, middle-sized volumes, and little catechisms, and is a compulsory subject in Soviet higher schools. But the authors of these handbooks scarcely merit consideration because, as we have pointed out, they merely repeat Lenin's and Stalin's exposition.

C. DEVELOPMENTS IN RUSSIA

Discussion of philosophy in the Soviet Union is in order here since Soviet Russian philosophy is identical with dialectical materialism, and its western European counterparts have significance only so far as they accord with Russian philosophy. The reason for this is the fact that the extension of the influence of dialectical materialism is channeled almost exclusively through the Communist party which is strongly centralized and tolerates only that philosophy which satisfies Russian norms.

There are four periods in the history of Soviet Russian philosophy. (1) After the brief war period from 1917 to 1921 when there was still freedom, relatively speaking, all non-Marxist philosophy was banned or liquidated in Russia. (2) From 1922 to 1930 there was sharp conflict between the so-called "mechanistic" and "Menshevistic-idealistic" schools. The former interpreted dialectical materialism as pure materialism, while the latter, under the leadership of G. A. Deborin wanted to hold both elements in equilibrium. (3) On January 15, 1931 both schools were condemned by the Central Committee of the Communist party. Thus began a third period, from 1931 to 1946, during which, apart from Stalin's essay of 1938, philosophy seemed to be practically extinct in Russia. Philosophers published no more than commentaries and popularized works. (4) The fourth period is ushered in by A. A. Zhdanov's ad-

---

[3] There are other interpretations of Marxist teachings but they are much less significant and cannot be considered here.

63

Philosophy of Matter

dress of June 24, 1947, presented at the request of Stalin and the Central Committee. Zhdanov attacked one of the leading Russian philosophers, G. F. Alexandrov, and called for more active and systematic effort by all Russian philosophers. In 1950 there were several conflicts over the interpretation of the "classics" in reference to certain technical fields about which Stalin's essay had afforded no guidance. Here we may note the attack on the *Logic* of W. F. Asmus as "apolitical" and "objectivistic," the recantation by B. M. Kedrov of his effort of 1949 to stem the unrestrained tide of nationalism, the attack of N. Rubenstein's *General Psychology* in 1950, and the extended discussion of M. A. Markov's *The Nature of Physical Knowledge* (1947) which was condemned as unorthodox by A. A. Maximov the following year.

There is a parallel development in psychology. While at an earlier time the very term "psychology" was regarded as unorthodox and the effort was made to replace it by "theory of response" (*Reaktologie*) or some similar term, psychology, like logic, has latterly been tolerated as a legitimate branch of study. In all these controversies, including the well-known one about genetics in 1948, the most fateful role was played by M. B. Mitin. He represented the views of the government and took part in all proceedings against colleagues who were too independent in their thinking. Mitin ranks as the most outstanding representative of contemporary dialectical materialism.

All these controversies have occurred entirely within the framework of dialectical materialism and do not touch the principal doctrines of the system as laid down by Stalin. Each antagonist seeks to demonstrate his opponent's defection from the Marx-Engels-Lenin-Stalin line. It is noteworthy that there is very little appeal made to Marx and much more to Engels and Lenin.

D. MATERIALISM

According to materialism the only real world is the material world, and the mind is simply the product of a material organ, the brain. The contrast between matter and consciousness has no value except for epistemology; really there is only matter. The dialectical materialists certainly criticize the older materialist schools, yet this criticism is not aimed against materialism as such, but exclusively at the lack of a dialectical element, and of a "correct" conception of evolution.

The import of dialectical materialism depends, naturally, upon the meaning one gives to the word "matter." In this respect certain difficulties are caused by Lenin's definition, for according to him matter is simply a "philosophical category serving to indicate objective reality"; and in his epistemology matter is throughout opposed to consciousness by equating "matter" and "objective reality." Still, we are not left in the dark upon this point, because in other places the dialectical materialists maintain that we can know matter by means of the senses, that matter underlies causal and deterministic laws, and that it is opposite to consciousness; briefly, it is clear that the usage of the word "matter" by the dialectical materialists differs in no way from the popular one. Dialectical materialism is classical and radical materialism.

Yet this materialism is not mechanical. According to the accepted teaching, only inorganic matter is subject to mechanical laws and not living matter, although the latter is certainly governed by the laws of causal determinism. Even in physics the dialectical materialists do not defend unconditional atomism.

E. DIALECTICAL EVOLUTION; MONISM AND DETERMINISM

Matter is in continuous evolution toward the formulation of ever more complex beings—atoms, molecules, living cells,

65

plants, men, society. Thus evolution is not regarded as cyclic but as linear. Besides, evolution is regarded optimistically—the latest stage is always the most complex, which in its turn is equated with the best and the noblest. The dialectical materialists still retain a thoroughly nineteenth-century belief in progress through evolution.

According to them this evolution consists in a series of revolutions—small quantitative alterations in the essence of a thing pile up, tension is produced, and a struggle takes place until at a fixed moment the new elements become strong enough to destroy the equilibrium and a new quality emerges from the previous quantitive alterations. Conflict therefore exemplifies the driving force of evolution which proceeds by leaps—this is the so-called "dialectical evolution."

The entire course of evolution is aimless, being achieved as a result of encounters and combats under the impact of purely causal factors. Strictly speaking, the world has neither a meaning nor a goal and evolves blindly in accordance with eternal, deterministic laws.

There is nothing permanent; the whole world and all its elements are swept along by the dialectical evolution; in every place and at all times the old dies and the new comes to birth; there are neither permanent substances nor "eternal principles." Only matter and the laws of its change exist externally amid universal movement.

The world must be conceived as a unified whole. In contrast to metaphysics which (say the Marxists) sees the world as a host of disconnected entities, the dialectical materialists are representative of monism in a twofold sense. They see the world as the unique reality (outside of it there is nothing, and, in particular, there is no God), and they see its principle as homogeneous (dualism and pluralism of any sort are rejected as false).

66

The laws which govern this world are deterministic in the classical sense of the word. It is true that the dialectical materialists do not, for various reasons, wish to be classified as "determinists," and for this reason teach that a plant's growth, for instance, is not entirely determined by the laws of this plant because an external factor, such as hail, can render them inoperative. But in relation to the whole of things the dialectical materialists firmly rule out accidents—the world's laws in their totality determine the entire process of the universe without exception.

F. PSYCHOLOGY

Mind, or consciousness, is nothing but an epiphenomenon, a "copy, a reflection, a photograph" of matter (Lenin). Consciousness cannot exist without the body and is a product of the brain. Matter is the primary datum, and consciousness (or mind) is secondary; consequently consciousness is not the determinant of matter but, vice versa, matter of consciousness. Psychology is thus materialistic and determinist.

Nevertheless, this determinism is subtler than the earlier materialist version. For one thing the dialectical materialists do not wish to be out-and-out determinists, as we saw in relation to chance. Freedom, to them, consists in the possibility of deriving benefit from the laws of nature; even man, of course, is subject to these laws but he is aware of the fact and his *freedom* lies in the simple *awareness of necessity* (as with Hegel). Furthermore, they maintain, matter does not determine consciousness directly but works through the medium of society.

Thus man is essentially social, unable to live without society; only in society can he produce the necessities of life. But the means and methods for such production first of all determine interpersonal relationships and these in turn determine man's consciousness. This is the theme of *historical materialism;*

everything that a man thinks, wishes, or wills is in the final analysis a consequence of his social needs, just as they in turn result from methods of production and the social relationships created by this production.

These methods and relationships are continually changing and thereby society becomes subject to the law of dialectical evolution which comes to light in the class struggle. The total content of human consciousness is determined by society and changes along with social progress.

G. EPISTEMOLOGY

Since matter determines consciousness, knowledge must be conceived in a realistic fashion; the subject does not create the object, for the object exists independently of the subject; knowledge results from the fact that copies, reflections, or photographs of matter are present in the mind. The world is not unknowable but is thoroughly knowable. Naturally the true method of knowing consists solely in science combined with technical practice; technical progress shows well enough the degeneracy of all agnosticism. Though knowledge is essentially sense knowledge, rational thought is necessary to organize these experiential data. Positivism is "bourgeois charlatanry" and "idealism," because we do actually grasp the essences of things through phenomena.

So far Marxist epistemology sets itself up as absolute naïve realism of the usual empiricist type. The peculiarity of Marxist materialism lies in the fact that it combines this realistic outlook with another one, the pragmatic. From the notion that all contents of our consciousness are determined by our economic needs it follows equally that each social class has its own science and its own philosophy. An independent, nonparty science is impossible: the truth is whatever leads to success, and practice alone constitutes the criterion of truth.

68

Both these theories of knowledge are found side by side in Marxism without anyone trying very hard to harmonize them. The most they will concede is that our knowledge is a striving for the absolute truth, but that for the moment it is simply relative, answering to our needs. Here the theory seems to fall into contradiction, for if the truth were relative to our needs then knowledge could never be a copy of reality—not even a partial copy.

H. VALUES

According to historical materialism all contents of consciousness are the result of economic needs which, in turn, are continuously changing. This applies particularly to morality, aesthetics, and religion.

In regard to morality historical materialism recognizes no eternal code whatever and teaches that each social class has its own morality. The highest moral rule for the proletariat—the most progressive class—is that only that is morally good which contributes to the destruction of bourgeois society.

In aesthetics things are more complicated. It must readily be admitted that in reality, in things themselves, there exists an objective element which acts as the ground of our aesthetic appreciation and permits us to see things as either beautiful or ugly. But on the other hand this appreciation also depends upon evolution; each class having its own special needs, each has its own scale of values. Consequently art should not be cut off from life but must portray the heroic efforts of the proletariat in its fight to establish a socialist world (socialist realism).

Finally, a very different temper prevails in its theory about religion. Dialectical materialism treats religion as a conglomeration of false and fantastic statements which science has condemned, and science alone is the way to knowledge. Religion originates in fear; in their powerlessness before nature, and later before their exploiters, men have defied these powers and petitioned them, finding in religion and otherworldly beliefs a consolation which their exploited and slavish existence could not afford them. However, the exploiters (feudalists, capitalists, etc.) regard religion as a superb means of keeping the masses under their yoke; firstly, it makes them obedient to their exploiters and, secondly, it prevents the proletariat from revolting through promising them a better lot after death. The proletariat exploits no one, and so needs no religion. While morality and aesthetics are only subject to change, religion must vanish completely.

CONCLUDING CRITICISMS

At the basis of all the described systems lies an intuition, an awful realization of the overwhelming size of the universe, in which man seems an insignificant speck abandoned to the indifferent, or even hostile, cosmos. It is understandable that this fundamentally materialist intuition should be combined with an heroic romantic attitude. Lost in the boundless universe man has to assert himself by his own strength, through his own science, and this occasions the cult of science and technics and the enthronement of human reason.

Although this intuition is shared by all empiricists, their individual systems differ so widely that their movement is generally difficult to characterize. The majority of its representatives extol the objectivity and comparative power of human knowledge. On the whole, though some are less emphatic than others, they assert that mind does not create the world, that the world exists independently of consciousness and that a comprehensive knowledge of the world is possible. By advocating these conceptions, they deserve credit for opposing the threat to Western culture from deadly irrationalism and subjectivism. Many of the thinkers spoken of—above all the analytical phi-

70

losophers—have rendered great service to the progress of logic and the methodology of natural science.

Nevertheless, the negative aspects of the systems are yet more obvious. (1) They are all inclined to return to a position which the intellectual life of Europe has long since superseded, and so they constitute the reactionary philosophy of our day, which is particularly true of dialectical materialism. (2) On the side of theory they are extremely weak. Not to speak of the almost pre-Socratic level to which dialectical materialism frequently restricts itself, even neopositivism relies upon a primitive ontology and upon dogmatic presuppositions which its representatives never reëxamine. The one-sidedness of these systems is stupendous. (3) But most important of all, none of these philosophical systems have any answer to the great human problems with which contemporary thought is wrestling. In the face of suffering, morality, and religion, they usually content themselves with declaring that these do not offer problems, or even, that it would be nonsense to pose such problems. On account of their reactionary tendency, their theoretical weakness, and their failure before the great questions of human destiny, these philosophies are the least valuable in contemporary thought—with the exception of the purely methodological results of the analytical philosophers. Taken as a whole, contemporary philosophy has rendered obsolete not only their conclusions but even their way of formulating the problems.

τὸ γὰρ αὐτὸ νοεῖν ἐστίν τε καὶ εἶναι.

PARMENIDES

III

Philosophy of the Idea

As pointed out, idealism constitutes the second philosophical stream which carries typically nineteenth-century thought into the twentieth century. Despite the great power which it showed during the first quarter of the twentieth century its influence at the present day has waned so much that it has less energy than empiricism and is to be regarded as the weakest movement of contemporary thought. In England, for instance, it is almost nonexistent; in Germany, where about 1920 the Neo-Kantian schools were still flourishing, they are today only of second-rate importance; idealism has had no outstanding representative in France since the death of Brunschvicg; even in Italy, where the brilliant schools under Croce and Gentile held the field for a generation, idealist thought appears to be a thing of the past. But its influence was once really great and is still effective in many forms, for example, in Jaspers and certain Thomists; and so at least a brief account of some representative figures is necessary. Our selection includes Benedetto Croce, Léon Brunschvicg, and some German Neo-Kantians. They constitute an ascending series—Croce being nearest to positivism, and certain Neo-Kantians approaching the threshold of phenomenology. The differences between them are considerable. Croce is fundamentally Hegelian, Brunschvicg very subjectivist, while the Neo-Kantians' devotion to Kant still does not prevent serious dissension among themselves. One feature they share: they are all idealists—objective idealists—in their theories of knowledge, that is, they regard the whole of reality as immanent in the objective spirit, whose appearances include both nature and the human soul, or may even be identical with both of them.

8. BENEDETTO CROCE

A. ITALIAN PHILOSOPHY AND CROCE'S POSITION

The picture of Italian philosophy at the end of the nineteenth century is not essentially different from the general picture of philosophy in other European countries at that time. It is true that Carlo Catteneo (1801-1869), Giuseppe Ferrari (1812-1876), and Enrico Morselli (1852-1929) staunchly upheld positivism, which found such an influential spokesman in Roberto Ardigo (1828-1920) as to become the predominant force in Italian intellectual life. But next to it came idealism, which Augusto Vera (1813-1885) and, even more so, Bertrando Spaventa (1817-1883) brought into relationship both with Hegelianism and with the historicism of the Italian Renaissance. There were also a number of Neo-Kantians, among whom Alfonso Testa (1784-1860) stood out; he was the inspiration of Alessandro Chiapelli (1857-1932) of Croce's generation. Idealism in the broad sense was represented by

Bernardino Varisco (1850-1933). Yet it was positivism that held sway at the end of the nineteenth century, not only among philosophers but among cultured Italian circles in general.

The change in the intellectual situation was effected primarily by Benedetto Croce. As a pupil of Spaventa he came into contact with Hegelianism, but while he adopted its most essential theses he gave it a personal interpretation. Furthermore Croce underwent powerful positivist, and even pragmatist, influences. In his youth he had become absorbed in Marxist teaching under the direction of A. Labriola (1843-1903) while at the same time he brought the long-forgotten Giovanni Battista Vico (1668-1744) back to fame and studied the latter's historicism along with similar currents in the latest German philosophy. Yet Croce integrated all these varied influences into a powerful synthesis eloquently and persuasively elaborated.

B. LIFE, WORK, CHARACTERISTICS

Benedetto Croce (1866-1953) was born at Pescasseroli (in the Abruzzi) and spent all his life in Italy. He was twice Minister of Education, the second time in the liberation government. He remained faithful to his liberal and democratic convictions unlike his friend Giovanni Gentile (1875-1944) the other prominent Italian idealist, who entered the service of Fascism and was shot by the patriots. The year 1903 marks the most important date in Croce's life for it was then that the first issue of his periodical, *La Critica*, appeared, for which he himself wrote most of the articles. This periodical exercised a decisive influence upon Italian intellectual life, not confining itself to philosophy but broaching questions of universal history, the history of art, literary criticism, and even politics. Croce has an unusually catholic mind and has enriched all of these subjects with a wealth of original ideas. Yet it is not unjustifiable to say that Croce is really much more a historian of art and literary critic than a philosopher. In spite of this his great quadrilogy (published between 1902 and 1917, under the title *Filosofia dello Spirito*) containing an Aesthetic, a Logic, a Practical Philosophy, and a Philosophy of History, has strongly influenced not only the whole of Italian philosophy, but the whole of European philosophy as well. A symptom of this is the fact that the *Breviario di Estetica* (1913) has been translated into English, French, German, Spanish, Hungarian, and Czech, and is among the most famous works on aesthetics; while the *Filosofia della Pratica* has even a Japanese version.

Croce writes in a very clear, but very sweeping style. On this account he is frequently suspected of being so concerned to express himself in beautiful language that he leaves little room for the scientific qualities which specifically philosophical work requires. For example, in contrast to the German Neo-Kantians, Croce's definitions are usually imprecise, his arguments frequently obscure and supported by mere assertions containing violent abuse of his opponents. Once these limitations are conceded it must be recognized that Croce's work opens up a wealth of problems and contains many original and interesting solutions. For all his literary polish, and in spite of his inexact formulae, he exhibits a fundamentally consistent train of thought and provides a genuine synthesis of Hegelian idealism, historicism, and positivism. Though his philosophy no longer occupies the predominant position even in Italy, his work will certainly go down as one of the classics of twentieth-century idealism.

C. MAIN THESES

Croce's system has its logical foundation in his unmistakable conceptualism and his theory of a dialectical *a priori* synthesis.

Philosophy of the Idea

According to Croce's *conceptualism* (though he does not describe it by this name) there are two, and only two, ways of knowing—the intuitive, or aesthetic, and the conceptual, or logical. The first pertains to the senses and has the singular—the individual thing—as its object, the second is rational and refers to universals. In a remarkable series of arguments Croce attacks and condemns the positivists' nominalism, which would confine knowledge to sensation. Yet he himself admits only universal concepts as relational; the intellect can have no grasp of a thing's content, but seizes exclusively upon the relations between things, which are for their part sensuous intuitions. In other words, exactly as in Kant, there is no intellectual intuition, and the intellect's sole function is to link sensuous intuitions together; the world has no intelligible content. Croce's very radical conceptualism is therefore laid bare.

Croce's *dialectic* teaches principally, that there is nothing fixed and permanent in the world, which is simply an eternal stream of events. It teaches next that this process culminates in a synthesis—not a synthesis of opposites (as in Hegel) but of differences which retain their characteristics in the synthesis. Thirdly, the process (*svolgimento*) is not linear but circular, because every determinant is also in its turn determined. Lastly, the cosmic process is simply the manifold appearance of a unique reality, the spirit. These fundamental concepts obviously correspond to Hegelian doctrine with mere alteration in details.

Spirit differentiates itself in numerous ways. The basic division is between its *theoretical* and its *practical* activity, which again divide themselves according to whether they have a singular or a universal object. Within theoretical activity comes *aesthetic* activity which refers to singulars, and *logical* which refers to universals; within practical activity is found *economic* activity concerned with individual aims and *moral*, determined by the general good. Therefore philosophy, despite being the science of the one reality (that is, of spirit), must be arranged in sections to correspond with these four modes of its appearance.

D. THE AESTHETIC SYNTHESIS

Aesthetics is the science of sensuous intuition. As such it conditions logic, without itself being directly conditioned by logic, because there are no concepts without intuition, whereas there are intuitions without concepts. One symptom of aesthetic intuition is that it cannot be separated from expression—intuition instantly provokes creative expression. Thus no essential difference exists between the artist's aesthetic activity and that of the nonartist. However, Croce in his *Breviary of Aesthetic* does indicate a certain shade of difference with his thesis that art is a twofold *a priori* synthesis; firstly, it is a synthesis (and not merely a conglomeration) of intuitive images; it is equally a synthesis of image and sensation. Art is a lyrical intuition in the sense that it is synthetic and organic.

Croce's aesthetic constitutes the most original section of his work, along with his philosophy of history, and contains a host of interesting observations and daring theses. Here it must be sufficient to point out that art, for Croce, is not a physical fact (because art is a reality whereas physical facts are mere mental constructions)—that it is not a practical activity, as such, and is entirely alogical. Art is a unity or, more precisely, a manifold *a priori* synthesis of form and content, of intuition and expression, of expression and beauty. It is a perfect whole and the divisions into individual arts or individual artistic and literary genres are quite arbitrary.

E. THE LOGICAL SYNTHESIS

Logic provides a synthesis of a superior order. For Croce (as for idealists in general) the concept in a logical process is

77

identical with the judgment, and with a synthesis of subject and predicate. But as its mode of expression does not always make this clear, formal logic (more exactly 'formalistic logic') must be abandoned because it has been identified with modes of expression, from Aristotle's day until the age of logistic. Judgments which are freed from verbal form may be split into two types—definitional judgments, in which subject and predicate are universal concepts, and perceptual judgments (historical judgments) by which a universal predicate is attached to an individual. Only the latter is a genuine judgment. Yet if one looks more closely one realizes that not all elements in a definitional judgment are universal, for the simple reason that this judgment is always provoked by a historical investigation or question, and so is bound to the concrete. One sees, therefore, that a judgment, by its very nature, is a logical *a priori* synthesis of universal and singular, of concept and intuition. This synthesis remains obscure, unless one recognizes that the two elements constituting it are but two manifestations of one and the same spirit which, although clearly different, are not opposites. Aesthetic and logic are merely two forms of the dialectical evolution of one and the same reality. Furthermore, as in Hegel, since the whole of reality is spiritual the real is identical with the rational.

Logic is the critique of the natural sciences. From this emerges the logical assertion that the so-called concepts of these disciplines are plainly *pseudoconcepts*, and of two kinds. The first kind, empirical pseudoconcepts (such as the pseudoconcept of the cat), are only empirical approximations, while the second kind, abstract pseudoconcepts (such as the pseudoconcept of the triangle) have no content. Since the natural sciences, (and even mathematics) have no truly universal concepts at their command and rest entirely upon arbitrary conventions, they are nothing but pseudosciences. In this respect,

Croce is a representative of a most radical positivism and pragmatism. According to him, it is true, the natural sciences are not subordinated exclusively to practical ends, but their activity places them in the province of practice and not of theory.

No more is to be hoped from metaphysics and religion as means of real knowledge than from the natural sciences. Metaphysics is plainly impossible because we have no intellectual intuition (Kant); Religion, which is nothing but myth, is simply a false philosophy. Among all contemporary idealists, Croce is perhaps the one who shows least sympathy for religion. The only science worthy of this name, he says, is the philosophy of the spirit. Yet the natural sciences, metaphysics, and religion do interest him so far as they are real manifestations, or 'moments' of the spirit and have to be treated as the steps by which the spirit ascends toward philosophy.

F. THE PRACTICAL SYNTHESIS

Besides the theoretical activity proper to the spirit there is a practical activity further divided into the *economic* and the *moral*. The former corresponds in the domain of practice to aesthetic intuition in the theoretical domain, and is determined by the individual; it aims at whatever is useful, including politics and economics in the current meaning of these terms. Moral activity is distinguished from it by directing the spirit toward the universal, or the whole. After making penetrating criticisms of them, Croce rejects hedonistic, utilitarian, and similar doctrines because they provide no basis for that moral activity without which life becomes a disconnected series of single actions devoid of deeper meaning. Similarly Croce will have nothing to do with the doctrine that economic activity should be repudiated or should be reduced to the moral type; far from it, for economic activity is independent of moral activity while the latter is inconceivable without the former,

79

just as aesthetics is independent of logic although the latter itself depends on sensuous intuition. It is impossible to apply moral judgments to the practical man, who acts from the point of view of the useful as such; for such a judgment is obviously impossible from any other point of view but the moral one. There is, however, no opposition between the economic and the moral from the latter angle because they are combined in a higher synthesis. Moral man, that is, man as he is ordered toward a universal and spiritual end, does not in the least cease to be motivated by the useful, to tend toward joy, for example, which, by the way, coincides with this very activity. Moral and economic activity, then, are not so much opposites as one more distinction within the realm of the spirit.

A work of this kind cannot present Croce's moral teaching in all its richness. But it should be pointed out how Croce expressly denies that emotion can act as the moral criterion and regards moral activity as belonging to the province of the will; how he refutes the distinctions between motive and act, between means and end, and rejects material morality, especially that of 'religious utilitarianism' or altruism; how his profound concern for freedom leads him eventually to countenance the Hegelian thesis in which the will is simultaneously free and determined. The will is determined because it would be unmanageable without its determining conditions, and it is free because its creative act transcends all previous realities by the very fact of being creative.

Regarding the relationship between practical and theoretical activity, the first point to realize is that the two alternatively spring from and follow each other. Practical activity requires an initial knowledge, but knowledge, in its turn, is impossible without some act. Once more we encounter the cyclic movement of the spirit—intuition passing into a judgment, which provokes practical activity and this, again, confronting us with new matter for the exercise of intuition. In spite of the fundamental unity of the stages of the spirit's ascent Croce firmly insists that nothing could be more false than to interchange these stages—for example, to condemn the artist, as such, from a moral standpoint. By his very creative acts every poet is moral because he is performing a holy function.

This assertion makes it sufficiently obvious that Croce will have no more to do with religion in his practical system than in his theoretical synthesis. He will not recognize religion as a specific form of the spirit and invokes the support of Pascal's *Provincial Letters* in order to repudiate "Jesuitical morality"; yet in spite of all this he comes forward as the champion of religious morality, which he contrasts with the parrot-like superficiality of the various secular moral codes. The Catholic moral teaching seems to him so full of riches as to contain nearly all the true morality of the spirit.

G. HISTORY AND PHILOSOPHY

History, according to Croce, must be distinguished from chronicle, which is both dead history and practical activity. True history is contemporary history, issuing from the spiritual structure of the present and harmonizing with the creative becoming of the spirit. Admittedly a historical judgment is an individual judgment. Yet, although it refers to the particular, it not only contains universal predicates but has a proper object which is universal. It is poetry, for example, and not Dante which is the concern of literary history. History is identical with philosophy and philosophy with history, because the concrete and historical nature of philosophy does not permit it to be separated from becoming. Thus Croce asserts the complete *identity of philosophy and history* whose separation for purely didactical purposes allots philosophy the task of examining historical method. In fact, says Croce, every philosopher is, at the same

81

time, a historian and every historian equally a philosopher; for a man's philosophy reflects all history and the whole story of his life.

Individual men, like individual disciplines (art, philosophy, and science in general) are only transitory "moments" of that one reality—the unity of spirit which comprehends all the different elements. From the preceding accounts of its individual provinces it becomes obvious that, for Croce, no reality exists apart from the spirit. The world is the spirit, in which are united both subject and object, singular and universal, theory and practice; for spirit is the *a priori* synthesis of all synthesis, the pure infinite and eternal evolution (*svolgimento*) which proceeds from one stage to another and transcends them all. This infinitude presents us with a mystery, the mystery of the *actus purus*, the true Absolute, a mystery which is nothing other than that goal which the cosmos has not yet reached. Everything is enclosed in it and all being is simply its manifestation; the latter is real so far as it constitutes a "moment" of its eternal evolution.

9. Léon Brunschvicg

A. HISTORICAL BACKGROUND AND CHARACTERISTICS

In the van of nineteenth-century French idealism appears Charles Renouvier (1815-1903), a Kantian and an original thinker. He was followed by a series of noteworthy representatives who in general, however, did not write very much. Among those of the first rank was Octave Hamelin (1856-1907), the author of penetrating studies about several great philosophers, but whose only systematic work was *Essai sur les éléments principaux de la représentation* (1907). Belonging to the same movement was Jules Lagneau (1851-1894) whose influence was primarily personal and whose writings did not appear in accessible publications until 1924-1925. Also noteworthy are Dominique Parodi (b. 1870) and Émile Chartier (1868-1951), the latter known under the pseudonym "Alain." Nevertheless the most important French idealist and, after Bergson, still the most influential French philosopher, is Léon Brunschvicg (1869-1944). His first work, and the most important as regards his own system, *La Modalité du jugement*, appeared in 1897. After this came the *Introduction à la vie de l'esprit* in 1900, the monumental historical work *Les étapes de la philosophie mathématique* in 1912, and an equally significant volume *Le Progrès de la conscience dans la philosophie occidentale* in 1927. Brunschvicg continued publishing a further series of works until the Second World War. His influence proved to be strongest during the years 1920 to 1939.

Brunschvicg is an idealist in a double sense. In the first place, he attempts to extend Kant's and Hegel's teaching to their utmost conclusions and, secondly, he draws upon Plato, Descartes, Spinoza, and Pascal; some of the latter's thoughts are adopted in his system and given an idealist interpretation in his epistemology. Strong positivist influence is also traceable in his work. In the field of natural science he represents a radically *mathematical* and *conventionalist* viewpoint, regarding mathematics as the highest level yet reached by human thought. Quite obviously he has the same notion of a synthesis as Croce, with whom he also shares a special interest in history, even though his knowledge of this subject does not appear to be so broad as that of the Italian idealist. On the other hand, Brunschvicg expresses himself more precisely than Croce and his differences of opinion from other thinkers are always conducted with supreme politeness—in contrast, once more, to Croce; above all, his references to religion and morality indicate a noble disposition which has won him universal respect.

83

B. IDEALISM

At the very beginning of his main work, *La Modalité du jugement*, Brunschvicg dogmatically asserts the basic thesis of idealist epistemology, "knowledge gives birth to a world which for us is the only world. Beyond that there is nothing; if there were anything beyond (*au delà de*) knowledge, its definition would be in terms of the inaccessible and the indeterminable, which would amount to nothing for us." Thus philosophy must be the criticism of thought, all the more so because only thought is transparent to thought; yet the main object of thought is not the concept but the spirit's own activity, which leads us to define philosophy as an intellectual activity attempting to become conscious of itself.

As usual this idealism is combined with a conceptualism which maintains that judgment precedes all other activities of the mind. For, no matter how simple a concept may seem, it is already, by its nature, a synthesis of form and content; it assumes an act which combines these two. Therefore it may be said that conceiving and judging are one. The task of the understanding consists ultimately in the act of judgment, which represents the fundamental and unique act of the spirit. In this context Brunschvicg takes issue not only with the realistic intellectualism of Plato and Descartes, who attempted to found the synthetic activity of the mind upon some kind of transcendent reality, but also with Kant, because Kant was unable to free this activity from subordination to the category of relation, and therefore to the concept. True philosophy, says Brunschvicg, must be freed from all that is presupposed in the judgment.

Judgment itself consists in affirming an existent as either necessary or contingent, and its essential constituent is the verb which is called the "copula" in reference to the content of the judgment. Thus the fundamental object of philosophical investigation is to be found in the modalities of the verb.

C. THE MODALITY OF THE JUDGMENT

On closer observation two forms of this modality stand out, the form of internality (*forme d'intériorité*) and the form of externality (*forme d'extériorité*). The form of internality lies in the reciprocal immanence of ideas and is particularly characteristic of mathematical judgment, in which the subject and the predicate are meaningless if they are considered apart from each other. This form is the unity of the spirit which determines its own laws. Judgment becomes intelligible through the form of internality with which it is essentially connected. The form of internality is peculiar to ideal judgments and affords a basis for the modality of necessity. Yet it does not suffice on its own and there is also another form of externality, since judgment, in certain essential aspects, must be a manifold. The form of externality is conditioned by a certain irrational element which the spirit encounters; this element, however, is neither a being independent of spirit nor an external projection of this spirit, but is simply the spirit's limitation by itself. When the spirit meets this limit and encounters a check to its own activity, it suffers a violent shock which is commonly attributed to the action of some being outside the mind; therefore the form of externality is proper to judgments about reality. There are thus two constituents of mind, (1) the form of internality (with which the rationality and necessity of mathematical judgment are bound up), and (2) the form of externality (to which belongs the irrationality of the impenetrable and the reality in existential judgment). Brunschvicg recognizes yet another form between these two, a mixed form corresponding to contingency.

Since spirit is a unit, the perfection of human thought is

85

found in mathematical analytical judgment which displays the form of internality at its purest; this judgment is *a priori.* The science of mathematics is specified by its form and not by its object, of which it is completely independent. There is no such thing as mathematical—that is, intellectual—intuition. The other judgments, (geometrical, physical, and probability judgments), despite their increasing irrationality, are not parts of the world of perception but form a different world, the 'world of science,' which cannot be reduced to the world of perception. The question as to which of these worlds is the true world cannot be solved theoretically, and one has to acknowledge a dualism. The same applies to practical life, where the interior moral laws are opposed to external activity and resist disharmony among individuals. There are two mankinds, just as there are two worlds, but this dualism is ultimately resolved through the history of the spirit aspiring to unity and internality.

D. THE LEVELS OF THE SPIRIT'S LIFE

In his learned studies on the history of the human spirit, Brunschvicg sketches its evolution in bold strokes; in this we may distinguish two essentially different ages; childhood and full maturity. The first is the age of externality, of the *acousmatic*, who accepts what issues from the voice of authority, while the second is that of the *mathematician*, the man of rational science. Rational science was discovered by the Pythagoreans, the creators of mathematics, and by Socrates, the master of reflection; unfortunately Aristotle thrust spiritual life back into the age of childhood and in consequence Europe has remained fixed in the acousmatic groove for twenty centuries. Descartes was the first to rediscover the mathematical route and restore to mankind the full enjoyment of its right to truth; along the road which he had opened up progress was but slowly achieved because thinkers were unable to liberate themselves from realist prejudices such as regarding the spirit as dependent upon the external world. Later the Romantics threatened to plunge mankind back into the Middle Ages. But finally science helped the spirit on to victory when Einstein eliminated the idea of intuitive qualities. There are grounds for hoping that, although faith is dying out, a glorious future awaits the reason. We shall come to see that nothing exists apart from the freedom of the spirit, of pure consciousness.

Yet this evolution should not be conceived in a Hegelian sense as a necessary unfolding of the spirit, for the spirit is free and contingent and its progress is comparable to the winding course of a stream. But despite this element of contingency, history reveals a continuous progress of consciousness toward its perfect fulfilment in reason, whose prototype is found in the science of mathematics. As a further symptom of the spirit there is revealed in history something uniquely flowing, mobile, and in no wise rigid. Brunschvicg has even insisted upon the similarity between his own doctrine and Bergson's upon this point.

E. THE RELIGION OF THE SPIRIT

In contrast to Croce, Brunschvicg shows a lively concern for religious questions as he has always been profoundly interested in Pascal; ultimately his whole thought moves toward a philosophy of religion. According to him secular thought provides no basis for a defense of religion, which must be built up from its own resources. Unfortunately there is not one religion but many, all of them fighting each other on specifically religious territory. Nor can philosophy acknowledge a double truth, one religious and the other scientific; religious truth has to be the truth pure and simple. This truth was long since discovered in the religion of the Word of the inner light, and

Philosophy of the Idea

consists in the assurance that God is present in our thinking and in our love. But this God is not transcendent, not God the creator of the world. Nor is he an object or a concept, or even an object of love which could be set over against another object; he is whatever enables us to live the life of the spirit. To put it briefly, God is the Word and, one can even say, *the copula of judgments*. This conception of God not only releases us from mythology, but at the same time frees us in a moral sense —we expect from God nothing but a free and pure comprehension of the divine. We must do the same in the moral sphere as Galileo did in the theoretical by renouncing the primacy of the earth. Such a renunciation would throw into relief the character of human reason, its unselfishness and genuine humility. This purification will lead us to a "Third Testament". Thus consciousness will rid itself of its own past, yet, far from ungrateful toward this past, it will prove to be faithful to it. Just as the New Testament is the fulfilment of the Old Testament so the religion of the spirit (which should be identical with scientific investigation) is the fulfilment of the Gospel.

Obviously in this doctrine we are dealing at bottom with an utterly immanentist, monistic philosophy, according to which there is nothing apart from freedom, from the creative sweep of the spirit which unfolds itself in ever superior forms until it finally achieves complete unity in consciousness.

10. NEO-KANTIANISM

A. THE NEO-KANTIAN SCHOOL

During the last thirty years of the nineteenth century, German idealism normally took the form of Neo-Kantianism. Seven great schools can be counted, each giving a different interpretation to their master's thought: (1) the physiological movement (Hermann Helmholtz, 1821-1894; Friedrich Albert

Lange, 1828-1875) which interpreted Kant's *a priori* forms as physiological dispositions; (2) the metaphysical trend (Otto Liebmann, 1840-1912; Johannes Volkelt, 1848-1930) who maintained the possibility of critical metaphysics; (3) the realists (Alois Riehl, 1844-1924; Richard Hönigswald, 1875-1947) emphasizing the existence of things-in-themselves; (4) the relativist trend exemplified by Georg Simmel (1858-1918) for whom the *a priori* in Kant is of a psychological and relative nature; (5) the psychological school (Hans Cornelius, 1863-1947) which moved even closer to positivism. These five schools were unorthodox Kantian and have now been superseded. By contrast the two remaining and most important schools have maintained their fidelity to Kant's spirit and have been very much alive between the two wars. These are (6) the logistic (or Marburg) school, and (7) the axiological (or Southwest German or Baden) school. Finally a first-rate thinker, Bruno Bauch, put forward a kind of synthesis which both supersedes and develops these two last-named schools.

The Neo-Kantian movement is almost exclusively German, but after having reached the peak of its influence in the period immediately after the First World War, it is today on the wane even in Germany, where it is being replaced by phenomenological, existentialistic, and metaphysical schools. The rule of National Socialism dealt it a fatal blow because its representatives, largely of Jewish extraction, were fiercely persecuted.

In this section we shall deal with the main points in the teachings of the Marburg school, the Baden school, and Bruno Bauch. The number of important Neo-Kantians is too large and yet their general influence is too small to warrant a section for each one of them. Fortunately, as with neopositivism and Marxism, we are dealing with a genuine school possessing common principles and employing a common procedure throughout its various branches.

Philosophy of the Idea

B. THE THINKERS

The founder of the Marburg school in Hermann Cohen (1842-1918) who made his name by his works on Plato, on the history and principle of the infinitesimal method, and on Kant, all of which are difficult works to understand. His outstanding pupil, Paul Natorp (1854-1924) became famous for his book on Plato (*Platons Ideenlehre* 1903) and had a remarkable capacity for presenting his ideas in a clear and comprehensible form. His *Philosophie, ihr Problem und ihre Probleme* (1911) is the best introduction to Neo-Kantianism after Rickert's *Der Gegenstand der Erkenntnis* (1892). Other important Marburgers are Ernst Cassirer (1874-1945) and Arthur Liebert (1878-1947) who are both known for their wide international influence. Karl Vorländer (1860-1928) attempted a synthesis of Kantian and socialist ethics. Finally, the philosophy of law within the Marburg school is represented by Rudolf Stammler (1856-1938), its most distinguished figure.

Wilhelm Windelband (1848-1915), a pupil of Rudolf Lotze and one of the most important historians of philosophy, founded the Baden school. Windelband was endowed with a gift for brilliant exposition and his *Präludien* (1884) have seldom been surpassed for clearness and beauty both in style and in language. Windelband's successor as head of the school was Heinrich Rickert (1863-1936), another master of clear and precise thought. The work of Emil Lask (1875-1915) marks him as the Neo-Kantian whose doctrine is the closest to a phenomenological position; he was killed in the First World War leaving little of the posthumous work that many had hoped for. Another notable representative was Hugo Münsterberg (1863-1916) who was primarily concerned with psychology.

Bruno Bauch (1877-1942), who also began in the Baden

school, was a pupil successively of Rickert, Windelband, and other Neo-Kantians. However, his philosophy burst the framework of this school, attempted to synthesize the Baden and Marburg schools, and contributed fresh elements from its own resources. He is regarded as one of the most difficult of present-day philosophers.

C. GENERAL FUNDAMENTAL ASSUMPTIONS

All Neo-Kantians profess several fundamental conceptions which characterize the school as a whole. First, they all appeal to Kant, who in their eyes is the greatest philosopher, and almost *the* philosopher, of modern culture, and they are agreed in accepting a number of his assumptions. Like him, they repudiate the psychological method and metaphysics, regarding the latter as an impossibility; they employ the *transcendental method* in philosophy to replace the psychological, or indeed any empirical, method. The method which they employ makes it the essence of philosophy to analyse the logical conditions of knowing and willing. Second, following Kant once more, they are *conceptualists;* they deny intellectual intuition (though in different ways since the break-up of the school); they regard reason as potentiality for constructing a whole from its parts, as the simple capacity for synthesis; there is no knowledge of contents and essences. Emil Lask seems to form a partial exception to this generalization because he has been influenced by phenomenology. Thirdly, their theories of knowledge are *idealist;* Knowledge is not the grasp but the construction of an object. "Being does not exist in its own right: it is the creature of thought."

Nevertheless, to understand Kant is to transcend him, says Windelband, and the Neo-Kantians, in the words of Natorp, do not hesitate to bury the corpse of this philosophy in order that its spirit may live. As a matter of fact they transcend Kant in

91

several respects. For example, their idealism is more radical than Kant's because they repudiate the existence of things-in-themselves; also they contest the claim of experience to be an independent source of knowledge and are therefore more radical rationalists than their master. These are only the main points of divergence for they have extended Kantian doctrine along many other lines and have given it new and different form. The most significant changes will be discussed later in this chapter.

For a genuine understanding of the idealism of this school, one must bear firmly in mind that it has nothing to do with subjective idealism such as Berkeley's, and that here the question is one of a "transcendental" idealism. The Neo-Kantians energetically repudiate the notion that the world is to be found "inside the head" of the thinking subject, which would be a complete misunderstanding of their doctrine. Similarly they are not prepared to grant any importance to the "System C" of Avenarius, an epitome of consciousness and the nervous system. As they conceive it, the subject is not that consciousness which constitutes the object of psychology; Rickert first excludes from the concept of consciousness everything that has to do with the body and, second, all mental elements; all that remains is "consciousness pure and simple," which has no more reality than a mathematical point. Once this conclusion is granted, everything that exists must be immanent, and the acknowledgement of this latter thesis means that the Neo-Kantians have no need to deny empirical realism: although everything that exists is plainly immanent to consciousness there remain numerous elements transcendent of human, empirical, and concrete consciousness. This provides a way of overcoming solipsism. Then the problem arises of explaining the basis upon which objective data, which the Neo-Kantians never deny, are founded. Since there is no other reality but the contents of consciousness it is impossible to have recourse to a transcendent reality. Objectivity and truth are to be found only in judgment, and so the question now centers on the problem of judgment. The Neo-Kantians attempt to seize upon whatever makes the judgment objective and true while maintaining its immanence intact. The schools split up in attempting to solve this problem.

D. THE MARBURG SCHOOL

The representatives of the "logistic" Marburg school take their lead from the exact sciences of nature, and even when they turn toward ethics or, indeed, the philosophy of religion, their central interest still remains that of theoretical reason. It is the critique of pure reason, and the transcendental deduction in particular, which they regard as the decisive part of Kant's work. They develop an extremely radical type of idealism which reduces absolutely everything to the immanent logical laws of pure reason. In company with all other Kantians, they refuse to treat sensation as an independent factor of knowledge; sensation is not an element foreign to thought, but is more of an unknown, comparable to a factor to be determined, such as the mathematical x; it is not a datum of but a problem for knowledge, (*Sie ist nicht gegeben, sondern der Erkenntnis aufgegeben*). Knowledge must itself determine sensation. There is no intuition, since reason is a progressive unfolding of judgments and the object a "product" of this activity; yet the latter should not be thought of as a psychological activity because it is a purely conceptual combination of concepts. These concepts themselves are logical relationships; consequently all existence, the whole of reality, is reduced to a web of logical relations to the exclusion of every irrational element. "Logical idealism" or "panlogism" is the name given to this theory.

93

Philosophy of the Idea

On such a basis, how is objectivity of judgment to be explained, and how can the word 'truth' have any meaning? The Marburg idealists answer these questions by referring to the categories. They regard the latter as perspectives and as methodic rules of an entirely *a priori* nature, which means that they are independent of experience and determine the truth values of judgments (a judgment is both true and objective if it is made in accordance with the categories, and is false if it contradicts them). The categories are the conditions of knowledge, and outside them knowledge cannot exist, even though thought certainly does so. In this way they explain objectivity in the act of knowing without invoking any transcendent or irrational elements whatever.

The Marburgers consider that the norms in the moral sphere are also of an *a priori* nature because they do not spring from experience. Ethics is fundamentally a logic of duty and is purely formal (that is, without content), as in Kant. But the Marburgers are distinguished from the founder of the Critical Philosophy by the social character of their doctrine, which leads them to oppose Kant's individualism; they even go so far as to attempt a synthesis of Kantianism and Marxist socialism. In the eyes of the Marburgers religion has no unique character and is simply one form of morality so that, for Cohen, God himself is no more than an ethical ideal, the goal presented as the fulfilment of one's own moral task. Natorp originally at least subscribed to these notions, but opinions differ as to whether he underwent a change of mind toward the end of his life. In general the Marburgers are more faithful to Kant than other idealists, thus maintaining the nineteenth-century attitude. This is still more distinctly emphasized by the monistic character of their philosophy, which seeks to explain reality by means of a single logical principle.

Though both the Baden (or Southwest German or axiological) school and the Marburg school adopt the basic attitudes of Neo-Kantianism, there are differences between them on many essential points. The members of the Baden school do not take their bearings exclusively from the natural sciences but begin with the unity of culture, whose development along with the study of history is their guiding interest. The influence of German historicism upon them is clearly visible. Naturally the decisive feature of Kantianism in their eyes is to be more in the critique of practical reason than in that of pure reason. Their idealism is just as radical as that of the Marburgers but they are not radical rationalists because they recognize the existence of an irrational element in reality. They maintain that the grounds for objective being are to be found not in logical laws but in axiological laws resting upon values. Again, their theory is pluralistic and exhibits a deeper understanding of specifically religious values.

There is no transcendental reality in relation to pure consciousness. If, in spite of this, there are judgments based upon immanent realities which still lay claim to objective truth, this is to be accounted for by the existence of transcendental values containing an imperative; thus a judgment is true if it corresponds to an obligation, that is, if it conforms to a transcendental imperative. One can see that this doctrine assumes the existence of irrational content and does not attempt to reduce the whole of being to logical method, for what constitutes the ground of being are values independent either of reason or of "pure consciousness." Such values as are found in science, logic, ethics, aesthetics, are not entirely relative; they possess absolute validity and are immanent, ideal laws. They belong to an unchanging and eternal realm of their own; yet, without either

95

existing or being real, they are valid. There are three classes of them, those belonging to truth, to morality, and to beauty, but Windelband places the religious values above all these.

It is the peculiarity of religious values that they are inconceivable without some relation to a transcendent reality. A transcendent God cannot be reached by means of syllogistic, noncontradictory thought; but we do not need to comprehend such a God in order to believe in him, and we are driven toward such a belief by the very existence of religious values. Thus the bounds of total immanence are transgressed, though only at the price of religious irrationalism.

Apart from their theory of value, in which the Badeners can be reckoned as founders of a new philosophical discipline, they have also notably contributed toward making the social sciences (*Geisteswissenschaften*) better understood. Just as the natural sciences are "nomothetic" (that is, law-giving, according to Windelband) and "proceed by generalization" (according to Rickert), the social sciences, on the contrary, are ideographic and individuating. Their aim is not to establish general laws but to describe the individual. But because the historian cannot turn his attention toward any given individual, he has to make a choice; this choice presupposes a judgment about values, and therefore valuation is the basis of all social science.

Rickert set himself the problem of explaining the relationship of these two realms toward each other, the realm of reality and the realm of values. According to him the relationship only becomes possible through the medium of a sphere which is different from both of them and which he calls 'the third realm' (*drittes Reich*), while his name for the relationships which constitute it is 'significant patterns' (*Sinngebilde*). Culture corresponds to this third sphere.

Through extending the ideas of the Baden school and

through contact with phenomenology, Lask achieved a synthesis which recognized intuitive contents and treated them as genuinely immanent. This did not prevent his adopting an attitude which was in radical opposition to the Marburg conception of them.

F. BRUNO BAUCH

Bauch began in the Baden school but diverged from it on many points. While the Marburgers started from the first, and the Badeners from the second, of Kant's *Critiques,* Bauch considers the third *Critique* to be Kant's chief work, and to contain the kernel of his philosophy. His basic position is extremely transcendental. He does not speak of an *a priori* synthesis, but rather of a law of synthesis; this brings him to a much more pronounced objectivism than the other Neo-Kantian idealists are ready to acknowledge. Thus he comes to distinguish between the validity (*Gültigkeit*) characteristic of judgments and the actuality (*Geltung*) of objective relationships; the latter is the foundation for the former. The transcendental subject is no longer conceived, in Rickert's fashion, as an indispensable residue of consciousness but simply as a system or epitome of the conditions necessary for the object; it is an objective subject which in the last resort bears no resemblance to a subject except in name. The title of Bauch's main work, *Wahrheit, Wert und Wirklichkeit* (*Truth, Value and Reality,* 1923) expresses very well another of his distinctive tendencies; by this tendency the three problems are regarded as three aspects of one and the same question in which reality is conceived to be like truth and, furthermore, as identical with value, because truth (truth value) is fundamentally pure actuality (*Geltung*), that is, reality, while all other values are participations in it. This makes it clear that Bauch reduces everything to transcendental relations (in the Marburg style),

97

Philosophy of the Idea

yet thinks of relations as real connections (*Geltungszusammenhänge*) in similar fashion to the Baden school.

Having stated his idealistic objectivism, Bauch develops a doctrine of the dialectic which is in a certain way reminiscent of Hegel's. His 'concepts' (*Begriffe*), that is, the formative laws of the object, are not stiff and motionless, but eternally mobile; there is continuous evolution not only in the material world, but also in those laws of our world which determine essences. As a whole they bear the name 'idea,' but this is not simply a regulative concept, as it is for Kant, because it is the objective unity in the infinite totality of logical laws.

CONCLUDING CRITICISMS

There are three fundamental ideas characteristic of contemporary idealism—uniqueness of spirit, the idea of objective law, and the recognition that there is a creative aspect to knowledge. The members of this movement see some things in sharp outline to which the empiricists are blind—that the spirit is something utterly different from matter and cannot be reduced to it; that neither the logical nor the moral law can be made to rest upon a mental process (at least according to the Neo-Kantians); and that knowledge is not merely a passive reception of images. These ideas of the idealists unquestionably rise above the primitive level of materialism, positivism, and psychologism as well theoretical and axiological subjectivism. With equal determination the idealists oppose vitalistic irrationalism. They are responsible for a number of very valuable contributions such as Croce's aesthetics, the Baden school's theory of value, and their penetrating and often astonishingly subtle analyses of knowledge.

Yet their ideas remain one-sided and so exclusively rationalistic that they do not do justice to certain other aspects of reality. It is a characteristic of all idealists that they fail to appreciate the material world and ultimately reduce it to a mere appearance. Again, the majority of them, at least, show no feeling for the real and the concrete and have a noticeable tendency to replace being by logical functions devoid of content. This is largely due to two fundamental principles which they adopt without proof—the principle of immanence, and conceptualism. In the final analysis they resemble the empiricists in their inability to answer the concrete and pressing questions of human existence as such. This is particularly striking with respect to religion; apart from the Baden school none of them show any real understanding of this subject. So here once more we have representatives of a typically nineteenth-century mentality; their philosophy is today threatened by new and more concrete tendencies ever more bent upon the wholeness of being.

... ὅτι πάντα χωρεῖ καὶ οὐδὲν μένει ....
... ὡς δὶς εἰς τὸν αὐτὸν
ποτα μὸν οὐκ ἂν ἐμβαίης.

HERACLITUS

IV

Philosophy of Life

While scientific knowledge of matter was central to the empiricism and materialism discussed in chapter ii and while the idealism described in chapter iii revolved around the idea, the philosophers whom we are now about to meet attempt to explain all reality in terms of life. Another feature which distinguishes them from the idealists and empiricists is the fact that they are striving to break away from the general framework of "modern" (1600-1900) philosophy, and especially of Kantianism. They wish, above all, to avoid both mechanicism and idealism. However much they differ from each other in details they are at one on the following issues:

1) They are absolute *actualists*. For them there is only movement, becoming, life. So far as they recognize matter or being at all, it is only as the by-product of movement; in this

respect each of them echoes Bergson's verdict "there is more in becoming than in being."

2) Their conception of reality is an *organic* one, in which biology enjoys a status comparable to that of physics among the representatives of scientific materialism. History also plays an important role with some of them, especially for Dilthey's school. At any rate, none of them think of the world as a machine, but as pulsating life.

3) They expound their own philosophy of knowledge in the light of this biological attitude; without exception they are *irrationalists* and resolute empiricists. Concepts, *a priori* laws, logical deduction are an abomination to them; they consequently will not accept rational method as the touchstone of philosophy but replace it by the test of intuition, practice, and a vital understanding of history.

4) For all this they are but rarely subjectivists and they assume the existence of an *objective reality* which transcends the subject; therefore they will have nothing to do with transcendental or absolute idealism.

5) Finally the majority of these philosophers betray a marked inclination toward *pluralism* and personalism. If this inclination does not entirely harmonize with their basic teaching concerning the evolution of life, it may perhaps be explained as a reaction from materialistic or idealistic monism; in any case this has been one of the movement's most powerful tendencies.

Four different schools of life-philosophy may be distinguished; Bergson's philosophy of the life-impulse, American and English pragmatism, the historicism inaugurated by Dilthey, and German life-philosophy. It is convenient to deal with historicism and German life-philosophy in one chapter and to treat Bergsonism separately from Bergson; hence the exposition of life-philosophy is split into three chapters—Berg-

Philosophy of Life

son, pragmatism and Bergsonism, German life-philosophy and historicism.

11. HENRI BERGSON

A. ORIGINS AND CHARACTERISTICS

Henri Bergson (1859-1941) is the most important and original representative of the new "life-philosophy," and it is at his hands that it has received its most perfect formulation. But though he later became its leader, he was by no means its founder, since in France itself Blondel's *L'Action* (1893) appeared quite independently of Bergson's *Données immédiates*, and Le Roy also had held out against mechanism even before becoming Bergson's pupil. This whole movement has many links with the spiritualist, voluntarist, and personalist tendency of French philosophy inaugurated by Maine de Biran, whose principal representatives were to be Felix Ravaisson-Mollien (1813-1900), Jules Lachelier (1832-1918), and Bergson's master, Émile Boutroux (1845-1921). Yet these philosophers were not the only ones to influence Bergson—he learned a great deal from the critique-of-science movement and even from English utilitarian and evolutionist doctrines. As he admits, Herbert Spencer's teaching at first seemed the only one adapted to reality, and his own philosophy was born of the effort to provide deeper foundations for Spencer's system.

But this attempt eventually led him to reject Spencerism absolutely, then to attack it all along the line. Bergson's speculative energies have been largely crystallized into four works which clearly illustrate his spiritual development; the *Essai sur les données immédiates de la conscience* (1889) contains his epistemology, *Matière et Mémoire* his psychology, *L'Évolution créatrice* (1907) his metaphysics based upon biological speculation, and *Les Deux Sources de la morale et de la religion*

(1932) describing his ethics and his philosophy of religion. Each of these works achieved an altogether unprecedented success, due partly to the fact that Bergson elaborated a really novel philosophy answering to the deepest needs of the times, but just as much because he presented it in uncommonly beautiful language. In 1927 he was awarded the Nobel prize for literature. His incomparably incisive arguments and rare philosophical earnestness are combined with imaginative illustrations which are impressive both on account of their startling clarity and the artistic manner in which they are expressed. In addition, his work is supported by a profound factual knowledge which he has gained at the cost of extensive and painstaking research. All this equipped Bergson to overthrow nineteenth-century positivism and, to a large extent, nineteenth-century idealism also. Bergson has acted as one of the pioneers for the new spirit of our age.

B. DURATION AND INTUITION

According to popular notions which have become incorporated into science, the world is characterized by *extension*, numerical *diversity*, and causal *determinism*. The world is composed of rigid, extended bodies whose parts are spatially separate; it is marked by precise divisions and a completely *homogeneous space*, and its whole behavior is predetermined by fixed laws. Natural science does not take movement into account, but simply deals with the successive locations of bodies; nor does it investigate the forces at work in nature but simply their effects; the natural scientist's picture of the world lacks dynamism and life of any kind; the time of the scientist is ultimately sheer space, for whenever he claims to be measuring time, he is simply measuring space.

Yet within ourselves we are able to detect an altogether different reality once we take the pains. This reality exhibits a

103

purely *qualitative intensity* and is composed of utterly *hetero-geneous* elements which are so involved in each other that it is difficult to distinguish them clearly; finally, this inner reality is free. Far from being spatial or numerical, it actually endures, it even *is* pure duration and, therefore, is different from the space and time of natural science; it is a single, indivisible act, an impulse (*élan*) and a becoming, which cannot be measured. From its very beginnings this reality is in constant flux; it never *is*, it is always *becoming*.

The human faculty adequated to spatial matter is the intel-lect (*intelligence*), which in its nature is directed toward use; once the use is given, the form taken by the intellect is also given. Since we require clearly defined things for our use, the intellect concentrates upon whatever is corporeal, unorgan-ized, and partially fixed because the intellect can only lay hold upon immovable things. It can only conceive of matter, which it constructs for the purpose of turning bodies into tools; it is the organ of *homo faber* and its essential function is to fashion tools. Because of its essential connection with matter, the in-tellect in this sphere is not restricted to phenomena, but can grasp the essences of things. Bergson outstrips the phenomenal-ism of Kant and the positivists, and acknowledges that the in-tellect has a capacity for penetrating into essences; he also re-gards the intellect as analytical, which means that it can dissect things and recompose them in accordance with some law or system. Clarity and a capacity for making distinctions are the characteristic features of the intellect.

However, it is equally characteristic of the intellect that its very nature prevents it from comprehending real duration, or life, because it is formed to correspond with matter and trans-fers to the world of duration the clearly defined forms of the extensive, quantitative, material world. It interrupts what is all one stream of life by introducing discontinuity, spatiality, and necessity; thus even the simplest movement in space overtaxes the comprehension of the intellect, as Zeno's paradoxes show.

We can only know duration in virtue of intuition, but this enables us to grasp it both intimately and directly. Intuition displays features opposite to those of the intellect for it is the organ of *homo sapiens* and is free from subordination to practice; its object is the fleeting, the organic, and the continuous and it is its monopoly to grasp duration. While the intellect analyses and dissects things in preparation for their use, intuition consists of a simple glance in which the reality of duration is experienced without dissection or composition. Intuition is not come by lightly, because we are so accustomed to using our intellects that the exercise of intuition requires a powerful interior effort which does violence to our natural inclinations; we are only capable of this at most favorable and transitory moments.

To sum up briefly, there are *two spheres*, one the sphere of spatial and rigid matter, which is the concern of the practical intellect, the other the sphere of life and enduring awareness, the province of intuition. Since the intellect is exclusively determined by practical ends, philosophy can only make use of intuition; but the insights which it attains in this manner are not susceptible of formulation as clear and precise ideas and so cannot be incorporated in logical proofs. If one philosopher wants to help another the only thing he can do is get him to reproduce an intuition similar to his own. This accounts for the wealth of suggestive imagery in Bergson's writings.

C. EPISTEMOLOGY AND PSYCHOLOGY

Bergson applies his intuitive method in the first place to epistemological problems. He argues that previously there have been three classical solutions to these problems, conventional dualism, Kantianism, and idealism. However, all three solutions depend upon the false presupposition that perception and memory are purely speculative and independent of practice, though, in fact, they are thoroughly practical and are directed toward action. On its own side the body is simply a center for action. Once these points are established it follows that perception apprehends only one facet of reality, and that its essence is actually to choose those aspects which are useful in order to complete some task. Idealism is therefore in error because the objects of which the world is composed are "true pictures," not merely constituents of consciousness. Equally mistaken are conventional and Kantian realism in that they posit a homogeneous space between consciousness and the external world and treat it as undifferentiated. In fact, space is no more than a subjective form adapted to man's acts.

Bergson supports his epistemology by a very definite theory of psychology. He rejects materialism, which derives its whole strength from the fact that consciousness is dependent upon the body—as if the fact that a piece of clothing moves and falls along with the hooks on which it hangs would lead anyone to infer the identity of clothing and hooks. There is not even a parallelism between psychological and physiological phenomena, though it would prove nothing if there were. This can be shown from the case of pure memory. Two kinds of memory have to be distinguished, a mechanical, corporeal memory which simply consists in the repetition of functions that have become automatic, and pure memory by which images are remembered. Here there can be no question of a localization in the brain such as materialists use as their main argument, for if there were such localization an injury to part of the brain would eliminate definite parts of the memory, but in fact it often produces only a general weakening of the memory. A much more convincing comparison is with the kind of office that performs the transference of messages; the specifically mental life is not its function. Nor is memory a decayed perception; it is an essentially different phenomenon.

Associationist psychology is rooted in a double error by making duration spatial and by turning the self into a combination of things in the pattern of matter. These same errors also lead to psychological *determinism*, which conceives of motives as co-temporal things and of time as a path through space, whence it proceeds to deny freedom. The truth is that behavior issues from the whole personality, that a decision creates something new, that action springs from the self, from the self alone, and is therefore completely free. If freedom is so often denied in spite of being immediately evident, this is due to the fact that the intellect constructs a superficial self similar to a body, and thereby conceals the deeper real self which is creative and enduring.

D. LIFE AND EVOLUTION

The two classical doctrines in which attempts are made to explain life are the *mechanistic* and the *teleological*, and both end in the same way by ultimately denying duration. According to the former, organisms are machines functioning in conformity with predetermined, calculable laws; according to the latter, there already exists a finished world plan. Both of them illegitimately extend the concept of the intellect in certain respects, forgetting that the intellect is for action and not for the understanding of life. Philosophy must transcend these doctrines, particularly mechanism, which simply denies quite obvious facts.

The observation of a certain phenomenon in the problem of life, like a similar observation on the psychophysical problem, permits the conclusion that materialism is false. This phenomenon consists in the fact that organs of an entirely similar structure are generated along very different lines of

Philosophy of Life

evolution; the evolution of the eyes, for instance, in the molluscs and the vertebrates must have diverged long before they began to enjoy vision. Relying upon these facts and some other considerations Bergson rejected Darwinism and Neo-Darwinism and, therefore, the mechanistic conception of the living organ. A living organ must be regarded as the complex expression of a simple function and may be compared to a picture which results from a thousand strokes of the artist's brush yet expresses one simple inspiration of the artist.

An organism seems to be a mechanism because it possesses a mechanism. But just as a curve split into very small segments only appears to conicide with its tangents, similarly life appears to be a mechanism if it is examined in detail by the methods of natural science—yet it is not so.

Life as a whole is no abstraction. At a determinate point in time and at a certain location in space, a stream of life welled up, passed from one spore to another through developed organisms. The stream of life seeks to overcome the obstacles presented to it by matter; it does not flow logically, but occasionally errs, is sometimes hemmed into a blind alley and even swirls backward. Yet the universal urge of life persists, and in order to be able to deploy itself, the life impulse (*élan vital*) divides itself into different streams. This is how the great split between the plant realm and the animal kingdom came about— the plants directly accumulate their energy so that the animals may draw upon it and then let it off as if it were gunpowder expendable at will. Consequently plants are earth-bound and consciousness is only latent in them, but consciousness is awakened in the animal world.

The life impulse within the animal kingdom again takes two different directions as if it were experimenting with two methods; it reaches completion in one direction through the social insects and in the other direction through human beings. In the first direction, life is striving toward movement and flexi-bility by means of the *instinct*, which means the capacity to use, or even to create, organic instruments; instinct knows its object inside out through sympathy and handles it unerringly, though always according to the same pattern. The vertebrates, on the other hand, develop the *intellect* which is a faculty for constructing and using inorganic instruments. By its very es-sence the intellect is directed toward relations and the forms of things and not toward things themselves, so that it only knows its object in an external fashion; on the other hand it can pack its empty forms with an unlimited number of objects of any kind that it likes. The finished intellect overcomes its original limitations and can even be turned to ends other than the prac-tical ones for which it was created.

Finally, among men, instinct becomes detached and able to reflect upon itself, if only at fitful intervals, and this constitutes *intuition;* man is moreover free. This whole course of evolution thus results in the liberation of consciousness in men, and man is seen to be the ultimate goal of organized life on our planet.

E. METAPHYSICS

Once the philosopher allows himself to be plunged into the sea of life surrounding him he is in a position to grasp the origin of bodies and of the intellect; this intuition shows that not only life and consciousness, but the *whole of reality is a becoming;* there are no things, only actions, and being is funda-mentally becoming. Thus "there is more in becoming than in being." It is merely our intellect, and consequently science, which presents us with fixed bodies. The material world is really movement and impulse, though it is only a declining and disintegrating impulse. There is accordingly a double movement in the world, that of life which is ascending, and that of matter which is descending; the law of matter is the law of diminishing energy against which life is struggling in vain, for it can only delay its fulfilment. To make this process comprehensible one might compare it with steam of a high pressure which is escaping through cracks in the side of a vessel; in the open air it forms into drops which fall down, though there is a small quantity of the vapor which does not liquefy for some seconds and even attempts to bear up the drops which are falling. Similarly, the massive container of life is ceaselessly giving off a sort of vapor which is turned into a world of its own as it falls; the falling drops are matter. To give another illustration, the world might be compared with the quick upward movement of an arm which drops as soon as the muscular tension is relaxed; matter is like the exhaustion of a creative movement. Yet even these illustrations are inadequate because life belongs to the sphere of psychology and is not spatial.

A similar process takes place in consciousness. Intuition follows the same direction as life, but the intellect pursues the opposite one, being conformable to matter. Intuition, however, shows us genuine reality wherein life appears as an immense wave which unfurls and then becomes dammed up at nearly every point; the obstacles are overcome only at a single spot, and there the impulse breaks through into freedom. Mankind is the form of this freedom, and so philosophy has been right in asserting the freedom of the spirit, its independence from matter, its unbridgeable separation from animality and, perhaps, even its survival beyond death.

Nevertheless, philosophy has fallen into error through its use of the intellect and its concepts. By means of extended analysis Bergson shows how the *idea of disorder* arose (namely from the contingency between two different orders, the geometrical and the vital) and how the *idea of nothing* was formed (which is actually a pseudoidea). He attacks the most celebrated philosophical systems of the past including the metaphysics of Plato and Aristotle; the latter have eliminated duration by following the intellect's natural inclination for employing concepts which conform to language. Though they have changed some details, the same applies to the modern systems created by Descartes, Spinoza, Leibniz, Kant, and, above all, Spencer. Spencer is notorious for affirming *the cinematographic nature of our thought;* he tries to visualize and expound evolution as though it were a succession of states in the evolutionary process, thus utterly misunderstanding true duration.

F. ETHICS

According to Bergson there are two types of morality, the closed and the open. A *closed morality* is derived from the most general phenomena of life; it arises from the pressure exercised by society, and its appropriate behavior is performed automatically and instinctively. The individual self and the social self clash only in exceptional circumstances. This impersonal closed morality is closed in three ways; it wishes to preserve social conventions; it almost identifies the individual and society, so that the mind always revolves in the same circle; lastly, it is always the product of a limited group and can never be valid for all mankind because the principle of the social unit which produced it is the need for self-defense.

Besides this closed morality of sheer duties there is an *open morality* which receives enbodiment in outstanding personalities, saints, and heroes, and is human and personal instead of social. It does not result from pressure but from an inner vocation, and, far from being fixed, is essentially progressive and creative. It is open in the sense that it embraces life with love, and, even more, supplies the sense of freedom and harmonizes with the life principle. It is born of a deep emotional experience which is similar to that afforded by music through having no object.

In reality neither the closed nor the open morality is found in a pure form since every aspiration tends to crystallize into a corresponding obligation, and the latter tends to envelop the former. Both these forms, the subintellectual and the super-intellectual, are worked out on an intellectual level and so moral life is rational life. But at bottom the closed and the open moralities are complementary manifestations of one and the same life impulse.

G. PHILOSOPHY OF RELIGION

The distinction made in the moral sphere is equally valid in the religious, since there is a static and a dynamic religion. *Static religion* consists of nature's defensive reaction against the effects of intellectual activity, which threaten to suppress the individual or to dissolve society; in reply to them static religion reconciles man to life and the individual to his society by means of myths, which act as lullabies. Static religion is the product of the "myth-making function" (*fonction fabulatrice*) of the intellect. The intellect in its narrow sense threatens to destroy social unity and nature cannot use the instinct to oppose it since the latter's role in man has been usurped by the intellect. But nature defends itself by generating the myth-making function. Thus an animal has no anticipation of death, but a man's intellect tells him that he will die and that a sickening gulf of indeterminacy lies between an undertaking and its desired result. So that he may endure this bitter knowledge nature manufactures gods by means of the myth-making function. The role of the myth-making function in human societies corresponds to the role of instinct in animal societies.

Dynamic religion, or mysticism, is something entirely different. It comes from a return to the original direction of the life impulse and from anticipating the unattainable goal toward which life is struggling. Thus mysticism is only found in unusual men; there is no sign of it among the ancient Greeks; and in India it failed to achieve a fully developed form through remaining purely speculative, but it certainly comes to life in the great Christian mystics who were endowed with almost perfect spiritual health. The Christian religion appears to be the crystallization of such mysticism but, even more, it provides its basis, because for all their unique qualities the mystics are but imperfect imitators of the one who preached the Sermon on the Mount.

The experiences of the mystics not only provide support for the likelihood of the assumptions made as to the origins of the life impulse, but equally for asserting God's existence, which cannot be proved on logical grounds. The mystics also teach that God is love, and there is nothing to prevent a philosopher from amplifying the idea which they have propagated, that the world is a concrete manifestation of this love and of the divine need for love. The experiences of the mystics, which psychological conclusions have confirmed, provide a probable—almost, indeed, a certain—basis for maintaining survival after death.

12. Pragmatism and Bergsonism

A. PRAGMATISM

While pragmatism is primarily an American and English movement it has by no means remained confined to these lands. About 1900 it had many followers, especially in Germany, where there were signs of it in the empiriocriticists, Karl Marx and Lenin, in Georg Simmel and Hans Vaihinger (1852-1923); the positivists in general maintained parallel viewpoints. Pragmatism found many points of agreement with certain French representatives of the critique of science, especially with Abel Rey. However all these thinkers advocate several other doctrines and not just pragmatism.

Epistemologically the main point of pragmatism consists in denying that there is a purely theoretical knowledge and *in reducing the true to the useful*. Yet these fundamental theses are represented in different degrees by individual pragmatists; while the most radical section maintains that each statement which leads directly to success is true, the most moderate teaches that whatever can be verified by objective facts is true. But usefulness, value, and success are universally regarded as the unique criteria of truth and generally as its very essence; differences are found only when it comes to determining this usefulness more precisely.

For Anglo-American pragmatism, however, the question is not simply one of epistemology, since it usually involves a whole life philosophy similar to Bergson's; consequently reality to them is not something fixed—it is freely creative and flowing, beyond the grasp of the intellect; therefore all knowledge is based on experience. Most Anglo-American pragmatists also maintain a personalistic and humanistic attitude in common with Bergson, and the main difference between their leaders and the French philosopher is that intuition remains essentially theoretical in his account, while according to the pragmatists all knowledge is practical by definition.

Pragmatism springs from the same causes as Bergson's philosophy, develops along parallel lines, and plays a similar role in intellectual history. It has now been superseded, however, in Europe and only partially survives in other movements (neopositivism, existentialism), so that here we need do no more than give short accounts of the three leading pragmatists, James, Schiller, Dewey. William James and John Dewey are Americans, but their influence upon European thought has been so important that they at least deserve touching upon.

The American logician and philosopher Charles Sanders Pierce (1839-1914) was the first to suggest pragmatist ideas, but pragmatism was most fully worked out by William James (1842-1910), the founder and chief representative of this school. James was an extraordinary personality; he was a physiologist and an eminent psychologist, deeply religious and endowed with great feeling for art, as well as a brilliant writer who exercised a striking influence upon contemporary philosophy as a whole. His own philosophy has its roots, on the one hand, in the reaction against the idealism of Bradley and of the great American idealist Josiah Royce (1855-1916), and, on the other hand, in his fight against scientific monism and determinism, for which he brought the critique of science into play and extended its application. A *dynamic* and *pluralist* conception of reality underlies all his arguments. Nothing in the world is finished; it contains no substances, is in constant change and is not one being but composed of multifarious individuals. All these ideas prompt him to confess a definite inclination for polytheism; monism he rejects as an abomination. His philosophy is likewise very anti-intellectualist and denies even the antithesis of subject and object; it is described by James himself as "*radical empiricism.*" He takes the notion of the contingence among beings to its utmost extreme (*tychism*). Another famous doctrine is his psychophysical "*neutral*" *monism*, according to which there is no essential difference between mental and physical phenomena. Still James's best known doctrine is his *pragmatism*—an idea is true if it leads to the perception of an object, and a statement is true if its adoption produces satisfactory results, if it vindicates itself in practice. The word which James applies to this practical verification, "cash value" has often been misunderstood, since James

Philosophy of Life

does not simply take "usefulness" to mean the satisfaction of an individual's material needs but everything which serves the development of man and society. In this sense he regards religion as supremely true; it must be judged by its results and James says that he does not know whether religion has any bearing upon metaphysics but that in any case it is a fruitful hypothesis. This short sketch gives only the slightest impression of James's rich teaching but a more detailed examination is not possible here because this philosophy really belongs to an earlier epoch.

C. ENGLISH PRAGMATISM

Pragmatism developed in Great Britain under the influence of James and the anti-associationist psychology which was represented both by James and by George Frederick Stout (1860-1944). Ferdinand Canning Scott Schiller (1864-1937) was the leader of this movement, which was also indebted to the logician Alfred Sidgwick (1850-1943) who always insisted that a purely formal logic was impossible. English pragmatism first came to light in 1902 with the publication of a book entitled *Personal Idealism*, the work of eight young philosophers. The contributors to this volume, including among others Henry Sturt (1863-1946), Hastings Rashdall (1858-1924), and Schiller himself, were not all pragmatists but all of them describe themselves as pluralists, in opposition to Bradley's idealism and Spencer's monism. Like many other publications of this time *Personal Idealism* signified much more the nineteenth-century intellectual crisis than the advent of a new and united movement.

Schiller had already come to the fore in 1891 with his *Riddles of the Sphinx: A Study of Evolution Written by a Troglodyte*, a curious work in which he advocated pluralism and personalism and developed the doctrine that God is a finite personal being. This work belongs to the time when Schiller was not yet a pragmatist.

In 1903 he first announced his adherence to pragmatism, which he described as "humanism." He adopted the dictum of Protagoras that man is the measure of all things and defended the Greek sophist against Plato's intellectualism; indeed, he even strengthened the Protagoras formula by declaring that man is not only the measure of reality, he is in fact its creator. According to Schiller this reality is an unshaped but shapeable mass which requires human action (*Tat*) before it becomes actual (Schiller uses the German word *Tat-sache*, "fact"). The question as to what it is, is utterly meaningless and the only question which we have ever to ask is, what can we make of it?

Under Sidgwick's influence Schiller concentrated his attention mainly upon logic which, he says, can never be formal and abstract—*expellas hominem logica, tamen usque recurret* (you may drive the human element out of logic, but it will always return). Logic is a human thing, the servant of man, a concrete instrument of labor. It is false to treat the principle of identity and the rest as universally valid logical laws.

The same applies to *truth*, because all truth is human and none is absolute. Schiller does not exactly maintain that every useful statement is also true but he certainly maintains that a statement has to be useful in order to be true, and that a true statement does exhibit a value. The truth is not fixed but dynamic, perpetually becoming. Schiller gives to truth a wholly Darwinian interpretation by plunging it into the stream of life; and so his doctrine is not a logic, but a "biologic," of knowledge.

Schiller never secured much following in English philosophical circles, where he was regarded as an extravagant sophist, a title of which he himself boasted. After his death in 1937 no

117

successor appeared to carry on his work but his numerous well-written publications have exercised a considerable influence. A number of widespread ideas of the present day are attributable to Schiller.

D. JOHN DEWEY

American pragmatism received a unique expression in John Dewey (1859-1952) who combined scientific materialism with James's ideas. While the teaching of James was eminently religious, and while Schiller attempted to establish a philosophic humanism, Dewey turned exclusively toward the natural sciences. He proclaims his adherence to Watson's *behaviorism*, according to which mind is simply a function of the body. There is no real knowledge other than the knowledge gained by the methods of natural science. In previous ages, before mankind possessed our modern techniques, the bases of behavior were sought outside the realm of experience, but now it is high time to cast aside all transcendental thinking and to rely exclusively upon *experience*.

This experience teaches us that all things change and that there is nothing permanent in either the material or the intellectual sphere. Thought itself is merely an instrument of action and man first begins to think when he encounters material difficulties which have to be overcome. Therefore an idea has only an instrumental value (*instrumentalism*) and is a function worked out by practical experience in order to serve this experience. The whole value of an idea consists in its success, and truth is ultimately but a form of the good.

Dewey's fame is due, above all, to his deep concern with social reform, but his philosophy itself has also exerted profound influence in the United States. For a long time it was the dominant intellectual force in a country which has put all its stock in technical achievement and has not yet undergone the bitter experience of scientific "progress" known to Europe. Thus James's doctrines, which arose as a protest against attaching exaggerated value to technics and the natural sciences, have suffered an astonishing inversion at Dewey's hands, and have become the main prop of a materialistic-scientific outlook.

E. THE DIALECTICAL SCHOOL

Let us recur briefly to the so-called dialectical school which took some of its basic ideas from pragmatism. The organ of this school is the journal *Dialectica*, founded in 1947 and published in Zurich. Its leading spokesman is Ferdinand Gonseth (b. 1890). Gaston Bachelard (b. 1881), a prominent French philosopher of science, and many other scholars and philosophers are in more or less active sympathy with this school. According to Gonseth all human knowledge is dialectical. It must rely upon rules and theories which are provisional only and are based upon the live, collective thought of the investigators. There is no absolute criterion of truth. Propositions, rules, and theories are to be adhered to only as long as their scientific utility justifies it, and this holds for all fields of study. Nor is there an absolute logic. There are only alternative logics which are likewise to be accepted or rejected on the basis of utility. But the dialectical school repudiates the charge of relativism, holding that it is not truth which is relative but rather that nothing can be accepted as absolutely true. It likewise repudiates the nominalism and sensationalism of the neopositivists because dialectical methods are said to prove themselves in all fields, even in introspective psychology and theology. The school nevertheless appears to be similar to neopositivism in regarding the method of the inductive sciences to be the only way to knowledge. At the Tenth International Congress for Philosophy in 1948 the dialectical school emerged as one of the

119

largest and most dynamic. It has succeeded in attracting to itself many European thinkers who had been neopositivists. It exerts a strong attraction for numerous natural scientists and mathematicians interested in philosophy and for those philosophers who are concerned with the methodology of natural science and mathematics.

F. BERGSONISM

At the beginning of the twentieth century in France a widely influential school had been formed under Bergson's influence. It was affected simultaneously by the critique of science and by Anglo-American pragmatism, and went even further along the vitalist and irrationalist path than Bergson himself. Almost all its representatives are declared pragmatists and the remainder are voluntarists, for whom will is superior to the intellect and truth is a vital value, as for Schiller.

It would be transgressing the limits of this exposition to pursue these systems in detail, systems which, incidentally, are more noteworthy for their radicalism than for originality. Nevertheless the development in some of them is worth mentioning. The philosophers of this group, still very radical before the First World War, have now shown so much more moderation that they are almost regarded as intellectualists. With the single exception of Blondel, however, they have actually remained open opponents of the intellect's claims to knowledge and, as pragmatists, treat truth as adaptation to life. Their philosophy is biological but without the profundity that their common mentor, Bergson, exhibited in formulating this attitude.

The contemporary philosophers of this group, include the psychologist Maurice Pradines (b. 1878), a very radical anti-rationalist, the moralist Jean de Gaultier (1858-1942), who combines irrationalism with subjective idealism, and, finally, the group of Catholic thinkers formed under Bergson's influence from among the pupils of Léon Ollé-Laprune (1839-1899). Some of them, such as Alfred Loisy (1857-1940) and Lucien Laberthonnière (1860-1931) have scarcely any significance as philosophers although they played leading parts in the modernist movement. There are others who are still esteemed in contemporary philosophy, particularly Edouard Le Roy (b. 1870) and Maurice Blondel (1861-1948). Yet Blondel was not a convinced irrationalist and even took long strides toward metaphysics. We would call attention, nevertheless, to his dictum that "at the start of every scientific procedure . . . a decretal is inserted," and that "science provides us with no information whatever about the ground of things" because "its freedom is unlimited." Therefore Blondel is even more sceptical in regard to science than Bergson, who does admit its capacity to penetrate to material essences. Le Roy is yet more radical. According to him science as such is purely conventional, and a purely conventional character is all that can be attributed to the scientific expression of facts themselves, to say nothing of scientific theories. The scientist creates the order of things by tracing out facts upon the formless matter which is given to him. Science is but a formal word game devoid of inner significance, a mere mental device for mastering the world. The same is true of religious dogmas in which no conceivable meaning can be discovered; they are simply formulae, practical rules of life. Le Roy assumes the existence of God but denies that it can be proved.

13. HISTORICISM AND GERMAN LIFE-PHILOSOPHY

A. CHARACTERISTICS. HISTORICISM

The movements of thought in Germany which correspond to French life-philosophy and English pragmatism, are the two

121

movements of historicism and biologistic philosophy. These have one decisive feature in common despite their fundamental differences, namely their profound understanding of living processes and their denial that the procedure of the natural sciences has any value when life is in question. In addition, both are strongly influenced by Friedrich Nietzsche (1844-1900).

Historicism, the more important of the two movements, owes its main inspiration to the powerful development of historical science in Germany during the second half of the nineteenth century; its outstanding philosophical godfathers, after Nietzsche, include Georg Simmel (1858-1918), originally a Kantian relativist; in a greater degree Rudolph Eucken (1846-1926), the philosopher of spiritual life; and, above all, Wilhelm Dilthey (1833-1911), the great historian and theorist of history. As its name indicates, historicism is connected particularly with the study of history and, consequently, of spiritual development. History lies at the heart of philosophizing, according to the representatives of this school, and is not manageable either by the methods of natural science or by any rational procedure; its range already encloses the whole of thought. This notion gives rise to radical irrationalism and to a more or less avowed relativism.

The other tendency is less dominated by history but forms a pure life-philosophy and is in fact biologistic philosophy; it does not conceive of becoming as a historical spiritual process, but as the broad flow of vital elements. Its most eloquent and influential representative between the two wars was Ludwig Klages.

The following passages present concise summaries of the main points of Dilthey's theories, of his principal disciples, and of Klages.

B. WILHELM DILTHEY

Wilhelm Dilthey belongs to an earlier and superseded period but deserves a place here because his influence reached its peak after the First World War. A most eminent historian, he began as a positivist and had also been strongly influenced by Kantian currents—a typical start for a nineteenth-century thinker. He must, however, be counted among the foremost representatives of the crisis at the century's end because he managed to transcend the two already mentioned currents in the name of an irrationalistic relativism. Life and the *understanding of life* (*Verstehen*) is his central problem, and he conceives of it teleologically as the integration of all aspirations and as a perfect unit, as "a context embracing the human species." Each event in life has a meaning so far as it is a symbol of what belongs to life. In his epistemology he attacks the intellectualist standpoint, because knowledge does not come from an intellectual operation but from the whole person, and we affirm the existence of an external world because our will meets resistance. Dilthey works out a penetrating epistemology for the social sciences called hermeneutics whose three fundamental principles are these: historical knowledge is self-awareness; explanation (*Erklären*) is not the same as understanding (*Verstehen*), which is not a rational function but involves all the emotional and spiritual forces of the soul; understanding is a communication from life to life, because reality itself is life. We can only grasp the total situation by the combined effort of all our nature's forces as they are integrated within ourselves.

Toward the end of his life Dilthey arrived at *a doctrine of the world view (Weltanschauungslehre)*; any world view may be traced back to man's perspective and his various attitudes toward life; thus the man himself and his philosophy must be

Philosophy of Life

placed into their historical context. History allows us to discern three types of philosophers who correspond to three attitudes —the reign of reason gives birth to positivistic materialism; that of emotion to objective pantheistic idealism; while the predominance of will produces idealistic freedom, whether Platonic, Christian, or Kantian. Philosophy, like all human things, is entirely relative. "The final pronouncement of the historical world view is that human accomplishment of every sort is relative, that *everything is moving in the process and nothing is stable*." Dilthey's philosophy has many further aspects but it is particularly his relativism and his replacing reason by life which have come to exercise such great influence upon contemporary thought; of the other aspects only his theory of time should be mentioned which anticipates Heidegger's philosophy.

C. DILTHEY'S SUCCESSORS

A number of thinkers were influenced by Dilthey, but they exhibit many considerable differences from each other. One of them is Ernst Troeltsch (1865-1923), a Protestant theologian, philosopher of religion and history, and historian of culture. There is, in addition, a genuine Diltheyan school whose members devote themselves to very varied aspects of Dilthey's system but share allegiance to historicism. The first place among these goes to Eduard Spranger (b. 1882) who is famous for his works in pedagogy, psychology and the philosophy of culture; next come Erich Rothacker (b. 1888), Georg Misch (b. 1878), and Hans Freyer (b. 1887). Theodor Litt (b. 1880) stands somewhat apart from Dilthey but may be placed in this school. These are only the leading figures in a movement which has many branches.

Some thinkers, who are not strictly speaking Diltheyans and stand outside this school, have at least felt the effects of historicism, as is revealed in their keen interest in the philosophy of history. Foremost among them is Oswald Spengler (1880-1936) whose work *Der Untergang des Abendlandes* (1918-1922) became widely known after the First World War. Spengler's philosophy is avowedly indebted to the thoroughly irrationalist thought of both Nietzsche and Dilthey. He is known largely for his theory of culture cycles, to each of which he attributes a life span of some one thousand years. Spengler is radically relativist, maintaining that there are no eternal truths and that each philosophy is an expression of its own time and only its own. Truth is relative to a determinate human type. It is not without some justification that Arnold J. Toynbee (b. 1889) has sometimes been described as a Spenglerian in his philosophy of history. Toynbee, however, has far more knowledge at his command and comes to less pessimistic conclusions than Spengler. In *A Study of History* (10 volumes, 1934-1954), a work distinguished by its vast historical materials and its wealth of ideas, Toynbee seeks to establish laws of the development and decline of civilizations. It is noteworthy that he replaces the concept of progress, so widely held in the nineteenth century, with a concept of cultural and historical cycles. This idea is already at the base of Spengler's work and through Toynbee has now attained very wide currency. In the work of the school of sociologists led by Pitirim Sorokin it has achieved notable scientific success. Another adherent of historicism, the English philosopher of history Robin George Collingwood (1891-1943), might also be mentioned here.

D. GERMAN LIFE-PHILOSOPHY

Except in the particular instance of historicism, the influence of life-philosophy has never achieved the same degree of success in Germany as it has in the Anglo-Saxon countries and in

125

France. Its German representatives are philosophers only in the popular sense. Mention must be made of Keyserling (1880-1946), the well-known graphologist and characterologist, leader of a school of wisdom and author of the much-read *Travel Diary of a Philosopher* and many other works, who professes an irrationalism which is bound up with a radical pragmatism. Ludwig Klages (b. 1872) is a much more original mind. In his principal work *Der Geist als Widersacher der Seele* (3 volumes, 1929-1932) he develops a radical antispiritualism. On his view soul pervades all things, and in such a world there prevails a natural harmony. Unfortunately, "because of man" an extraspatial (acosmic) power, called mind (*Geist*), has intruded into this world and it has the capacity to sunder off body from soul and thus to destroy the life cell. With mind there appears the person, the will, and the eccentricity of striving. The mind commits murder against life through the deed—it is the adversary of the soul, of all that is natural, loyal, and valuable. We are advised to take decisive measures against the mind and return to the world view of Pelasgianism, that is, to a primitive-unconscious life free of the mind.

CONCLUDING CRITICISMS

The philosophers discussed here have seen clearly that life contains qualities which make it fundamentally different from matter. The intense experience of this idea and the fact that it has been expressed so forcefully has enabled them, Bergson and James especially, to stand out successfully against the prevailing positivism and idealism of the nineteenth century. It is also symptomatic of the revolutionary force which initiated a new direction in European thought. Because of this vision the life-philosophers were able to analyze the factors of life and movement in a frequently astonishing fashion, and to burst the narrow framework of scientist rationalism in favor of a more organic and concrete conception of reality. The life-philosophers at the same time restored man and his vital problems to their rightful place. For all this they deserve great credit as well as for their success in overthrowing the tyranny of nineteenth-century prejudices; as a matter of fact it is difficult for us today to appreciate how much we owe to them in this respect.

Historicism has the special merit of drawing attention to the uniqueness of historical event and process and thus of stimulating the study of a series of problems of historical method and also of questions about the very nature of temporality itself.

Unfortunately their efforts to understand living reality more fully are strongly prejudiced by their one-sided basic assumptions and by an attitude toward reason which they inherited from the older doctrines of the past century and which they were never able to transcend. Their philosophy is actually a biologistic philosophy, which fixes its whole attention upon life and is in no position to grasp superior realities. Their philosophy is no less one-sided than that of the idealists. It is even more dangerous because normally it is sheer animal life which acts as the focus of their attention and provides their ultimate term of explanation, whereas the idealists accord this function to the spirit. Furthermore the conception of reason formed by these philosophers, is just as narrow and limited as that of the nineteenth century, because what they are attacking is deductive reason such as we find in the theorizing of modern physics. They reduce reason to this kind of meager skeleton, they deny intellectual intuition (thus remaining faithful to Kant), and they limit the whole range of the spirit to the bare performance of inferential thought. So it is not surprising that they are all blind to the existence of objective laws and, for the most part, to the difference between spirit and the mental functions of animals, and that usually they end up as radical irrationalists. This is why they remain nominalists or psychologists, unable to rise to the conception of anything supersensible.

Stated briefly, life-philosophy still remains imprisoned to a great extent in the old mentality, even though it is acknowledged to have entered modern philosophy as one of its greatest liberating forces. This is one reason why its previous brilliant ascent does not prevent it from being replaced today by equally concrete and more illuminating philosophies, existentialism and a new metaphysics.

Erit igitur veritas, etiamsi mundus intereat.

ST. AUGUSTINE

V

Philosophy of Essence

Phenomenology is the second great philosophical current which, along with life-philosophy, brought about the break with the nineteenth century, though under quite different auspices. More exactly, it is but one of two movements of the same type which issued from the teaching of Franz Brentano (1838-1917). The other is represented by Alexius Meinong (1853-1921), and his followers, Alois Höfler (1853-1922) and Christian Ehrenfels (1850-1932); these thinkers developed a theory of objectives (*Gegenstandstheorie*) similar to phenomenology in many respects. Of a different order of importance is phenomenology itself, founded by Edmund Husserl (1859-1938), who won the adherence of a great school of eminent followers, first in Germany and later in every part of the world.

Two fundamental features of phenomenology need to be underlined. In the first place, it is a method which consists in describing *phenomena*, that is, anything that is immediately given; on this account it turns away from the natural sciences and places itself in opposition to empiricism while, in contrast to idealism, it refuses to take epistemology as its point of departure. Considered as such a method it presents a complete antithesis to all the dominant features of the nineteenth century. Secondly, its object is essence (*Wesen*), that is, the ideal intelligible content of phenomena, which is seized immediately in an act of vision—in the intuition of essence (*Wesensschau*). Here again it is in opposition to the nineteenth century which recognized neither the self-subsistent being of such essences nor the possibility of knowing them. Husserl later developed a theory closely akin to Neo-Kantianism but did not persuade his school to follow him along these lines. Phenomenology and the theory of objectives have both contributed largely to the formulation of neorealism (Moore), existentialism (Heidegger), and metaphysics (Hartmann).

Among phenomenologists should be noted Alexander Pfänder (1870-1941), Oskar Becker (b. 1889), Moritz Geiger (1880-1937), Edith Stein (b. 1891; she entered the Carmelite Order and lost her life in 1942 in a Nazi concentration camp), Roman Ingarden (b. 1893),[4] H. Conrad Martius, and Adolph

---

[4] Roman Ingarden's main work *The Controversy over the Existence of the World* (until now two volumes have appeared, 1946-1948) is one of the most significant publications of the present time. Unfortunately we could not consider it in this study nor even include it without reservation in contemporary European philosophy since it has appeared only in the Polish language which is not known to the great majority of European philosophers. We mention this here solely in order to protest against the unfortunately widespread custom of issuing serious philosophical works in languages which are known only to more or less minor groups, for example, Finnish, Polish, and Dutch. The decision should be made to issue all such works in *one* language, and in the present state of things English would doubtless be most suitable. Apart from this, the serious study of philosophy presupposes a knowledge of Greek and Latin. If we add to this the three major European languages, we have a total of five languages recommended for the study of philosophy and then there seems little reason for not extending this list ad infinitum.

Reinach (1883-1916); of the phenomenologists in France reference should especially be made to Alexander Koyré and Emmanuel Levinas; the United States possesses an outstanding representative and publicist of phenomenology in Marvin Farber (b. 1901). These are overshadowed by Max Scheler (1874-1928), the most original and influential thinker after Husserl.

14. EDMUND HUSSERL

A. DEVELOPMENT. IMPORTANCE

Edmund Husserl (1859-1938), who has exercised the deepest and most enduring influence upon present-day thought after Bergson, and is still doing so, was a pupil of Franz Brentano and also studied under the psychologist Carl Stumpf (1848-1936). He taught at the universities of Halle, Göttingen, and Freiburg im Breisgau. He combined a capacity for work with a singular gift for analysis and the keenest of intellects. His voluminous works provide an extremely stiff task for the reader, not so much because of any inadequacy of expression as from the aridity of their theme. He is a model of precision as a philosophical writer and reminds one of Aristotle in this respect. His system is affiliated to those of Brentano and Stumpf and, through the former, to scholasticism, but a certain Neo-Kantian strain also shows through.

Husserl began his career with mathematical studies; during that period he published the first volume of his important *Philosophie der Arithmetik*, a work giving no indication of the future course that his philosophy was to take. In 1900-1901 appeared his major work, *Logische Untersuchungen*, in which he concentrated his attention upon the foundations of logic. This monumental production is divided into two parts. The first, *Prolegomena zur reinen Logik*, affords a criticism of psy-

131

Philosophy of Essence

chologism and relativism from an intellectualist and objectivist standpoint, while the second, *Untersuchungen zur Phänomenologie und Theorie der Erkenntnis*, provides an application of the previously established principles to particular problems in the philosophy of logic. In 1913 Husserl published his *Ideen zu einer reinen Phänomenologie und phänomenologischen Philosophie*. Phenomenology there receives the status of a "first philosophy" and is related to the study of knowledge in general; idealistic conclusions may already be discerned in it. These conclusions are fully developed in the two following works, *Formale und transzendentale Logik* (1929) and *Erfahrung und Urteil* (1939). Husserl's career may be broadly summarized by saying that he sets out from the philosophical study of mathematics and then elaborates an objective and intellectual method, whose application to consciousness eventually leads him to idealism.

Husserl's influence flows along diverse channels. To begin with, the penetrating analyses contained in *Logische Untersuchungen* strike a hard blow at the positivism and nominalism which had dominated the nineteenth century. At the same time his method contributed vitally to the formulation of anti-Kantian thought by stressing the content and essence of the object. In both respects he is one of the pioneers of recent thought. Furthermore, the phenomenological method which he created is now very widely employed by philosophers; lastly, his works contain such a host of penetrating and subtle analyses that it seems doubtful whether this wealth of knowledge has yet been completely utilized, or even put in circulation. His works may come to rank as a classical source for future philosophy. Husserl was the founder of an important and extensive school that, however, by no means represents the limits of his influence, which extends over the whole of contemporary philosophy.

It is impossible to summarize here even one of his many significant works and so it is more necessary than elsewhere to refer the reader to the texts themselves, especially to *Logische Untersuchungen*. All that can be presented here is a bare outline of his method, of his theory of logic, and of the route by which he was led to idealism.

B. CRITICISM OF NOMINALISM

In his *Logische Untersuchungen* Husserl carries out a devastating criticism of the nominalism which had spread over the whole of philosophy since the days of Locke and Hume under the names of empiricism, psychologism, and others. If this nominalism were true then logical laws would be empirical and inductive generalizations comparable to those of natural science, while the universal would simply be a schematic image. Husserl shows that logical laws are not in any sense mere rules, any more than logic is in any sense a normative science, although it provides a basis for a normative doctrine, just as every other theoretical science does; in fact, logical laws have nothing to say about what should be, but have plenty to say about what is. For example, the law of contradiction does not lay down that two contradictory statements are not expressible, but that one and the same thing cannot have predicates which contradict each other. On the strength of these assertions Husserl turns against psychologism (according to which logic would be a branch of psychology), because it is guilty of a double error. If it were true, then logical laws would bear the same vague stamp as those of psychology; they would only be probable and would presuppose the existence of mental phenomena, which is absurd; in fact logical laws belong to another and entirely different order through being ideal and *a priori*. Second, psychologism perverts the meaning of logical laws completely because these laws are specified by something objective and have nothing at all to do with thought, judgment, and the like; the object, in logic, is not the concrete judgment made by a person, but is the content of this judgment; it is its meaning and belongs to an ideal order. Finally, his theory of abstraction leads the founder of phenomenology into conflict with nominalism by showing that the universal has nothing to do with a generalized image; what we imagine when we think of a mathematical proposition, for instance, does not matter. Because they could not imagine ideal objects, Locke, Hume, and their successors have hypostasized the universal by erroneously treating it as a mere image. But this is an error, because the universal is really an object of an altogether different type; it is an ideal universal content.

C. DOCTRINE OF MEANING

The preceding criticism constitutes one of the most valuable enrichments of twentieth-century thought and a return to the great ontological thought of the ancients and the medievals. It gives support to the thesis that logic has its own allotted province—namely, meaning. Whenever we understand a name or a statement, the significance of neither the one nor the other of these expressions can be treated as though it were in any way a part of the corresponding act of understanding; it is, much more truly, its meaning. What is meant by such expressions in relation to the manifold of individual experience is an identity in the strongest sense of the term. But the term "to mean" is ambiguous and it can be seen to serve at least three different functions. (1) What the expression "manifests" (i.e., mental events, experiences). (2) What it "signifies"—which itself splits up into (a) the sense, or the content of the concept, and (b) what is denoted by the expression; in conjunction with this distinction, Husserl isolates three elements of the act, namely its *quality* (as conception, assertion, doubt, belief, etc.); its *matter* (the same matter—that is, content—can have different qualities; for example, one may imagine the content of a sentence, then doubt it and then assert it, etc.); the *object of the act*, which is what the expression denotes, in contrast to the content, which is the sense (*Sinn*) of the expression. Finally (3) Husserl distinguishes between acts which bestow meaning and those which fulfil meaning, the latter providing the act with its intuitional fullness while the former simply contain the bare essentials of the expression and do not provide the intentional meaning with its intuitional fulfillment.

This theory of meaning is connected with a *pure grammar*, the philosophical theory of grammar. Here again, as in so many other fields, Husserl has sown precious seeds which are now coming to fruition in mathematical logic. For example, mathematical logic is indebted to him for the concept of the category of meaning (*Bedeutung*). Another interesting and important aspect of the *Logische Untersuchungen* is the doctrine of the whole and its parts. Even though it is one of the most valuable achievements of contemporary philosophy it would be impossible to go into the details of this theory here because it is too abstract, and also because it has not exercised such an influence as Husserl's other views.

D. THE PHENOMENOLOGICAL METHOD

Husserl's aim is to establish an ultimate basis, free from all presuppositions, on which to erect all sciences, especially philosophy. The ultimate legitimate source of all rational statements is seeing, or, as he puts it himself, "that prime consciousness which presents the given immediately" (*das originär gebende Bewusstsein*). It is imperative to get at *the things themselves;* that is the first and fundamental rule in the phenomenological method. "Things" are simply taken to mean whatever is given, that which we "see" in consciousness, and this "given"

Philosophy of Essence

is called "phenomenal" in the sense that it appears (φαίνεται) to our consciousness. The word does *not* indicate that there is an unknown thing behind phenomena; such an unknown does not come into question for phenomenology, which is content to start with whatever is given without trying to decide whether this given thing is a reality or an appearance—at least it is there, it is given.

The phenomenological method is neither deductive nor empirical, but consists in *pointing* (*Aufweis*) to what is given and *elucidating* it; it neither explains by means of laws nor deduces from any principles, instead it fixes its gaze directly upon whatever is presented to consciousness, that is, its object. Consequently its whole direction is toward the objective, and although the activity of a subject can itself become an object of investigation in its own right, it is neither this activity nor the subjective concept which immediately interests the phenomenologist but rather *what* is known, doubted, loved, hated, and so forth. Even in the case of pure fancy, the act of imagination must be distinguished from what it imagines; when we imagine a centaur, for example, this centaur is quite distinguishable as an object from our mental act. Similarly the tone quality *c*, the number 2, a figure or a circle, and so forth, are objects and not mental acts. But Husserl rejects Platonism, which would only be true if these objects were realities, and he even calls himself a "positivist" on the ground that he requires all knowledge to be based upon the given.

Yet in order to lay hold on reality itself, it is necessary to correct the many gross errors of which positivists are guilty. The fact is that positivists equate vision with sensible or experiential visual perception and do not realize that every sensible, individual object possesses an *essence* (*Wesen*). Though each individual is a contingent reality, even this contingent owns an essence or, as Husserl says, "a pure *eidos*" (*ein rein zu fassendes Eidos*). Thus there are two kinds of science—a factual science, which rests upon sensible experience, and essentialist or eidetic science which aims at the *intuition of essence*, the vision of the *eidos* (*Wesenschau*). But all factual sciences are founded on the essentialist sciences, in the first place because they all make use of logic, and generally of mathematics also (eidetic sciences), and second, because every fact includes an essence among its constituents.

Mathematical sciences are specifically eidetic sciences and phenomenological philosophy belongs to the same class, taking essential structures instead of contingent facts for its object; it is purely descriptive, its proper task being to describe essence. The procedure consists of point-by-point elucidation, which advances from one stage to another by means of the intellectual intuition of essence. It attacks the foundations of science without any aid from presuppositions and is thus a "first philosophy," as well as being a rigorously apodictic science. Although not easy to practice, the use of the phenomenological method by Husserl and his pupils has shown that it provides wide scope for extraordinarily fruitful research.

E. REDUCTION: BRACKETING

The proper object of phenomenology, the eidos, has to be attained by what Husserl calls *Epoche* which, without being Cartesian doubt, is a suspension of judgment. It means that phenomenology "brackets" certain elements of the given, and takes no more interest in them. Such reductions can be split up into different types. The historical *Epoche*, first of all, sets aside every philosophical doctrine, because the phenomenologist is not interested in other people's opinions but grasps the things themselves (*die Sachen selbst*.) Once this initial elimination has been carried out, the *eidetic reduction*, follows, by which the individual existence of the object in question is

137

Philosophy of Essence

"bracketed," since it is essence which phenomenology is searching for. The elimination of individuality and existence involves the abandonment of all sciences of nature and of the spirit, their factual observations no less than their generalizations; even God, conceived as the ground of being, has to be set aside. Logic itself and all other eidetic sciences are subject to the same condition, for phenomenology places itself in the presence of pure essence and ignores all other sources of information.

This eidetic reduction is accompanied in Husserl's later works by yet another which bears the name "transcendental reduction." This consists in not only bracketing existence, but also everything that is not a correlate of pure consciousness. As a result of this last reduction all that remains of the object is what is given to the subject; but in order to understand this theory of transcendental reduction more fully it is necessary to turn to the doctrine of intentionality in which it is grounded.

F. INTENTIONALITY. IDEALISM

The transcendental reduction applies the phenomenological method to the subject itself and its acts. Husserl had previously maintained that the province of phenomenology is made up of different regions of being, and he now allots one of these regions—and a peculiar region of being at that—to *pure consciousness*. One arrives at this pure consciousness by means of the concept of intentionality, a very difficult notion which Husserl takes over from Brentano, and so, indirectly, from scholasticism. It is the essential quality of certain experiences to be experiences *of* an object; these experiences, so far as they are a consciousness (or love, appreciation, etc.) of anything, are said to be "intentionally related" to it and are called "intentional experiences." By applying the transcendental reduction to such intentional experiences one comes to recognize consciousness as a pure reference point for intentionality to which the intentional object is presented and one sees the object as intentionally given to the subject, because the reduction does not leave it any other kind of existence. One recognizes experience itself as pure act, which seems to be nothing more than the intentional relationship of pure consciousness toward the intentional object.

Thus phenomenology becomes the science of essence in pure experience. The whole of reality appears to be a stream of experiences interpreted as pure act. Yet it cannot be overemphasized that this stream is in no way mental, that it is merely a question of pure, ideal forms, and that pure consciousness (which is termed *"cogito"* when actualized) is not a real subject, because its acts are only intentional relations, and what is given to this logical subject ultimately constitutes the whole of the object. Within the stream of experience Husserl distinguishes between sensual *hyle* (matter) and intended *morphe* (form); *noësis* is the name he gives to that which forms matter into intentional experiences, while by *noëma* he means the manifold of data to be found in pure intention. In considering a tree, for example, one must distinguish between the meaning (*Sinn*) of the perception of the tree (its noëma) from the meaning of this perception as such (noësis); similarly in a judgment one can distinguish between the promulgation of the judgment (i.e., the essence of this promulgation, "judgment noësis") and the promulgated judgment ("judgment noëma"). The latter could be termed a "statement in the purely logical sense" except for the fact that the noëma contains a constituent essence apart from its logical form.

The most important of all these analyses demonstrates the bipolarity of intentional experience; the subject, in its very essence, is related to the object, which, by its own essence, is present to the pure subject. Because an intentional act can be

Philosophy of Essence

produced without a real object, as sometimes happens, the existence of reality is not absolutely necessary before there can be pure consciousness; on the other hand, the world of transcendent *"res"* is wholly referable to active consciousness. Thus reality, in its essence, is relieved of its independent and absolute character and becomes merely something intentional, something that appears, a content of consciousness.

And so Husserl's philosophy finally comes round to a transcendental idealism in many ways similar to that of the Neo-Kantians. The only vital difference between himself and the Marburg school is that he will not allow the object to be dissolved into formal laws, and that he recognizes a plurality of what appear to be *existent* subjects. This idealist trend did not commend itself, however, to his school.

15. MAX SCHELER

A. PERSONALITY. INFLUENCE. DEVELOPMENT

Among the philosophers under Husserl's influence, one has to take special account of Max Scheler both because of his originality and of his speculative ability. He was born 1874 in Munich, became a pupil of Eucken, and then taught in the universities of Jena, Munich, and, after 1919, Cologne. From Cologne he was called to Frankfurt a. M. but died there in 1928 before resuming his teaching.

Endowed with an unusual personality, Scheler was also beyond doubt the most brilliant German thinker of his day. His main strength lay in the field of ethics but his interest in religious philosophy, sociology, and other problems was no less intense. At all times his thinking is purposeful and close to life and his writings abound with problems. He is certainly the most original figure in ethical studies during the first half of the twentieth century.

The most varied currents afforded him inspiration. His first two books bear witness to the influence exercised on him during his earlier years by his teacher Eucken, whose thought centers upon spiritual life, who accords supreme place to the spirit, despite being a sort of life-philosopher, and who has a profound admiration for St. Augustine. Both these features reveal themselves in Scheler, for whom St. Augustine is the great doctor of love, a love which the great saint conceives in an original manner such as the Greeks had never known; that is the line which Scheler chose to develop in his second period. After St. Augustine, Scheler received the most lasting impressions from life-philosophy, Nietzsche, Dilthey, and Bergson, which accounts for his title "the Catholic Nietzsche" (Troeltsch). Meanwhile he moved into the orbit of Husserl so that today he is considered to be the chief phenomenologist after the founder of the school, although his application of phenomenological methods to fresh problems leads him to modify the views of Husserl.

Scheler's life may be divided into three periods. As pointed out, the first period is dominated by Eucken. The next phase is that of his maturity (1913-1922) in which he produces *Der Formalismus in der Ethik und die materiale Wertethik* (first published in Husserl's Year Book, 1913-1916), the most fundamental of his books; and then two collections of essays entitled *Vom Umsturz der Werte* (1919) and *Vom Ewigen im Menschen* (1921). During this time Scheler is a personalist, a theist and a convinced Christian. Then a profound change takes place within him, partly, it would seem, through his own restless nature and the violent crisis in his life; not only does he lose his previous faith, he even repudiates his theistic tenets. This conversion is already announced in *Die Wissenformen und die Gesellschaft* (1926) but receives its most pointed expression in *Die Stellung des Menschen im Kosmos* (1928). If

Philosophy of Essence

his philosophy up to this point had turned upon the notion of God's personal love, now he maintains that man is "the unique locus of the realization of the divine." An early death robbed Scheler of the opportunity to amplify this latest phase of his thought.

B. EPISTEMOLOGY

Three types of knowledge are granted to man. The first is the *inductive knowledge* of the positive sciences, which is rooted in the urge for power and never attains to cogent laws; its object is reality. Scheler assumes the existence of reality but agrees with Dilthey that a creature which merely knew would have no reality because reality is whatever presents obstacles to our effort, and its existence is proved by our colliding with these obstacles.

The second type of knowledge enables us *to know the essential structure* of everything there is, the "whatness" of things. As a condition of this knowledge we have to eradicate instinctive attitudes and to ignore the real existence of things, since such knowledge takes the *a priori* as its object. Along with Kant, Scheler asserts that there is *a priori* knowledge, interpreting as "*a priori*" all those ideal statements and units of meaning which are given to the thinking subject without his making any assumptions whatever. Nevertheless Scheler is led to contradict Kant upon several points at issue here. One is that what is comprised in the primary *a priori* is essences and not propositions. The sphere of *a priori* evidence has nothing to do with the formal sphere; there is an essential *a priori* which has content independently of experience and induction. Scheler rejects idealistic conceptualism and positivistic nominalism with unusual acrimony. Again, he will not concede to Kant that epistemology provides the fundamental theory of the *a priori;* he says that the basic error of the Kantians consists in asking "how can anything be given?" instead of the fundamental question "what is given?" Thus he treats epistemology as but one chapter in the theory of objective interconnections of essence. Finally, he considers the Kantian doctrine upon the spontaneity of thought to be radically false since it attributes all unification to the work of the understanding (or in certain cases, of the practical reason), whereas there is no such understanding which acts as law giver to nature. Convention is all that we can draw up, never laws. But the greatest error committed by Kant and all modern rationalist philosophers is to have equated the *a priori* with the rational; in fact, the whole of our spiritual life has *a priori* features—even the emotional faculties of the spirit such as feeling, loving, hating, and so on; there is an "*ordre du coeur*," a "*logique du coeur*" (Pascal) in the deepest sense. By treating Husserl's phenomenology from this angle Scheler has extended it along original lines and opened up new vistas for it. He calls this doctrine "emotional apriorism."

The third type of knowledge is *metaphysical* and salvational and is arrived at by combining the results of the positive sciences with a philosophy centered upon essence. Problems on the borders of science (e.g., "what is life?") form its initial object, whence it proceeds to a metaphysic of the absolute. But the way to such a metaphysic cannot begin with objective being. It originates in philosophical anthropology, which sets itself the question, "What is man?" Modern metaphysics has to be meta-anthropology.

C. VALUES

Values are the *a priori* grounds of emotion, the intentional objects of feeling. Though reason is blind to them they are as directly given to intentional feeling as colors are to vision. They are *a priori*.

143

Philosophy of Essence

Scheler carries out a devastating critique on the one hand of axiological nominalism, for which values are simply empirical facts, and on the other hand of ethical formalism. In this way he manages to achieve liberation from the dominant nineteenth-century prejudices very much as Bergson was able to do in the realm of theory. A presentation of this critique cannot here include the details, but has to limit itself to sketching the ground plan.

In human conduct Scheler distinguishes between the aspiration, the aim, the end, and the value. *Aim* is a content offered for realization; it is contained within the sphere of imagination and so it is always represented in consciousness. Not every aspiration necessarily has an aim. On the other hand, every aspiration does have an *end*, which is found in the very process of aspiration and is not conditioned by an act of imagination. In every end there is a *value*, which is its most intimate content. The assertion that man always aspires to pleasure is completely incorrect; ultimately, in fact, he never aspires to pleasure, nor to any emotional state whatever, but to values. And even when he takes pleasure as his end he does so under the impression that it is a value. However, to present a value does not imply producing an aspiration, because one can be aware of values (even ethical ones) without aspiring to them. It therefore follows that values are not dependent upon aim but are already present in the ends aspired to. Indeed values form the basis of our ends and only thereby can they form the basis of our aims. Furthermore one should not interchange value and obligation (*Sollen*). Ideal obligation is to be differentiated from normative (imperative) obligation; in the latter there is an ideal obligatory content related to aspiration as its condition. Value generates ideal obligation which in its turn generates normative obligation. To use the latter as a basis for ethics betrays a profound misunderstanding.

Values are anything but relative, they are absolute in the double sense of the word; their content is not relational; they belong to the category of quality, and they are unchanging. It is not the values themselves but our knowledge of them which is relative. There is an unmistakable vigor in Scheler's attack upon the various forms of relativism and particularly of relativist ethics. He subjects to examination first subjectivism, which traces values to human sources, and then relativism, which reduces them to mere life or regards them as conditioned historically. In this enquiry one discovers variations in the feeling for, and therefore knowledge of, values (ethos); variations in judgment upon value (ethics) in the models for institutions, ownership, and commerce; variations in practical morality concerned with the value of human behavior; and, lastly, variations in custom and traditionally accepted habits. These are all subject to constant change, which nevertheless fails to disturb the ethical values; the latter may be clearly or less clearly conceived, defined, and formulated, but in themselves they remain absolute and unchanging.

Values form a closely knit realm held together by formal *a priori* laws and the interconnections of essence. Accordingly all values are classed either as positive or negative; the existence of a positive value is itself a positive value, its nonexistence a negative one; the existence of a negative value is a negative value, its nonexistence a positive one. The same value cannot be both positive and negative, every value that is not negative being positive and vice versa. The values are also classified into higher and lower. The most permanent ones, the least "divisible" ones, those which generate others, those which produce a deeper satisfaction, and, finally, those which are least relative, are all higher values. The values are placed in their *a priori* hierarchy as follows: (1) values of sensible feeling, pleasant and unpleasant; (2) values of vital feeling, noble and vulgar; (3) spiritual values, beautiful and ugly, just and unjust, the pure knowledge of truth; (4) values of the holy and the unholy. Truth is not a value. This outline does not include the ethical (moral) values because these consist in the realization of other values which are relatively higher, or relatively lower, ones.

Finally, values are classified according to their subjects, the main division allotting some values to persons and others to things; the latter are all valuations of valuable things (goods), including among others cultural goods. Personal values are attached to the person himself and to his virtues and by their very essence are higher than those attached to things; ultimately the person alone is either good or evil. The secondary division of these values corresponds to tendencies in ethical capacity, the third one to the acts of a person. The ethical values are therefore personal values par excellence.

D. PERSON AND COMMUNITY

At the heart of Scheler's system lies the problem of the human person. To be a person is not the same as to have a soul or even to have selfhood; all men are not necessarily persons in the deepest meaning of the term, because the concept of person involves maturity and complete powers of judging and choosing. The person is not identical with the substantial soul, is not mental, and has nothing to do with phychophysical problems, character, or the health (as opposed to the sickness) of the soul. Neither substance nor object, it is much rather *the concrete unity of acts*, which is not in itself objective; the person is only revealed in its actions. But this does not mean to say that it is a vacant spring board (*Ausgangspunkt*) for acts, and still less that it consists in the sum of such acts, as Kant thought. The fact of the matter is that the whole person is

146

committed in each act and varies in each act without exhausting its being in any one of them; and since the entire realm of action is spiritual, the person is essentially spiritual. *Spirit*, according to Scheler, does not consist of intelligence and the faculty of choice, for in this respect Edison and a clever chimpanzee differ in degree only, not in essence; it is a new principle, and is totally different from nature. The acts which the spirit generates are not functions of a self—they are nonmental (but not thereby physical) because acts are committed whereas mental functions occur. It is the act of ideation, that is, the ability to separate essence and existence, which constitutes the fundamental sign of the human spirit. Spirit is therefore objectivity (*Sachlichkeit*), the capacity of being determined by the objective nature of things.

The person is eminently *individual;* every man, in the degree to which he is a person, is a unique being and a unique value. (The contrast which Scheler is stressing is between individual and general, not between individual and common). To talk of a general person, or "consciousness in general" (Kant) is nonsense. The person is doubly autonomous, firstly through autonomous personal insight into good and evil and, secondly, through autonomous personal volition for the good and the evil concretely given. Although the person is bound to his body he does not stand in a dependent relationship toward it because control over the body is one of the conditions for personal existence. Finally the person is never part of a "world" but always its correlate, so that each person corresponds to a world (microcosm) and each world to a person.

But the person is differentiated into an individual person and a common person (*Gesamtperson*). The essence of the person is found in the fact that his whole spiritual being and activity is rooted both in individual reality (individual person)

Philosophy of Essence

and in membership in a community. Therefore every finite person "owns" both an individual and a common person, the latter springing from the manifold sources of experience which form the totality of shared experience. According to Scheler there are four types of social unity: (1) unity through slavish and infectious imitation (the masses); (2) unity through experiencing the same things together (*Miterleben*) or in retrospect; this produces an understanding between the members which, however, does not transcend the common experience (*Lebensgemeinschaft*); (3) artificial unity, in which all links connecting individuals have previously been shaped by particular and deliberate acts (society, *Gesellschaft*); there is no society, moreover, without a community (*Gemeinschaft*); (4) the unity of independent individual persons in an independent spiritual and individual common person. This latter unity is founded upon unity of essence in regard to a determinate value. Actually there are only two pure types of such common persons, (a) the church (salvational value) and (b) the nation or the cultural circle (the cultural common person, spiritual values of culture).

E. MAN AND GOD

The word "man" has two meanings. According to the first, man as *homo naturalis* is a small pocket, a *cul-de-sac*, of life, an isolated relic of incessant evolution; man, in this sense, has not raised himself out of the animal world; he was an animal, he is an animal, and an animal he will remain to eternity. The humanity of the *homo naturalis* has neither unity nor greatness, and there is no misconception worse than that which led Comte to worship this humanity as the "*grand être*." But "man" has still another meaning; man is the creature who prays, the searcher for God (*Gottsucher*), the ultimate image of the living God—the lightning flashing through the cloud of

148

mere natural existence and radiant with transcendent forms of meaning, value, and achievement: the "person."

Man enjoys an elemental and irreducible religious experience; the divine element belongs to the primitive givenness of the human consciousness. The formal designations of the divine essence are *ens a se*, infinity, omnipotence, holiness. The God of religion is a living God, he is a person, the person of persons; the God of pantheism is merely a poor reflection of theistic belief. The reproach of anthropomorphism against the latter is absurd and comical because it is not true that God is conceived according to man's image but rather that the only notion of "man" which makes sense is "theomorphism." In the last resort every soul believes either in God or in idols, and even the agnostic believes in nothingness; God responds to this faith by making a revelation from his own side, and so religion and belief are only granted as a result of the workings of a personal God.

Metaphysics, which is always hypothetical, can never provide a basis for religion. Furthermore the God of philosophy is nothing but an inflexible first cause, and the real reason why the medieval proofs of God's existence carried conviction was simply because the Middle Ages had a wealth of religious experience. Yet metaphysics is an essential preliminary even for religious knowledge, and a culture without metaphysics is a religious impossibility; but then religion gives a fresh interpretation to this systematization of the world's nature (*system of conformity*). Nevertheless Scheler himself suggests a fresh proof for God's existence; all knowledge of God is knowledge through God; now there is such knowledge, for example any religious act, therefore God exists. He is given as the correlate of the world for just as there is an individual person corresponding to each microcosm so the person of God corresponds to the whole of the world (macrocosm).

F. LOVE

The thoughts so far presented are revolutionary enough both in form and content but it was Scheler's extremely radical theory of love which he first used to shake the complacency of nineteenth-century thought. In the first place love is not sympathy because it is not a feeling at all; it neither presupposes a judgment nor is it an act of aspiration; it contains within itself no social element and can just as well be directed toward oneself as toward someone else. There was a serious misunderstanding in regard to this at the root of all relativist nineteenth-century theories; they identified love with altruism, an absurd notion by which the other had to be loved as other; they made it into a love of humanity alone, love for something abstract, a fresh monstrosity; they identified it with the inclination to help or improve others, a feature which may certainly result from love, but cannot account for its essence. Scheler's far-reaching analysis proves that altruism and similar forms of modern sentimentality are based upon resentment, upon hatred of the higher values and, in the last resort, of God. An attitude of envy toward those who are the bearers of higher values leads to egalitarian and humanitarian ideals and these are the fundamental denial of love.

Genuine love (like genuine hatred) is always love for a person and never love for a value as such; Scheler even maintains that one cannot love even the good. Love goes through and beyond the value of the person; it is directed toward the person as reality. When we analyze our love for a person it becomes apparent that the sum of values attached to the beloved person can never come near to accounting for that love; over and above it there always remains an "unaccountable." What is "over and above" is the concrete person of the beloved, the true object of love. The supreme ethical value of a person is only displayed to us when we share in the consummation of his loving act.

Love is a movement in which each concrete individual object that carries value achieves the highest possible value ideally destined for it. In striving to exalt the beloved it exalts the lover also. Understanding love is the plastic sculptor who in seeing a person's casual act or expressive gesture can bring out the highlights of his essential worth—unhampered by all that inductive and empirical knowledge which more often conceals the person's essence. For these reasons moral progress and the progress of values in general is bound up with the social exemplar, the genius, the hero and the saint.

The love of God, love at its highest pitch, is not to be thought of as love for God the all-bountiful, for it is participation in his love for the world (*amare mundum in Deo*). God is revealed as the supreme source of love; he endows the person with his ground of being, that is, his love. It is thoughts such as these which must in the end determine the theory of the community.

Toward the end of his life Scheler sketched out a philosophy which is largely a repudiation of his earlier notions. In his main thesis he insists that the higher levels of being are weaker than the lower ones, because the most primitive and powerful sources of energy are those of the inorganic world; blind to ideas and forms and shapes, they are a matrix of unconscious urges. On this basis Scheler traced out a theology strongly reminiscent of that which Alexander had developed previously. But this phase of his thought remained incomplete, and history will continue to regard him as a personalistic and theistic thinker. It will remain to his lasting credit that he broke away from nineteenth-century monistic prejudices and once more gave enhancement to the person; his wider significance is due to the fact that he made the transition to existentialism by emphasizing that the person could never be objectivized.

Philosophy of Essence

CONCLUDING CRITICISMS

The fundamental phenomenological intuition is that ideal essences are given. It has already been shown how this intuition helped Husserl and his pupils to overcome empiricism, idealism, and even conceptualism—that fundamental doctrine Kant's which denies the real existence of material essences. Furthermore phenomenological theory cleared the way to a recognition of two philosophical positions of capital importance: the objectivity of knowledge (distinguishing between the act of knowing and its object), and of the human spirit's true nature. All Neo-Kantians treat the latter as a purely discursive function, as the technical reason (*ratio*) of the sciences; the phenomenologists restored its character as a genuine *intellectus,* and *intus-lectio* which is not limited to connecting perceived phenomena but enjoys a capacity for grasping essences. The phenomenologists went one step further and came to recognize other aspects of the spirit, which they term "emotional." Having founded their philosophy upon the object they were well placed to rediscover a more vital conception of the human spirit and one that is closer to reality. Thus they appear to have overthrown Kantianism and with it the fundamental presuppositions of "modern" (1600-1900) philosophy; so phenomenology in this respect is one of the great liberating forces in contemporary thought. It also marks a deeper and more decisive break with the recent past than life-philosophy achieved; consequently it is much more important and more relevant to the present than the latter. Admittedly its technical and difficult character does not permit it to compete in popularity with the systems of Bergson and James, or even of Dilthey, yet it surpasses these philosophers as much on account of its inherent value as of its profound effect upon philosophers.

These facts would be sufficient to show the importance of Husserl and his disciples in their true perspective. But to say this does not end the matter, for by their decisive struggle against all forms of theoretical and axiological nominalism the phenomenologists have reopened the discussion of a number of the weightiest, long-forgotten problems as well as of new ones. Although their method is not new (all great philosophers have been phenomenologists in method), they have endowed it with remarkable refinement and purity, and have quite consciously employed it as *the* essential philosophical procedure. Scheler deserves special recognition for concentrating explicitly upon the human person; he is one of the philosophers representing that return to man which is so characteristic of our age.

And yet there is a certain sense in which phenomenology remains no more than a link between the nineteenth century and our own day. What it lacks is the capacity to grasp concrete being; it is a philosophy of essence and not of being. Even Scheler did not arrive at a genuine metaphysic despite the great progress he made in this direction; his "person" remains simply the nucleus of intentional acts and he still splits reality into the phenomenal and the transcendent. The phenomenologists did not press on far enough toward the concrete, toward real being.

The philosophers of two other schools, that of existentialism and that of contemporary metaphysics, which are both expressions of the same tendency, move somewhat further toward the problems of being and of man. Yet the representatives of both these schools, like the majority of contemporary philosophers, are aware of their dependence upon phenomenology. It is one of the main inspirations of philosophical thought today.

Philosophy of Essence

He looked around; he saw nothing there
but himself. First of all he cried out, "I
am!" . . . And then he became frightened;
thus one is frightened, when alone.

BRIHADARANYAKA UPANISHAD

VI

Philosophy of Existence

---

16. THE GENERAL CHARACTER OF EXISTENTIALIST PHILOSOPHY

A. WHAT EXISTENTIALISM IS NOT

After the second world war existentialism[5] became fashionable in many countries. The reading of Sartre's very difficult
work *L'Être et le Néant* presupposes so thorough a knowledge
of the history of philosophy that only professional, well-

---

[5] (Every existentialist develops his own terminology because he finds every-
day language inadequate, in the same way as he rebels against a day-to-day
view of the world. Consequently this chapter will prove to be exasperating—
though even this may be a blessing, because if one reads the existentialists
without exasperation one is almost certainly misreading them. It may help
English-speaking readers if we point out that Jaspers and Heidegger use the

trained philosophers can follow its line of thought; despite this it has gone into numerous editions of many thousands of copies. Moreover, French existentialists, especially Sartre, have met the public more than half way by expressing their ideas in novels and plays. This degree of popularity has led to various misunderstandings of philosophical existentialism which must first be disposed of. Therefore we shall begin by stating what philosophical existentialism it *not*.

Existentialism addresses itself to what are today called the "existential" problems of man—the meaning of life, of death, of suffering, to name but these. This is not to say that existentialism has originated these problems, since they have existed in all ages. But to call St. Augustine or Pascal an existentialist for that reason would be a mistake. The same holds of certain modern authors such as the Spanish critic, Miguel de Unamuno (1864-1937), the author of the great Russian "epic", Feodor M. Dostoievsky (1821-1881), or the German poet, Rainer Maria Rilke (1875-1926). These authors have, to be sure, discussed or given poetic embodiment to various human problems with great penetration. Nevertheless, they are not existentialist philosophers.

It would also be an error to designate as existentialists those philosophers who have concerned themselves with the idea of existence in the classical sense or with specific existing things. Those Thomists, therefore, who regard Thomas Aquinas as an existentialist are far off the track, and it is an equally grotesque

---

German word *Existenz* in rather different ways, yet for both of them it means the distinctive, unique, breath-taking, as opposed to what is common, placid, and hum-drum in human existence (the German word for the latter being *Dasein*). There is much to be said for treating Heidegger's philosophy as secularized Scotism, and the reader may find it valuable to compare Heidegger's vision with the Scotist vision of the poet Gerard Manley Hopkins. Hopkins's "in-stress," "pitch," "in-scape," "heaven-handling," etc., and the urgency of his "terrible" poems, all have their echoes in Heidegger.—*Tr.*)

Philosophy of Existence

error to number Husserl among the existentialists merely because he exerted great influence upon them. The fact is that Husserl "brackets out" existence.

Finally existentialism must not be identified with any one body of existentialist doctrine, for example, that of Sartre, for as we shall see there are profound differences between individual points of view.

In reply to all these misconstructions we emphasize that existentialist philosophy is a technical philosophical position which first came to its full development in our time and can be traced back no further than Kierkegaard, and that it has articulated itself into doctrines which diverge very widely—only those views which are held in common can be regarded as *the* existentialist philosophy.

B. ITS REPRESENTATIVES

Within the limits of the present account it seemed convenient first to enumerate the philosophers who are regarded as members of the school and then to bring out their common features. There are at least four contemporary philosophers who should undoubtedly be labeled 'existentialists,' Gabriel Marcel, Karl Jaspers, Martin Heidegger, and Jean-Paul Sartre. All of them invoke the name of Kierkegaard, who, in spite of belonging to an earlier period is generally regarded as an existentialist and exerts great influence in our own time. Besides these four leading thinkers there are not many real existentialist philosophers although existentialism interests and influences many philosophers. Among others, Sartre's co-worker Simone de Beauvoir should be mentioned but above all Maurice Merleau-Ponty, one of the ablest heads in contemporary French philosophy. Two Russian thinkers, Nikolai Berdyaev (1874-1948) and Leo Shestov (1866-1938), who became very well known through works written in French, must also be given

156

prominent mention. We note in this connection the famous Protestant theologian, Karl Barth (b. 1886) who has been markedly influenced by Kierkegaard. But it is a mistake to regard Louis Lavelle (1883-1951), an outspoken philosopher of being, as an existentialist. This outline confines itself to the views of the four philosophers mentioned first. Gabriel Marcel's views are considered only briefly since his major work had not appeared at the time this book was being prepared, and little insight can be gained from his other works into the main lines of his thought. The following dates are milestones in the history of existentialism. Kierkegaard died in 1855. Karl Jaspers's *Psychologie der Weltanschauungen* was published in 1919. Thereafter the following works appeared: Gabriel Marcel, *Journal métaphysique*, and Martin Heidegger, *Sein und Zeit*, in 1927; Karl Jaspers, *Philosophie*, in 1932; and Jean-Paul Sartre, *L'Être et le Néant*, in 1943. Existentialism has come to flourish only recently in the Latin countries, especially France and Italy, whereas it had already achieved its most significant development in Germany about 1930.

C. ORIGINS

During his lifetime the Danish Protestant thinker Søren Kierkegaard (1813-1855) aroused scarcely any interest, and his rediscovery in the twentieth century is attributable to the similarity between his own tragic, subjectivist thought and the spirit of our own day. Gabriel Marcel elaborated ideas of his own much akin to those of Kierkegaard, even before encountering the Dane's work. Kierkegaard never established a system of his own. He makes a fierce attack upon the Hegelian system on account of its "publicity" and objectivity, and denies the possibility of mediation, that is, the possibility of merging the opposition between thesis and antithesis into an all-embracing rational synthesis. He asserts the priority of

157

existence over essence and seems to be the first to have given the word "existence" an "existentialist" sense. He is radically anti-intellectualist, maintaining that God cannot be reached by any rational process, that the Christian faith is full of contradictions, and that any attempt to rationalize it is blasphemy. Kierkegaard combines his theory of dread with a theory concerning the utter loneliness of man in his relationship to God and the tragic destiny of man. He regards the instant as a synthesis of time and eternity.

Along with Kierkegaard, Husserl and his phenomenology have been profoundly significant for existentialism. Heidegger, Marcel, and Sartre make constant use of the phenomenological method, although they neither adhere to Husserl's conclusions nor even to his basic orientation—as a matter of fact Husserl's elimination of existence in his analysis sets him in opposition to existentialism.

Existentialism is also clearly indebted to life-philosophy and is in certain ways an expansion of the latter especially in its actualism, its analysis of time, and its criticism of rationalism and natural science. Bergson, Dilthey, and above all Nietzsche have supplied existentialism with many of its fundamental aims.

Lastly the new metaphysics has exercised a very powerful influence upon the philosophy of existence. All existentialists underline the typically metaphysical problem of being and some of them, such as Heidegger, display a profound acquaintance with the great ancient and medieval metaphysicians. In their efforts to arrive at a self-subsistent reality the existentialists have attempted a thorough-going refutation of idealism. Nevertheless, some of them, especially Jaspers, seem still to be very much under its influence.

Thus existentialism was born of the two great spiritual movements which led to the break with the nineteenth century and has come under the influence of yet another typical movement of our day, the new metaphysics.

D. COMMON FEATURES

1) The commonest characteristic among the various existentialist philosophies of the present is the fact that they all arise from a so-called existential *experience* which assumes a different form in each one of them. It is found by Jaspers, for instance, in awareness of the brittleness of being, by Heidegger through experiencing "propulsion toward death," and by Sartre in a general "nausea." The existentialists do not conceal the fact that their philosophies originate in such experiences. That is why existentialist philosophy always bears the stamp of personal experience, even in Heidegger.

2) The existentialists take so-called existence as the supreme object of inquiry, but the meaning which they attach to the word is extremely difficult to determine. However, in each case it signifies a peculiarly human mode of being. Man—a term which is rarely used and is generally replaced by "thereness" (*Dasein*), "existence," "ego," "being for oneself"—is unique in possessing existence; more precisely, man does not *possess*, but he *is* his existence. If man has an essence, either this essence is his existence or it is the consequence of it.

3) Existence is conceived as absolutely *actualistic;* it never *is* but freely *creates* itself, it becomes; it is a pro-jection; with each instant it is more (and less) than it is. The existentialists often support this thesis by the statement that existence is the same as temporality.

4) The difference between this actualism and that of life-philosophy is accounted for by the existentialists' regarding man as pure *subjectivity* and not as the manifestation of a broader (cosmic) life process in the way that Bergson does, for example. Furthermore, subjectivity is understood in a

159

creative sense; man creates himself freely, and *is* his freedom.

5) Yet it would be thoroughly misguided to conclude from this that the existentialists regard man as shut up within himself. On the contrary, man is an incomplete and open reality; thus his nature pins him tightly and necessarily to the *world*, and to other men in particular. This double dependence is assumed by all representatives of existentialism, and in such a way that human existence seems to be inserted into the world, so that man at all times not only faces a determinate situation but *is* his situation. On the other hand they assume that there is a special connection between men which, like the situation, gives existence its peculiar quality. That is the meaning of Heidegger's "togetherness," Jaspers's "communication," and Marcel's "thou."

6) All existentialists repudiate the distinction between subject and object, thereby discounting the value of *intellectual knowledge* for philosophical purposes. According to them true knowledge is not achieved by the understanding but through experiencing reality; this experience is primarily caused by the dread with which man becomes aware of his finitude and the frailty in that position of being thrust into the world and condemned to death (Heidegger).

Several other common features of minor importance may be discerned in existentialism, but deep differences between its individual representatives are equally evident. For example, Marcel is like Kierkegaard in being a confirmed theist whereas Jaspers adopts a sort of transcendence which should not be interpreted as either theism, pantheism, or atheism, because Jaspers repudiates all of these. Heidegger's philosophy at first seems to be atheistic but his very categorical though, unfortunately, unexpanded statements definitely exclude this interpretation. Finally Sartre tries to work out a professed and logical atheism.

The aims and methods of individual existentialist philosophers are equally different. Heidegger tries to establish an ontology in the Aristotelian sense, and his use of a strict method is copied by Sartre. Jaspers refuses to admit any sort of ontology as a means of elucidating existence but expands a metaphysical system, and the method which he employs seems to be a very flexible one.

17. MARTIN HEIDEGGER

A. ORIGINS. CHARACTERISTICS

Martin Heidegger (b. 1889) began his career as a Jesuit novice. He took his doctorate at Freiburg im Breisgau after studying under Rickert, and then attached himself to Husserl. Under the latter he prepared himself for a university lectureship with a thesis on categories and signification in Duns Scotus's teaching (1916), and became coeditor of the *Jahrbuch für Philosophie und phänomenologische Forschung*. In 1923 he was appointed professor at Marburg where he published his most important work, the first part of *Sein und Zeit* (1927). Soon after, in 1928, he returned to Freiburg as Husserl's successor and continued to teach there until 1946.

Heidegger is an extremely original thinker. The problem of his historical affiliations is not of primary concern here and we need only mention that he borrows his method from Husserl, that he is in many ways influenced by Dilthey, and that his general thesis is largely inspired by Kierkegaard. Heidegger is equipped with an unusual knowledge of the great philosophers of the past, among whom he frequently quotes Aristotle, although he interprets him in very arbitrary fashion. A stir was caused by the volume which he devoted to Kant, *Kant und das Problem der Metaphysik* (1929).

Few philosophers are so hard to understand as Heidegger.

161

The difficulty does not stem from inadequacy in expression or weakness in logical structure, for Heidegger's work always proceeds in very systematic fashion. The difficulty arises rather from the unusual and strange terminology which he has devised in the hope of providing a language for conveying his thoughts. This is a source of numerous misunderstandings and one of the reasons why his philosophy is often treated as a joke, particularly by the neopositivists.

B. PROBLEM AND METHOD

The aim of Heidegger's main work is to evolve a concrete answer to the question of the meaning of being. This question had not only fallen into complete oblivion but had generally been misstated under the impression that being is self-evident and obvious. As a matter of fact the average person does have a vague and middling understanding of being, but it is a very obscure concept all the same. In reality, being (*Sein*) is not the same as *a* being, the subject which has being or is in being (*das Seiende*), but is the determinant of such a being as a being. If we wish to find an answer to the question as to the meaning of being we have to search for a being which is just as accessible to us as it is in itself. But this search is itself a certain being's mode of being—of the being, in fact, that is ourselves; the latter is what Heidegger calls "human existence" (*Dasein*).[6] Therefore the analysis of being as human existence is declared to be the starting point of the investigation. It is the peculiar quality of human existence that it is a being which, in being, is interested in this very being. The understanding of being is in

---

[6] (Undoubtedly this rendering of *Dasein* is but an approximation but it has some currency in English versions of existentialist writings and may at least lead the reader on toward the correct meaning. For a discussion of this point see Heidegger's *Existence and Being*, Vision Press or Henry Regnery, pp. 396-397.—*Tr.*)

itself an element in the being of human existence, and for this reason human existence is said to be "ontological," while all other beings are only "ontic." The being itself to which human existence is specifically related is called *Existenz*. To determine the essence of human existence requires much more than a matter-of-fact answer to the question "What?" For the "essence" of human existence, is found in its existence, from which alone it can be understood. Only by existing do we understand existence in its purity; such an understanding is called by Heidegger "existential" (*existentiell*). On the other hand, the coherence peculiar to the structure of existence is known as "existentiality" (*Existentialität*) and its analysis, "existential understanding" (*existentiales Verstehen*); it is an elucidation of human existence through the qualities of its being, known as "existentials"—in contrast to the categories, which are qualities of being proper to beings other than human existence. Existential analysis is fundamental ontology; it forms the basis of every ontology and of all the sciences. Its only possible method is the phenomenological one; whatever displays itself as what it is, is a "phenomenon." This means that phenomena are not appearances in the common acceptation of the word. The word ending "-logy" in "phenomenology" comes from λέγειν, which implies raising a being out of its hiddenness, since many phenomena are either undiscovered or else recede into obscurity. Thus phenomenology in this sense is hermeneutics (Dilthey), and is applied to existence in order to reveal its structure. Philosophy, consequently, is *universal phenomenological ontology proceeding from the hermeneutics of human existence*, the analysis of existence which follows out the thread of all philosophical inquiry to that foundation from which it originates and to which it must always return.

But Heidegger has not yet carried out anything more than an analysis of human existence upon which a universal ontology

163

might be founded; so far the second half of *Sein und Zeit* has not yet appeared.[7]

C. BEING-IN-THE-WORLD

The mark of human existence is that it exists, that it has the character of being to each one his own (*Jemeinigkeit*), that is, it can never constitute an exemplar under a genus, and that it stands in various relationships toward its being. The ground for these modes of being is being-in-the-world. This in-dwelling is not a being-relationship between two spatially extended beings, any more than between subject and object; it finds expression rather as preoccupation with (*Besorgen*), if a being other than one having human existence is involved, and as concern for (*Fürsorge*), if it is directed toward another being which enjoys human existence. The world is not made up of things but of tools (*Zeuge*) which are always "for" something. Handiness (*Zuhandenheit*) is the mode of being appropriate to a tool, and what is handy always involves a connection with other handy things; each tool has a bearing upon another tool as well as having an owner and a user. The characteristic being of anything handy is to be found in its circumstances (*Bewandtnis*); the latter inevitably lead to the questions "for what?" and "to what intent?" and thus to human existence. Therefore, the possibility of discovering anything that is handy has human existence for its condition. Every tool has its place, that is, it is brought into line, set up, and so on. The potential place of a tool is its region. In human existence one notices an essential tendency toward proximity, that is, toward the drawing together of what is handy. Objective distances provide no

---

[7] The *Brief über den "Humanismus"* and other new writings of Heidegger contains indications of a fundamental change in his thinking. But since this latest phase of his philosophy is more suggested than explicitly set forth, it is not considered here.

indication of the proximity or remoteness of anything handy because it is preoccupation which constitutes the measure both of proximity and of remoteness. It follows that the world is an ontological determination of human existence, and exists only for a given human existence.

All earlier ontologies were guilty of assuming that handiness was the same as being present or at hand (*Vorhandenheit*), a mistake of which Descartes was particularly guilty (*res extensa*). In actual fact, not only is handiness not founded upon being-at-hand but, on the contrary, mere being-at-hand is no more than a defective mode of handiness.

The very fact that a tool is used for work means that other human existences are also given at the same time; the world of human existence is a world in which we are together (*Mitwelt*); the in-dwelling of human existence involves the coming together of various human existences, and human existence itself is essentially togetherness. Just as the model relationship of human existence in regard to a tool is that of preoccupation, similarly its relationship in regard to another human existence is that of concern for it. Concern may take charge of some matter with which this other is preoccupied, or it may help this other to achieve freedom in the welter of its concern. Empathy is only possible on the basis of togetherness.

D. "THERENESS" (DAS "DA") AND CONCERN

Not only is human existence in the world, it is essentially constituted by being-in-the-world; it is its "thereness," and as "thereness" it illumines itself—it is its own *disclosure* (*Erschlossenheit*). "Disclosure" does not signify the act of knowing; it signifies the "existential" at the root of the act. This mode of being contains three elements, realization of one's situation (*Befindlichkeit*), understanding (*Verstehen*), and discourse (*Rede*), all of which have the same origin.

165

In realizing one's situation one finds that an all-pervasive mood is upon one, by means of which human existence as a being is disclosed and its "facticity"—its "that it is"—unfolds itself. This "that it is" is the same as "being flung down" (*Geworfenheit*). It needs to be emphasized that "facticity" is not simple presence but is a being-characteristic of human existence.

Understanding is taken here in the same sense as one claims "a capacity for coming face to face with (*vorstehen*) a thing". Understanding is that mode of being of human existence which is capacity-for-being. Human existence cannot be equated with simple presence, but rather it always *is* what it *can be*; it is a "down-flung" potentiality. The essential structure of understanding is called "project" in Heidegger's terminology; by it one secures an existential grasp of the range of the capacity for being, and it is that aspect of human existence in which human existence *is* its potentiality. When the understanding expands it is called "exposition" (*Auslegung*), although this does not necessarily take the form of a statement.

Discourse is the foundation of language but is not language itself; it is the meaningful articulation of the discovered intelligibility of being-in-the-world. Man is ζῷον λόγον ἔχον, a being capable of discourse, which is so broadly interpreted that its modalities include both listening and keeping silent.

The integral structure of "thereness" (*Da*) is most readily conceivable when dread (*Angst*) is assumed as the ground of the phenomenon in question. The difference between dread and fear is that the threat which produces dread is nowhere. It is the world as such which inspires dread, and the reason for it is the possibility of being-in-the-world. But this being is always "self-transcendent" (*über sich hinaus*). Hence the structure of human existence appears to consist in the encounter of being as already-being-oneself-in-the-world with other beings. This is none other than anxiety (*Sorge*). Everything which human existence does or wishes or knows, its preoccupation and concern, its theorizing, practicing, willing, wishing, pushing, and struggling, is simply a manifestation of anxiety. Anxiety is the being of human existence.

E. MAN[8] AND BEING-UNTO-DEATH

This analysis is incomplete because so long as human existence exists it has not achieved "wholeness"; its essence remains unfinished. Death alone is the end of human existence.

Yet with death human existence can no longer be grasped as a being, and we can never have a genuine experience of another's death. But human existence is neither completed nor simply eliminated at death: by the ending brought about through death we mean being unto the end of human existence. Death is a possibility of being and, indeed, the most unique, unrelated, and unovertakeable of these possibilities. The very being of human existence is being-unto-death. Human existence is committed to this way of being from the moment of its inception.

It is this self-same fact which throws human existence into dread, and leads it to flee into the world; it seeks refuge in *"man"* through dread of its own being, through the fear of encountering dread. *Man* is an existential, a mode of being, the unauthentic (*uneigentlich*) being of human existence. Here it becomes slave to a neuter which forces its own viewpoint and behavior upon human existence. This *man* is neither a determinate man nor the aggregate of men; its most characteristic feature is that it induces mediocrity and tends to bring

---

[8] (As noted further on in the text *man* is the German term commonly translated "one" in English, as in "one never knows what will happen." Etymologically it springs from the same source as *Mann*, the German equivalent of "man" or "husband" in English.—*Tr.*)

Philosophy of Existence

everything down to one level. It relieves human existence of the necessity for decision and for the acknowledgment of responsibility—"one" (*man*) does this or that. *Man* is a seduction, a narcotic, and an estrangement; it externalizes itself in talk, in being-said, where the mere dictum passes for appropriateness of discourse, in restless curiosity, in distraction, haste, and, finally, ambiguity. It becomes impossible to decide what has been disclosed and what has not. These form the characteristics of day-to-day being, which is termed the "falling away" of human existence, because in this case human existence falls away from itself and falls into the world.

Dread of death produces this unauthentic, day-to-day being which is de facto *untruth*; *man* does not allow himself to think of his own death but simply says "one has to die" (*man stirbt*).

F. CONSCIENCE AND RESOLUTENESS

To snatch ourselves back again out of the grip of *man* is to make a choice, to commit ourselves spontaneously to the possibility of being arising from the most intimate self. Our conscience bears witness to such a possibility. *Conscience* is a mode of discourse, a call which unbinds the spell cast upon human existence by *man* and his idle talk. Conscience cannot be explained as a biological function, nor should it be regarded as the voice of an alien power (God); the call comes from anxiety, from human existence, which in being "thrown down," becomes anxious about its possibility of being. The call of conscience does not say anything which could be "debated"; its weird silence points toward guilt. Here there is no question of guiltiness in its common connotation but of the ground for that connotation, and that ground is nothingness. Guiltiness does not therefore in the first instance arise from wrongful behavior. On the contrary, nothingness belongs to the existential meaning of our being "thrown down;" not only does projection (*Entwurf*) derive from the nothingness of the ground of being—it is itself essentially null. Thus guiltiness belongs to the being of human existence and indicates the null being upon which its nullity is grounded.

When we deliberately choose the path of conscience we assert our readiness to face dread along with the silence in which it is completed. Heidegger calls it "resoluteness" (*Entschlossenheit*) when we silently project ourselves into our own guiltiness and are prepared to face the dread of it; it constitutes the loyalty of existence toward its own self, it is freedom unto death. It liberates human existence from *man* but does not free it from his world. The opposite is true, because only resoluteness enables other fellow beings to really "be" according to their own particular capacity for being. Resoluteness alone lays bare the situation by disclosing the insistent "thereness" present in it. It is the means by which men embrace their destiny and spontaneously accept their role in the world.

G. TEMPORALITY AND HISTORICITY

Resoluteness supplies the key to the problem of unity in human existence. The latter is not grounded in the "I," and the reason why *man* cries out "I, I" (*"Ich, Ich"*) so frequently and noisily is because fundamentally this cry does not refer to his proper self. Neither the traditional nor the Kantian theory managed to elevate itself above this viewpoint of the *man*. An analysis of the "I," however, shows it to be the expression of anxiety. The self, then, is constantly present as the ground of anxiety, and the self-dependence of the "I" is nothing other than anticipatory resoluteness. Now anticipatory resoluteness is identical with being unto that most intimate and absolutely unique potentiality of being, being unto death. But this is only so because human existence is able to come face to face with

169

itself, that is, because it has a capacity for endurance. The future is the readiness to face and endure the approaching possibilities. We find also that the only fact which makes it possible to be "flung down" is that future human existence can be its *past*—human existence can only come to itself so far as it comes back to itself. Finally, no situation affords the possibility of resolute being except in the "presentation" of what is in being. To anticipate this future coming-back-upon-ourselves is already to introduce resoluteness as a present factor in the situation; this phenomenon taken as a whole is named "temporality." Temporality is the meaning of anxiety and, therefore, of existence; it is essentially ec-static, a primordial "being beside oneself". The future, the past, and the present are all ec-stases of temporality. Among these the future is primary. But since human existence is being-unto-death our individual future reveals itself as finite. Primordial time is finite.

Every existential can be explained, and must be explained, through the temporality which makes it possible. But human existence does not exist as the sum of momentary realities; far from traveling a predestined route, human existence extends itself in such a fashion that from the very outset its being constitutes itself as something extended. "End" and "betweenness" *are* only so long as human existence exists. Heidegger describes the activity peculiar to extension which extends itself as the "occurrence" (*Geschehen*) of human existence, and the revelation of the structure of occurrence constitutes our understanding of historicity (*Geschichtlichkeit*). Primarily, it is human existence which is historical, but in a lesser way so are inward being and even the world. But the latter exists only through the maturing (*zeitigen*) of human existence. An historical occurrence is an occurrence of being-in-the-world.

This analysis enables Heidegger to develop a theory of time, in the light of which he subjects all previous theories to a critical examination, and in which he pays particular attention to the Aristotelian and Hegelian standpoints.

H. TRANSCENDENCE AND NOTHINGNESS

Heidegger has no more than sketched the main lines of his metaphysics, which is very difficult to interpret correctly.

The relationship of human existence to beings which do not enjoy human existence is transcendent in a double-edged manner. On the one hand human existence is thrown down into the world and is attuned to and utterly subject to the beings in it; in this way the world transcends human existence. On the other hand, human existence is really the "formative" agent of the world; it transcends the world; the domination which it exercises over things in being is so complete that it actually draws them out of their fundamental hiddenness and endows them with being, that is, with meaning and truth. There can be particular beings (*Seiende*) but no being (*Sein*) without human existence. This "domination" is the very self-hood of human existence; human existence is realized in transcending such beings. The "essence" of human existence is to transcend.

There remains human existence in its third transcendence, the transcendence of nothingness. Nothingness is not only a logical category, it is even primarily an ontological category, because instead of negation constituting a basis for nothingness, nothingness (ontic nothingness) provides the basis of negation. Human existence is related to nothingness as follows: first, human existence has no ground, it originates in the abyss of nothingness; second, it culminates in death, which is another abyss of nothingness; third, the very being of human existence is an anticipation of death, of nothingness: it is intrinsically void. Meanwhile, all those beings which do not enjoy human existence are brought forth out of nothingness. Heidegger

171

recognizes universal validity in the dictum, *ex nihilo omne ens qua ens fit*. Though on his own principles he should say, "nothingness exists," he attempts to avoid this nonsensical expression by saying, "nothingness makes nought" (*das Nichts selbst nichtet*)—a phrase which has caused much amusement, especially to the neopositivists.

The question now is, what meaning is to be attached to "nothingness." A tentative answer runs as follows: beings without human existence come to be out of nothingness through human existence, a process consisting in the bestowal of intelligibility (truth) through human existence; it is only being (*Sein*) and not beings (*Seiende*) themselves, which arises out of human existence; therefore Heidegger's thought may perhaps be expressed by saying that "nothingness" is conceived as a being without being, as an utterly unintelligible chaos. He treats human existence as the *lumen naturale* which alone supplies beings with their meaning and structure. If this interpretation is correct, Heidegger's philosophy must be interpreted as a radically immanentist philosophy according to which all meaning is dependent upon human existence. But though it is commonly supposed that this is his intention, it is sharply rejected by Heidegger. Nor should his philosophy be taken as a kind of subjectivism. Heidegger states emphatically that the world is involved in the original of both objectivity and subjectivity.

These arguments lead directly to Heidegger's teaching about freedom. Human existence establishes itself as a pro-ject by asserting its domination (*Uberstieg*)—domination is freedom itself. One can even say that human existence is freedom. And since all interpretations and all grounds come from human existence, it follows that freedom is the ultimate ground of all intelligibility: "Freedom is the ground of the ground" seems to be the last word in Heidegger's philosophy.

18. Jean-Paul Sartre

A. HIS WORK AND ITS CHARACTER

In the years after the Second World War Jean-Paul Sartre (b. 1905) was the most discussed philosopher of Europe. His fame in nonphilosophical circles is of course owing largely to his brilliant fiction and plays and to the superficial summary of his philosophy in *L'Existentialisme est un Humanisme*, 1946. But beyond this, Sartre is the author of a series of serious philosophical works and his *L'Être et le Néant*, 1943, a difficult and highly technical work of great scope, should earn a place among the philosophical classics of our time.

It would be a complete misunderstanding of Sartre to regard him only as a compiler of books. He is not only a professional philosopher with a precise, technical, and original mode of thinking but also, of all the existentialists, the one who comes nearest to having a philosophy of being. It is noteworthy, moreover, that as the only philosopher who openly avows existentialism he has nothing of the kind of poetic-romantic inclination which so often characterizes this philosophy. On the contrary, his system is developed with strict logic, and is thoroughly rationalistic and, one might almost say, aprioristic. What Sartre is doing is anthropology, but it is anthropology which rests upon an ontology, and it consists almost wholly in the consistent application of ontological principles to man and his problems. One may rightly see in this philosophy an expression of the despair of the post-war individual, especially the French, and find in it the "world-view of a man without faith, family, friends or a goal in life." It is also clear that Sartre's influence is not in the end to be explained only by his preoccupation with theological problems—in the atheistic sense, of course. Despite all this one cannot deny the first-rate importance of his philosophical system or the astonishing

173

acuity of his treatment of many fundamental metaphysical problems.

Sartre is obviously dependent upon Heidegger. But he is not necessarily a Heideggerian, and Heidegger has justly declined all responsibility for "Sartrism". Like all existentialist philosophers, Sartre is a follower of Kierkegaard, but he often propounds solutions of problems of existence which completely contradict those originally propounded by the Danish religious thinker. He seems also to be influenced in many ways by Nietzsche. Husserl's doctrines are everywhere built into the fabric of his system as its presuppositions. Some basic ideas derive from Hegel, for example the antithesis between being and nothing, though of course without the ensuing synthesis of these. In drawing out his metaphysical conclusions, Sartre works on the plane of the old Greek philosophers. His system can be looked upon as an attempt to develop a philosophy which both corresponds to and confutes Aristotelianism, and many of his theses remind one of Parmenides. Some of his ideas about empirical freedom (not discussed here) especially his treatment of contingency, come close to Thomism.

B. BEING-IN-ITSELF

Sartre's existential system is apparently far removed from Kierkegaard's line of thought which is "subjective" and based upon personal experience. It proves to be a strictly rational, aprioristic, system of ontology. Proceeding from an analysis of being, the most general principles derived from this analysis are applied in the strictest possible way to special fields, such as questions of the nature of man.

One of these principles involves a complete rejection of the Aristotelian doctrine of potentiality. Whatever is, manifests itself in actuality (*tout est en acte*). In what truly is, there is not and cannot be any possibility or potentiality or ἕξις. So, for example, it is meaningless to ask what the genius of Proust might yet have accomplished, for his genius consists in nothing more than the totality of his works as an expression of his personality and not in the possibility of composing this or that work. Of a given being we can say no more than that it is, that it is in itself, and that it is what it is. A being *is*: it does not have being nor has it acquired being. There is no ultimate ground for the existence of a being. It is radically contingent, inexplicable, absurd. Essences can no doubt be explained, as when one explains a circle by means of a mathematical formula, but existence could be explicable only through God and there is no God—even the very concept of creation is self-contradictory. It follows that existence is prior to the essence of any given being. Green shoots do not develop by virtue of a divine idea. First of all, they *are*. Further, a being is in itself. It is therefore called by Sartre "being-in-itself" (*l'en-soi*). It is neither passive nor active, neither an affirmation nor a negation. In itself it is massive, rigid and still. Finally, a being is that which it is. Here, other being is completely excluded. A being has no relation to other beings. It is beyond time. Of course Sartre cannot deny the becoming of being-in-itself, but this becoming, he holds, is conditioned by determining causes, and is thus likewise a rigid and immobile becoming. This analysis has a remarkable similarity to the Parmenidean ontology and the question naturally poses itself how in such a rigid, immobile, deterministic universe, a free and knowing being such as man could ever arise.

C. BEING-FOR-ITSELF

The answer to the latter question is that it is possible because there is in the universe in addition to these rigid and massive beings which are determined by being-in-itself still another and quite different type of being, namely, being-for-

175

oneself (*le pour-soi*) which is specifically human being. But since everything which is must be a being and thus be being-in-itself, Sartre concludes quite consistently that this other type of being can only be non-being and therefore must consist in nothing (*le néant*). The origin of human being is that particular being negates itself (*se néantise*). The nothing is to be taken quite literally here. Sartre says that the nothing *is not;* in fact one cannot even say that it negates itself—only a being can negate itself and the nothing can exist only in particular beings, for example in "a little lake", "a worm".

That man as such, that is, as being-for-himself, consists in nothing, is shown in the following manner. First, with Heidegger, Sartre begins by saying that negation does not provide the basis of the nothing, but contrariwise, that negation has a basis in the object itself, and thus that there are such things as "negative realities" (*des négatites*). So for example, when an automobile is out of order we can look at or investigate the carburetor and find that there is *nothing* there. But now, the nothing cannot derive from being-in-itself, for being-in-itself is, as already noted, filled to the full with being. Hence the nothing comes into the world through man. But in order for man to be the source of the nothing, man must already bear the nothing within him. And in fact the analysis of being-for-itself shows, according to Sartre, that man not only bears the nothing within him but consists in nothing. This is of course not to be understood as saying that man as a whole is nothing at all, for in man there is being-in-itself, his body, his ego, his habits, etc. Nevertheless, what is *specifically* human consists beyond all this in the nothing.

D. CONSCIOUSNESS AND FREEDOM

Sartre teaches that being-for-oneself is characterized by three ec-stases: to the nothing, to what is other, and to being.

The first ec-stasis is that of consciousness and freedom. Consciousness (*conscience*), which is the first thing Sartre analyzes, is not reflexive consciousness but that which accompanies every instance of knowing. For example, when I count my cigarettes, I am conscious only in an unreflexive manner of counting them. This kind of consciousness has no content, no essence; it is mere existence. For what appears to be its content derives actually from the object. It *is* not, really. For if it were a given being it would be dense and full and could not become that other thing which it becomes in being known, and this fundamentally is what knowing is. Consciousness is therefore a release of a being (*décompression de l'être*), a kind of fission of a being. Negating is evident in self-consciousness also, for between that of which we are conscious and consciousness itself there is only a segment of the nothing. Even a thing so typically human as asking a question is founded in the nothing, for, in order to ask, the questioner must first negate a particular being (for unless it were not negated, it could not be asked), and then negate himself, his being determinately so-or-so, for otherwise every question would be meaningless from the start.

The nothingness of being-for-oneself appears clearer in the case of freedom. If man were determined by his past, he could not choose. But the fact is, he does choose, and thus he negates his past. Likewise when he strives he strives necessarily for what *is* not. Hence freedom must not be thought of as a property of being-for-oneself, for it is identical with it. Exactly as in Heidegger, Sartre regards being-for-oneself as a pro-ject (*pro-jet*). It comes to be in due time, and here the basic ec-stasis is what is yet-to-come, the future (*a-venir*).

From this two important conclusions follow. First, man has as such no nature, no fixed essence. His essence is simply his freedom, his indeterminateness. Second, man's conscious ex-

177

istence is not only prior to essence as with being-for-itself: existence is the essence of being-for-oneself. Sartre formulates the basic contention of all existentialist philosophers more clearly than any of the others.

Freedom reveals itself in dread. This is man's becoming conscious of his own being, which appears as the nothing, or of freedom. Man flees from dread and with this he seeks to escape not only his freedom, that is, the future, but even his past. For he would like to look upon this past as a principle of his freedom although it is but a being-for-itself which is finished once and for all, an immobile and foreign being-in-itself. But man cannot escape freedom for man *is* his dread. Thus the first ecstasis of being-for-itself is necessarily condemned to shatter.

E. BEING-FOR-ANOTHER

The second ec-stasis of being-for-itself is being-for-another. Relationship to others is of the very essence of man. Sartre holds that we do not have sexual drives because we have sexual organs; on the contrary, we have sexual organs because it is of the essence of man to be sexually inclined, to be-for-another. The existence of others does not need to be demonstrated. It is immediately given in the phenomenon of shame. The other person appears to him who is-for-himself in the first place in the glance (*regard*). So long as there is no one else in our visual field we organize all things around ourselves as the center. They are *our* objects. But if another person enters this field and looks about him the situation is at once disturbed. He seeks not only to draw our things into *his* field but to make of us an object in his world.

Accordingly a fundamental relationship must prevail between beings-for-themselves. Each one seeks to make an object of the other. Of course it is not a question of overmastering the other as a mere thing, of killing him, for example. The being-for-itself wants to dominate the other as a free being, to possess him both as an object and as a free being. In his extended and penetrative analysis of normal and pathological sex life (no doubt the main source of his fame among nonphilosophers) Sartre attempts to show the centrality of this notion of domination of others. We do not desire the body of another, nor even our own pleasure, but the other himself. One means to this is the identification of oneself with the other in the erotic caress. But all this ends and must necessarily end in shattering, for its goal is contradictory. The second ec-stasis of being-for-itself is thus condemned to shatter.

F. POSSIBILITY, VALUE, AND GOD

There is no potentiality in being-in-itself. The only source of the possible is being-for-another for of course the possible *is not*. Even value is nothing, modality of nothing. The basis of all value is the free choice of a being-for-itself which chooses itself and its values. Hence there is but one fundamental moral law: choose thyself! This law is always followed, for man is condemned to be free (*condamné à être libre*).

The question now arises: What is it that man always seeks, in what does his basic resolve and his primary choice consist? Existentialist psychoanalysis provides the answer, namely that basically being-for-itself always seeks but one thing, being. It is naught in itself, but it would *be*. But it does not wish to become mere being-in-itself. In suggestive style Sartre describes that revulsion (*nausée*) which in the face of the sticky and clammy (*agglutinant, visqueux*) character of being-in-itself overwhelms man, and that dread at being choked by being-in-itself. What man wants is to become a being-in-itself which at the same time provides its own foundation, in other words, to become a being-in-and-for-itself. Man wants to be God. Man's passion is in a sense the reverse of the passion of Christ, for

179

man shall die that God may live. But God is impossible—being-in-and-for-itself is contradictory. So finally the third ec-stasis of being-for-itself, the quest for being, shatters. Man is a useless passion—*l'homme est une passion inutile.*

G. THEORY OF KNOWLEDGE

The basic ideas of Sartre's ontology and metaphysics which we have now sketched are supplemented and elucidated by an astonishing number of phenomenological and psychological analyses, and these may even be by far the most valuable part of the whole system. Sartre considers also a number of more special questions. Among these we shall only touch on the problem of knowledge, a problem which in part Sartre treats at the very beginning of his work although its solution obviously depends upon his ontology.

Sartre professes a radical phenomenalism. There is nothing but phenomena, and these only, in fact, in Husserl's sense. Behind them there stands no Kantian noumenon or Aristotelian substance—he seems scarcely to distinguish between these two concepts. The phenomenon of being is merely one phenomenon among others, for being, too, is given. But there is not just the phenomenon of being but also the being of this phenomenon. The phenomenon of being is therefore, in St. Anselm's sense, "ontological", that is, it evokes being, it is transphenomenal. The idealists, who seek to reduce being to being known, are not aware that in order to reach this conclusion, they should first have to establish the *being* of knowledge, for otherwise everything dissolves into a radical nihilism. But even classical realism errs when it regards knowledge as an attribute, a function of an already existing subject. The fact is that all that is is being-in-itself and knowledge is a *nothing*. Knowledge has no content. It is a being-present of what has being-for-itself for being-in-itself as something different. It follows that everything which coheres with knowledge (so also truth) is purely human. Even the world is human. It is formed by being-in-itself from rigid and massive being-in-self. Things which appear in such a world are always the tools (*Zeuge*) of Heidegger. For man is an eternal quest for being and for selfhood, a quest which reaches out toward the oncoming possibilities afforded by being; being-in-itself necessarily appears to him as a means to his ends.

It may safely be said that there has never been a more extreme form of realism in the history of philosophic thought. Not without justification has this existentialism, which by its very name ought to provide an explanation of human existence, been described as a meontology, a theory of nonexistence. We can merely mention, finally, the ethical consequences of his meontology, the denial of all objective value and law, the assertion of the total meaninglessness of human life (even death is not regarded as its meaning), and the rejection of any justification for taking life seriously.

19. GABRIEL MARCEL

A. DEVELOPMENT AND CHARACTERISTIC

Gabriel Marcel (b. 1889) and Karl Jaspers, with whom he is often compared, belong to the second group of existentialist philosophers. They go their own way, as compared with Heidegger and Sartre, to the extent that they recognize not only "horizontal" but also "vertical" transcendence (that is, toward God), and that furthermore they reject both rational analysis and ontology, in the classical sense of the term, and are content with loose description of existential experience. The position of Marcel is so expressly antisystematic that his views are more difficult to put together than those of any other existentialist. In fact no one has as yet succeeded in doing so.

Philosophy of Existence

For this reason and also because Marcel has given only a preliminary announcement of his principal work (*Research into the Essence of Spiritual Life*) which is to offer an attempt at systematization, it is wise to restrict the summation of his philosophy, admittedly of great significance, to the mere essentials.

In point of time Marcel is the first of the contemporary existentialist philosophers. As early as 1914 he enunciated existentialist theses in his article *Existence et objectivité*. He is perhaps the closest to Kierkegaard in the whole school, but it must be noted that he developed his basic ideas before he had read a line of Kierkegaard. The general lines of his development, as presented in his two "metaphysical diaries" (*Journal métaphysique*, 1914-1917, and *Être et avoir*, 1918-1933), parallel those of Kierkegaard. Just as Kierkegaard's point of departure was his opposition to Hegel, so Marcel freed himself from idealism only very gradually through long preoccupation with the English neo-Hegelians and with Royce (*La Métaphysique de Royce*, 1945), and arrived finally at a subjective, existential philosophy. He began with the idea that in order to demonstrate the existence of God one must first specify more precisely the concept of existence. His studies along this line led to the development of a "concrete" philosophy. Marcel was then converted to Catholicism, and he is today one of the most important Catholic spokesmen in philosophy in France. Yet his attitude toward traditional Catholic philosophy, especially Thomism, has been consistently negative. In 1949 he was named to the Gifford lectureship, the highest honor for a philosopher and one which only a few Continental philosophers (Hans Driesch, Étienne Gilson, Karl Barth, among others) have achieved. Marcel is as little an academic figure as Sartre. But through his wide contact with the younger generation he has exerted a marked influence

on French thought and is today one of the most prominent
European philosophers.

B. BASIC IDEAS

Marcel holds that being-an-object and existence are two
entirely different dimensions of being. This is seen most clearly
in the fundamental problem of embodiment (*incarnation*).
The relation between my body and myself cannot be described
as either being or having. I *am* my body, yet I cannot identify
myself with it. The question about embodiment has led Marcel
to a rigorous distinction between the *problem* and the *mystery*.
A problem concerns what lies wholly before me, something
which I can scan objectively as an observer. A mystery, on
the other hand, is "something in which I am involved (*en-
gagé*)". Only mysteries are of any philosophic relevance and
thus philosophy must be transobjective, personal, dramatic,
indeed tragic. "I am not witnessing a spectacle": we should
remind ourselves of this every day, says Marcel. The possibility
of suicide is the point of departure of every genuine metaphysics. Such a metaphysics must be neither rational or intuitive. It is the result of a kind of second reflection (*réflexion
seconde*).

Marcel has not worked out this metaphysics, but he has
adumbrated its methodology. It is to give an answer to the
basic ontological demand, namely, that there must be being,
there must be something which cannot be explained away in
some easy way as, for example, psychoanalysis explains away
psychic phenomena. We are certain that there is being through
the mysterious reality of the "I am"—not through *cogito ergo
sum*. In this way the opposition of subject and object, of idealism, is overcome. Human reality reveals itself as the reality of
a *homo viator*, of being which is always in process of becoming. Every philosophy which misinterprets this truth, which

183

tries to explain man by means of a system, is incapable of understanding man.

We are led to the understanding of human being above all through the study of human relationships which are signified by judgments in the second person, in the *thou*. These unobjective thou-relationships are creative, for through them I create myself and also help another to create his own freedom. Here Marcel is close to the Jewish philosopher Martin Buber (b. 1878) who had enunciated similar theses even before Marcel. The center of the thou-relationship is faithfulness (*fidélité*). It appears as the embodiment of a higher free actuality, since the faithful one creates himself in freedom. Hope is even more basic than faithfulness, for the latter is built upon hope. Marcel holds that hope has ontological significance. It shows that the victory of death in the world is merely apparent and not final. Marcel regards his doctrine of hope as the most important result of his work. Here he departs radically from Sartre and Heidegger and apparently even from Jaspers.

The human thou can also be objectivized and become an it. But for this there is a definite limit, behind which stands the absolute thou which can no longer be taken as an object, namely God. We cannot through reason prove the existence of God. One encounters God on the same plane as the other, the plane of the thou, in loving and in honoring through participation in true being which may already take its rise in the questioning attitude of the philosopher.

20. KARL JASPERS

A. CHARACTERISTICS AND INFLUENCES

One of the first people whose works brought the existentialist tendencies in philosophy before the public eye was Karl Jaspers (b. 1883). He is considered in the last section here because he has elaborated the most closely knit system of them all and the one which comes nearest to metaphysics. In his earlier years he was a psychiatrist, and his important work *Die Phychologie der Weltanschauungen* (1919) marks his transition to philosophy, which has subsequently been his chief preoccupation. His main work is in three volumes entitled *Philosophie* (1932) and expounds his elaborate system in all its minute detail. Besides these there are a number of other works, notably the first volume of his *Philosophische Logik* (1947), a work of monumental proportions totaling 1103 pages.

The thought of Karl Jaspers is on the whole much more balanced than that of the majority of his fellow existentialists; for example, he critically analyzes their view of science, to which he accords a far more important place than they do. His books contain a wealth of remarkable analyses and are written in comparatively simple language free from the characteristic neologisms which makes the other authors so difficult to read. An obvious concern for metaphysics and a sort of natural theology also serve to distinguished him from the others who share the same label. Even so, he exhibits the fundamental attitudes and convictions common to all existentialists.

Jaspers confesses that the author to whom he owes most is Kant, whose presuppositions he does, in fact, take over. Kierkegaard, Nietzsche, and the sociologist Max Weber also help to provide him with inspiration but special note should be made of four thinkers whom he is in the habit of citing—Plotinus, Bruno, Spinoza, and Schelling. These names show beyond doubt that Jaspers is not only an existentialist strongly influenced by Kant; he is also, and perhaps principally, a Neoplatonist.

Philosophy of Existence

B. THE SEARCH FOR BEING

Jaspers rejects rational ontology but his position is nevertheless ontological and metaphysical. According to his view philosophy is metaphysics by its very nature for it poses the problem of being. But the common assumption that being is given constitutes an error. "It would be madness to think that being is something that everyone knows." On this subject Jaspers proclaims his adherence to two fundamental theses that have been stated by Kant, whom he regards as peerless, "the philosopher par excellence." First, he takes the *maxim of consciousness* to be valid: no object without a subject, everything objective is categorically conditioned by consciousness, objective being (*Dasein*) is always an illusion. Second, he adopts the Kantian doctrine of *ideas* and amplifies it; we are never presented with the whole of reality, and so he turns Kant's three ideas (the world, the soul, God) into three "encompassers" (*Umgreifende*). Everything that we know is knowable within the boundaries of some horizon or other. The encompasser of all vistas is unknowable; the world is the first encompasser, I am the encompasser of myself, and, finally, transcendence is the total encompasser. These two basic features are inseparable from an existential experience which may very well constitute the kernel of Jaspers's thinking—the experience of the jaggedness and brittleness of all being. The world as such is a perpetual ruin; it provides no foothold; its reality is not whole. Existence is never realized, and man is real only as historical and potential existence. The reality of being itself recedes until it finds a foothold in transcendence. But transcendence is not objectively given, it becomes real to us only in the break-up of all existence. Through universal failure, including the failure of our search, we arrive at being. "Failure is ultimate."

One can speak of being in a threefold sense. First we find being as plain givenness (*Dasein*), as objective; then we know being as being-for-itself (*Fürsichselbstsein*) which is radically different from the being of things and is entitled "existence"; lastly we have whatever is intrinsically being (*das Ansichseiende*), which cannot be derived either from plain givenness or from myself and is transcendence. There are three poles of being within which I am situated, but I cannot discover being in its wholeness no matter which kind of being I set out from. Therefore a philosophical venture demands an act of transcending which is accomplished in three ways—by world orientation, by the elucidation of existence, by metaphysics. The first raises the world from its condition of inert objectivity and stretches out toward the uttermost limits of its range. In the elucidation of existence the transcending act begins from the plain self (*Ich als Dasein*), the object of psychology, and terminates in my authentic existential self. Lastly, the act of transcending in metaphysics is possible only for existence which, in turning to itself, passes over to transcendence. In all three ways it is a question of overcoming the antithesis of object and subject and discovering true being; naturally this process is not within the powers of reason. What Jaspers is searching for in his philosophy is the root from which both object and subject stem; at this level concepts are no longer available, words no longer have any sense and one propounds arguments that signify nothing. Words are sign posts indicating the direction that one must take, and nothing more.

C. WORLD ORIENTATION

Philosophical world orientation attempts to break through the closed system of empirical world orientation; its shows the *irreducible limits of proof*, which in mathematics are the axioms, in the empirical sciences the dependence of facts upon theories, in a world outlook the difficulty of communication

187

and the lack of systematic completion. It emphasizes particularly the antinomies which are to be met in all phenomena. It shows that a unitary world view is unattainable because there are four *spheres of reality* in the world—matter, life, soul, and spirit. Each of them is real, although in a different sense at each of the four levels; the spirit especially is real in the strict sense of the word not just intentionally; they are heterogeneous modes of objectivity, and there are gaps between them. For example, the idea of evolution is an evident one for empirical thought yet it contradicts the consciousness of spirit. There certainly does exist a tendency to make either the spirit or nature absolute and to deny any other reality, but an enlightened world orientation sticks to the facts as they are and recognizes the existence of four spheres of reality. None of these four, not even inorganic matter, can be subsumed under a single unifying principle.

This *lack of unity* shows up even in technical affairs such as administration, education, and politics; everywhere one encounters unsurpassable limits, which Jaspers illustrates by analyzing the different kinds of approach of a physician to his patient and showing that none of them is self-sufficient. Furthermore he investigates the meaning and value of the natural sciences by tracing the objections which have been raised against them. He goes on to examine the social sciences (*Geisteswissenschaften*) and the classification of the sciences, showing that each division into branches is relative and becomes inapplicable the moment that it claims universal validity. Because the world does not contain the ground of its own being it is incomplete, and in consequence scientific world orientation is equally incomplete.

The same applies to self-sufficient philosophical world orientations such as positivism and idealism. Positivism is an absolutization of mechanistic thought and of compelling certitude; it cannot comprehend itself. The positivistic view of life shows itself to be impossible by the mere fact that it tries to justify itself—a nonsensical procedure if one admits positivistic conceptions. Idealism is equally false and one-sided. Setting themselves the problem as to what truly *is*, both systems give as their answer: the whole and the universal. Both fail to appreciate existence and know the individual only as an object. They regard being as demonstrable, and, indeed, as demonstrated. Their ethical systems eliminate the grounds of human choice. World orientation, in short, shows that *a universally valid world view is impossible.*

But the very failure of these efforts prepares the way for existential philosophy by leaving only two ways out of their dilemma—either backward to authority and revelation or forward to philosophical independence. The opposition between *religion and philosophy* reaches its maximum tension in theological and philosophical thought. Since both are simply explications of a faith, neither of them can bring forward compelling certainties. And yet one is bound to make a choice between them; everyone must either sink into the bosom of authority or else launch himself into existence at his own risk. Although there is a continual struggle between religion and philosophy, and although they can never understand each other, the one can respect the other as possible truth so long as they are both genuine and are not flattened out into mere objective certitudes.

D. EXISTENCE

What mythical language calls "soul," is called "existence" in philosophical terminology; it is a being which stands out against the totality of the world's being; it *is* not, but it can be and should be; I myself am being so far as I refuse to become an object for myself; my being is a breach in the being of the

189

world and exists only in action. This breach is encountered in inescapable situations (death, suffering, struggle, guilt), in historical consciousness, freedom, and communication.

Elucidation of existence is the method by which thinking ascertains existence, but it requires media of a unique sort in order to do so, because existence is not an object; I could never draw upon myself for knowledge of what I am. Elucidatory thought can never grasp existential reality, which is only to be found in actual deeds. Nevertheless it is itself an actualization of existential potentiality and can grasp potential existence on condition that it is not only conceived, but is conceived as transcending in the direction of existence (which is in itself a transcending act.)

The methods of elucidating existence are these: reaching out to those limits beyond which there is sheer emptiness; objectivation in psychological, logical and metaphysical language; and coining a specific universal. The latter helps to create a language in harmony with existential possibility, and provides a formal scheme of existence which will still be thoroughly inadequate but will serve at least one purpose—to initiate intercourse with existence.

Such schemata enable us to describe existence by means of a system of special *categories* which are the opposite of Kant's and are applicable to existence: existential reality instead of simply being subjected to rules, is absolutely historically actual—its origins are within itself, that is, it is free: here, to be means to decide. Existence is not inert but asserts itself in time. Jaspers replaces reciprocal causality by communication. What is real in existence is not correspondence to sense perception but indeterminacy in the moment of decision. Magnitude in the given (*Dasein*) has its parallel in the order of existence. Objective possibility is contrasted with the possibility of choice through the indeterminacy of the future, which is my very existence. The necessity of the given is contrasted with the fulfilled time of the instant, while endless time is set over against the eternal present. Existence is neither objective nor measurable, nor can it be experienced; it is not a universal currency since freedom is its essence. Each existence enjoys a time of its own and is the source of fresh creation.

Jaspers maintains that it is really impossible to define existence but the following may be taken as the most adequate of his many pseudodefinitions: "Existence is that which never becomes an object, that which is the origin of my thinking and acting, and that about which I speak in noncognitive trains of thought. Existence is whatever refers itself to itself, and thereby to its transcendence."

It would be a dangerous error to identify existence with subjectivity, because it actually exists by cleaving through the circle of being which is set up by the object and the subject. It is beyond any such distinction, for by philosophizing we call into question both objectivity and subjectivity. Existence makes a two-pronged drive, toward the objective and toward the subjective; the tentative grasp of novel objectivity is the philosopher's aim. One can easily see that Jaspers himself does not manage to express himself in objective terminology even when dealing with the problem of objectivity.

If we are to acquire further intimations about existence we need to clarify the concepts of communications, historicity, and freedom, which "is" existence.

E. COMMUNICATION

Existence is certainly its own source but it is not exclusively so and it is not isolated. Existence is present only in self-conscious communication: I *am* only in communication. Jaspers distinguishes several kinds of empirical communication (*Daseinskommunikation*), in which man is at the level of giveness,

Philosophy of Existence

yet they all have their limits, and existential communication is found beyond all of them. This is a process of revelation and at the same time a realization of the ego as the self; in it selves reciprocally create each other. Communication is a loving struggle in which existence strives to achieve its own total manifestation. This struggle, however, is of a peculiar kind because neither domination nor victory is at stake and each party places everything at the disposal of the other. Love is not communication, but its source; love can be a matter for doubt when there is no existential communication. The loving struggle of communication never ceases so long as there is no break in the communication; it seems to arise from nothing, and its ultimate goal is unknowable.

Thus communication is revelaed in ruling and serving (as fidelity and goodness, humility and responsibility), in social intercourse (which is an empirical condition of communication), in discussion (so long as it promotes a deeper understanding), and even in political relations (provided that they are not taken to be absolute values). In philosophy communication plays an outstanding part; as Jaspers points out in the introduction to his main work, "We do not philosophize in isolation but in communication; as a starting-point it is necessary for us to behave as man to man, as an utterly unique person addressing an utterly unique person." Philosophizing is impossible without communication and a thought is philosophically true so far as it helps communication toward fulfilment; philosophical truth has its origin and its reality in communication. The reason for this is evident—philosophizing is an act of existence, which, in its turn, is rooted in communication. This being so, *no* philosophical system can rank as the *ultimate truth*, since even the system of truth is only slowly realizing itself through the process of self-becoming and cannot be completed until the latter day, when time and process cease.

192

Existence is always in a situation: Jaspers describes a situation as that reality which confronts the subject involved in virtue of his givenness (*Dasein*) and either restricts him or opens fresh vistas for him. Some situations can be altered or circumvented but there are also absolute situations; these are the inescapable situations (*Grenzsituationen*), which are ultimate, which we cannot change, and upon which we come to grief. These situations, being beyond knowledge, can only be felt by existence. They are these: to be always in a determinate situation as givenness, death, suffering, struggle, and guilt. It is through our reactions to the inescapable situations that our potential existence becomes actual—we become ourselves whenever we enter into the inescapable situations with our eyes open. The fulness of existence can only be realized in an inescapable situation; in other words, real existence is historical existence which is reduced to silence.

So existence is *historicity*. Through historicity the double nature of my consciousness is revealed to me—my givenness is only temporal but I myself am not temporal. These two aspects are originally one in existential consciousness. Historicity is the unity of givenness and existence, of necessity and freedom; therefore absolute necessity and absolute freedom are caught up and synthesized in historical consciousness. Existence without my givenness would be nothing for there is no existence apart from givenness. Yet I should not *be* without my existence. Thus historicity is the unity of time and eternity. Existence is neither timelessness nor temporality, but the one in the other. This peculiarity of existence is shown in the "instant," the identity of temporality and timelessness, which converts the actual moment into the eternal present.

"This illustrates how historical consciousness can grasp only individual being but never the universal." It follows that historicity is unthinkable but it does not follow that it is irrationality, since irrationality is something purely negative while historicity is thoroughly positive. It bears the burden of existential consciousness; it is a source and not a limiting factor, the producer, not the by-product.

G. FREEDOM AND GUILT

Existence "is" freedom. This freedom exists at a level where the theories of determinism and indeterminism are irrelevent, because these two theories both assume that objective being is the whole of being and thereby freedom is forfeited. Existential freedom is not objective, it can neither be proved nor disproved; it is identical neither with knowledge, nor with free choice, nor with law, though without these three there is no freedom. I am conscious of freedom through existential choice, that is, through deciding to become myself. Freedom is utterly inconceivable because it is the same as existence—I am aware of my freedom by existing and not by thinking. Therefore freedom is shown to be the reconciliation of necessity and free choice; I can because I must; though my choice is free I bind myself by it; I carry out and accept its consequences; it is not determined by empirical reality but through self-creation at the moment of choice. Therefore just as there is no existence without givenness, similarly there is no absolute freedom.

Because I know myself to be free I know myself to be guilty; for guilt is not alien to freedom—it is intrinsic to my freedom and comes from my being free. Our existence involves us in action which has its grounds within itself. I must will and act in order to live, so that even inaction is really action. By choosing and acting I grasp one possibility and have to throw the others aside; but since these others include men, my existential decision, my very givenness, implicates me in guilt. This guilt shatters every attempt at self-justification on the part of ongoing existence. At the roots of every existent lies this original guilt, which is inevitable because it is existence itself.

H. TRANSCENDENCE

Givenness is tattered and groundless, existence is an endless insufficiency—it either exists in relation to transcendence or it does not exist at all. All being as permanence and being as freedom is *a* being, not *the* being. The true being is transcendence, which is hidden and absolutely unobjective; it is the concern of metaphysics, which only deals in symbols and from a logical view point represents a break-down in thought. Metaphysics constantly alternates between the poles of being and nonbeing. Transcendence appears as metaphysical objectivity in myth, theology, and philosophy, which are perpetually contending with each other. The true metaphysical method, however, follows one of three ways, the way of formal transcendence, of existential relationships, and of cypher reading.

By *formal transcendence* we not only transcend the categories of givenness but also the categories of existence itself. There is no alternative but to conceive of God as personal and yet the godhead remains utterly hidden.

The *existential relationships* to transcendence are surrender and defiance, the rise and fall of existence, the passion of the night and the law of the day, the richness of the Many as against the One. The doctrine of the two laws has become the most famous of these relationships. Our givenness seems to be subject to two forces, *the law of the day* and *the passion of the night*. The former enforces order, demands fidelity and clarity, and seeks its realization in the world; the second is an urge to destroy itself and the world along with it; it violates all order, it is darkness grounded in earthiness, in the maternal womb, in

195

Philosophy of Existence

the race; its expression is eroticism. The two worlds are related to each other but cannot be completely synthesized within any existence. In his theory of the One and the Many, Jaspers maintains that it is impossible for us to apply to the godhead our notions of unity and numerical plurality or, for that matter, any other kind of unity and plurality known to us. The transcendent is the One, but monotheism is just as inadequate as polytheism. We cannot even attribute personality to God because personality implies other personalities and the godhead has no one comparable to it. All these aspects of Jaspers's philosophy show him to be a true disciple of Plotinus. His godhead is hidden, unknowable, the absolute unity beyond all categories; it is transcendence though simultaneously present as the given and the existential. Jaspers's theory of cyphers, on the other hand, does contain certain novel views, but even here he retains many links with the classic Neoplatonic tradition.

I. CYPHER READING AND FAILURE

The most vital task for metaphysics is the reading of cyphers. Cypher is being, as it presents transcendence to us, but it does so without perverting transcendence into the being of an object or the being of a subject (existence). In cypher it is impossible to separate the symbol from what is symbolizes. Cypher cannot be interpreted, even though it is the means of presenting transcendence. It remains ambiguous. It is even less true that there is a universal interpretation of cypher, for each explanation is an explanation within existence, and cypher reading takes place within existence. It is accomplished through our own actions; in such reading I apprehend a being by my very struggle toward it. This reading has nothing to do with ontology since it presents no compelling certitude.

There is nothing which could not be cypher; givenness,

nature, history, pure consciousness, man himself, his union with nature and with his own world, his freedom—all of these may constitute cypher for trancendence. Art is the language of cypher reading, but philosophical speculation also is cypher reading. Therefore proofs for God's existence are speculative cypher reading and spring from the consciousness of existence. There are no proofs of transcendence but there are witnesses to it. The supreme cypher of transcendence is the dissolution of givenness—being in failure.

Experience teaches us that failure is ultimate, that everything falls into disruption. But in human situations it is existence itself which fails. Still there is a genuine and an illusory failure so that if anyone actually desires it, and especially if he desires an end to all things, then it is a case of illusory failure. Genuine failure is accomplished through contributing to the given world in the desire that it should be ordered and permanent while daringly accepting the certainty that it will crumble. This genuine failure makes us eternal and can fulfil the cypher of being. Hence the awareness of failure only induces passivity if permanence is taken to be the standard of value and the given world to be the absolute.

Failure is necessary. Values and permanence have to be fragile if there is to be freedom. Since freedom comes through nature but is contrary to it, nature must either break down as freedom or as givenness. Cypher reading is only possible through the failure of given illusions, of all knowledge and philosophy. It is especially true that if the finite is to be the vessel of the ultimate, it will shatter to bits. Jaspers seems to believe that the failure of each finite being reveals and establishes the infinity of God, the sole true being, who only becomes visible when everything collapses. Hence this philosophy proclaims as its final solution "to philosophize is to learn to die," and its watch word "to encounter being by-means of failure."

Philosophy of Existence

CONCLUDING CRITICISMS

To give a fair picture of existentialism two different traits must be clearly distinguished. Existentialism first of all consists in a return to the burning and cosmically significant questions of human destiny, and, second, it joins to this a new analysis of human existence upon an ontological and metaphysical basis.

The return to human questions—let us call this the *tychic* element (from τύχη, that is, man's lot or fortune)—is of course to be welcomed because of its implications for European culture. For the interest in human destiny seems to be indissolubly connected with European culture as it has evolved from Greek, Roman, and Christian sources. But in the course of the "modern" centuries this tychic element has almost entirely disappeared from European philosophy. Spinoza already says, "the free man thinks of nothing less than of death," and in the nineteenth century the personal was regarded as "unscientific." The tychic element must not, however, be thought of as something religious. Nietzsche, for example, cannot be regarded as a religious philosopher, even though he is an outspoken tychic thinker. Nor is it to be identified with the existential. As we have noted, neither St. Augustine nor Pascal were existentialists. Just what this element signifies in philosophy can be shown by a comparison of Haeckel and Nietzsche. Both were atheists and determinists, and yet each of them goes his own way. So, for example, the nonexistence of God is for Haeckel a demonstrable thesis, for Nietzsche it is a drama. If European philosophy were to follow the lead of thinkers of Haeckel's type, it would collapse utterly along with European culture itself. In restoring the tychic element to a place of eminence existentialism has without doubt contributed to the recuperation of our life and thought.

As often happens, existentialism has gone too far in the rejection, inherently justified, of the past. For many existentialist philosophers there seems to be nothing in principle worth considering except those tychic questions and questions of fate we have already alluded to. Their whole philosophy seems to center on death, suffering, failure. Thereby they neglect another essential factor in European culture, namely that sense of the objective and scientific which the Greeks had in such eminent degree. Often existentialism goes so far in its emphasis upon the tychic that it seems to be more an Indian than a European philosophy, that is, a kind of thought which seems to be exclusively, even in its logic, a kind of therapeutic device. It is for such reasons that existentialism encounters justified reproach among many, perhaps most, serious European philosophers.

Another unique trait of existentialist philosophy in addition to tychism is its definite technical philosophical character. Here many valuable insights and results are discernible. Unquestionably philosophy has been enriched by numerous superior analyses in psychology and phenomenology, and some fields have in fact been subjected to study for the first time through these efforts, for example, pure personal relationships between human beings—"being-with-another," "being-for another," "thou," "communication." A study of problems has thus arisen which constitutes a definite advancement in philosophy. Equally fundamental are the critical attacks on positivism and on idealism by the existentialists. Against the first they have successfully defended the irreducibility of human existence to matter, and respecting the second they have asserted with great power and conviction the priority of existence to thought. They have occupied themselves with ontology in various ways and some have not only worked it out in detail but have capped their efforts with a metaphysics. Still

199

Philosophy of Existence

further, their understanding of various anthropological problems goes far beyond the achievement of the nineteenth century in the field. One cannot repeat too often, therefore, that existentialism is not only a prophetic outburst but also a valuable technical philosophy.

Yet it is precisely in this technical aspect that we find also the great weaknesses of the existentialists. These philosophers could scarcely overcome idealism altogether. They begin with the assumption that the objective is necessarily conditioned by the subjective and thus seek being in a putative "transobjective" entity which cannot be thought and hence cannot even be uttered. The concrete has become so insistent a demand that they seek to deal only with what is to-each-his-own (*jemeinig*). But moving in this direction philosophy often becomes mere autobiography which can express nothing more than mere feelings, in poetic, often in meaningless, rather than in scientific form. The achievement of existentialist ontology is even more questionable. From the standpoint of the renascent science of being it seems often a mere dilettantish play with inadequate concepts, especially in Sartre's treatment of the nothing. No existentialist has penetrated to being qua being, and all of them constantly confuse the particular level of being (*Seinsstufe*) which is proper to man, with the mode of being (*Seinsweise*) which they erroneously attribute to him. The Cartesian separation of human from nonhuman being, which has so faithfully determined all modern thought, has not been overcome by a genuine ontology but only exacerbated. Therefore, despite the great achievements of existentialism, its insight into the contingency of particular beings and the transcendence of God, among other things, it remains in the last analysis unconvincing. These problems undergo a much more serious and penetrating treatment in the philosophy of being.

Leva dunque, lettore, all'alte ruote
Meco la vista . . .
E li comincia a vagheggiar nell'arte
Di quel maestro che dentro a se l'ama.

DANTE

VII

Philosophy of Being

---

21. METAPHYSICS

A. THE CONCEPT OF METAPHYSICS

In this chapter we shall discuss under the heading Philosophy of Being the branch of contemporary European philosophy which may be the most significant of all. Most philosophers we shall consider are avowed metaphysicians though some would only describe themselves as ontologists. Since the term "metaphysics" has numerous meanings we shall begin by specifying the sense in which we shall here use the term.

The word originated with Andronikos of Rhodes who used it as the title for a collection of Aristotle's works when he was putting them in order; all he meant to say was "the treatises which were listed after the physics" (μετὰ τὰ φυσικά). During the course of the centuries μετά received another meaning; it no longer referred to what came "after" physics, but was "beyond" its scope. The final touch to the popular notion of metaphysics was given by litterateurs with a smattering of technical comprehension, by intuitionist philosophers, and by the positivists with their propaganda. As a result the common belief among nonphilosophers today is that "metaphysics" means an effort to attain otherwordliness, God, or something of that nature, achieved by the imaginative faculty soaring beyond the range of precise argument.

For most philosophers we are about to consider, the term "metaphysics" has, however, a quite different sense, and it is necessary to specify this if we are to try to understand them. They regard metaphysics as the science of being, of being qua being, and they seek to develop this science by *rational* means. They thus readily proceed beyond the bounds of the natural sciences but most contemporary philosophers agree that this is altogether necessary. Rationality for philosophers of being is something quite different from what it is for positivists. It does not signify confinement to the procedures of the natural sciences but it calls for a complete exclusion of fancy and feeling and usually also of the so-called existential method of thinking.

One nowadays construes the difference between metaphysics and ontology in such a way that ontology confines itself to the analysis of structure, while metaphysics produces existential propositions, that is propositions about the existence (*Dasein*) of what is in being (*Seiendes*). Accordingly, the problem of epistemology, for example, is essentially a metaphysical problem because we are here inquiring after the existence (*Existenz*) of what is in itself (*Ansichseiend*). A further distinction between ontology and metaphysics is that the latter does not just investigate particular problems but, in principle at least, addresses itself to the whole of reality. One would therefore be justified in classifying the work of Nicolai Hartmann as philosophy of being; although he considers himself only an ontologist he is also undoubtedly doing metaphysics, as for example in setting up the law of strength (*Stärke*).

The foregoing must not be interpreted as meaning that the philosophers of being confine themselves to the analysis of being. On the contrary, nearly everyone of them has also a philosophy of nature, a philosophy of man, an axiology, and so on. The difference between them and other philosophers is just that they base all special philosophical disciplines upon a general ontology and metaphysics.

B. THE METAPHYSICAL PHILOSOPHERS

The number of contemporary metaphysicians is much too great even to name here. Nor is it easy to classify them into groups since they differ markedly from one another on special points. We shall nevertheless put them into four groups. The first group will contain philosophers, Germans for the most part, who incline toward indirect realism but who yet develop a metaphysics, often on an inductive basis. Among these Hans Driesch (1867-1941) must be named first. Driesch began as a biologist. After developing a philosophy of organism, somewhat akin to Aristotle's, he erected a metaphysics upon it. Besides Driesch we must mention Heinrich Maier (1867-1933) and the prominent psychologist Erich Jaensch (1883-1940).

The religious, theistic philosophers who lean toward Neoplatonism constitute a second group. This position was especially developed in England. Its most outstanding representative was the well-known Plotinus scholar, William Ralph Inge (1861-1954). Certain neorealists are close to this position though with much less inclination toward Neoplatonism, for example, John

203

Laird (1887-1946) and expecially Alfred Edward Taylor (1869-1945). In France, Maurice Blondel (1861-1948) moves in a similar direction; beginning as a Bergsonian he later developed a metaphysics which contains elements of Thomism, Neoplatonism, life-philosophy, and even of existentialism. Although his thought in his many volumes is somewhat imprecise, he exercised a noticeable influence on the Catholic clergy in France and on religious people in many other countries. The German counterpart to this is so-called Augustinianism, represented especially by Johannes Hessen whose thought is more rigorous than that of Blondel and his pupils.

The third group comprises the French *philosophie de l'esprit*, whose principal contemporary representatives are René Le Senne (1882-1954) and Louis Lavelle (1883-1951). No other metaphysician goes as far toward idealism as do the members of this group. Le Senne in fact can be reckoned as well among the idealists as among the metaphysicians. But the center of interest for all of them remains being qua being, and also in other respects their views exhibit the typical traits of the philosophy of being of the present.

In the fourth group we could place a number of philosophers inclined toward naturalism, especially Samuel Alexander (1859-1938) and George Santayana (1863-1952).

Although this classification may seem arbitrary, there can be no question about the remaining metaphysicians. We note expecially the German ontologist Günther Jacoby (b. 1881), the Viennese sociologist Othmar Spann (1878-1950), Paul Häberlin of Basle (b. 1878), and the leading German mathematical logician and Platonistic metaphysician Heinrich Scholz (b. 1884).

Above all these representatives of the new metaphysics stand Alfred North Whitehead (1861-1947), Nicolai Hartmann (1882-1950), and the Thomists. We shall therefore treat these systems very extensively. In order to specify the characteristics of the other positions we shall first present the basic ideas of Alexander, Lavelle, and Häberlin. Our choice here is determined by the fact that these three philosophers can also be counted as representatives of three other metaphysical schools.

C. INFLUENCES

The different schools of modern metaphysics have very different origins. Alexander and Whitehead come from English neorealism, Hartmann began as one of the Marburg school but underwent strong phenomenological influences, while the Thomists owe allegiance to scholastic tradition. Life-philosophy and phenomenology, the two pioneering movements of recent times, have exercised considerable influence upon contemporary metaphysics.

A search for one force which has ultimately guided the whole movement would undoubtedly lead to Plato and Aristotle. They enjoy a varying importance with each thinker, Whitehead being more a Platonist than an Aristotelian, the Thomists and Hartmann turning more to Aristotle. But Aristotelian influences are plainly detectable in most of them, especially in the way they combine intellectualism and empiricism with a predilection for explaining all reality in rational terms—a combination only found among Aristotelians. As a result of this Aristotelianism and their common devotion to the Greeks they are at the opposite pole from the Kantians.

But even though they have jettisoned Kantianism and most modern (1600-1900) philosophy along with it, this does not mean that they remain outside its influence; none of them has made a complete return to an earlier position. Whitehead does indeed describe himself as a Platonist in the strict sense, and the Thomists insist that they are reëstablishing the doctrines of St. Thomas Aquinas (1224-1272)—but in fact they both

205

greatly enrich the doctrines which they adopt because they integrate them with more recent problems. Thus Kant's concentration upon epistemology plays its role in all these systems even though they propose anti-Kantian solutions to it. Again, natural science enjoys a high status in the eyes of modern metaphysicians; it is true that none of those discussed in this chapter take natural science as their starting point but this is because their goal lies outside its domain. On the other hand many scientific theories, the doctrine of evolution particularly, receive their most adequate philosophical expression in contemporary metaphysics, above all in the English thinkers.

The metaphysicians have recently felt the impact of existentialism and it seems likely that the problem of existence will soon come to be dealt with from that viewpoint.

All in all the metaphysicians have shown themselves susceptible to the same series of influences as the existentialists. Most of them, however, go one step further than the latter by drawing upon the philosophical treasury of ancient, medieval, and modern (pre-Kantian) thought.

D. CHARACTERISTICS

The fundamental characteristics of contemporary metaphysics are as follows:

Empiricism. The thinkers in this group are of the opinion that experience alone provides a basis for philosophy. Consequently they unanimously reject *a priori* knowledge in the Kantian sense. If we do enjoy knowledge which is not purely sensible, this still does not mean, according to the metaphysicians, that we can know anything at all except from experience.

Intellectualism. The major difference between this type of empiricism and that of materialists or life-philosophers lies in the fact that the metaphysicians (and indeed the phenomenologists) admit the possibility of intellectual experience. Knowledge does not consist exclusively of sensible experiences linked together in logical relationships; there are intelligible contents in reality which are just as obviously factual as the sensible contents themselves.

Rational Method. Most metaphysicians reject Bergson's intuitive method and seek to vindicate their theses with the aid of rational argumentation. They are convinced rationalists who agree with Hegel that all reality is rational. In every sphere they make use of this method.

Ontological Tendency. Distinctive of the metaphysicians, as opposed to the phenomenologists, is the stress which they lay upon being. Their philosophy does not take phenomena or bare essence as its object but concrete being in its totality, in its existence as well as in its essence, and they study all the modes of being (*Seinsweisen*).

Universality. Just as they study the modes of being, they include also all of its *levels* (*Seinsstufen*) in their scrutiny. They do not grant a monopoly to any level because they view the whole of reality in the light of being. One sign of their universality is found in the fact that, unlike almost everyone else, they are prepared to undertake an explanation of all reality. This is the reason why most of them apply themselves to the problem of natural theology and try to suggest some theory about the world's ultimate principles.

These two latter features are not equally strongly marked in every metaphysician. Alexander, for instance, scarcely betrays any tendency toward ontology, and Hartmann's principles, no matter how universalist, do not permit him to offer any explanation for reality as a whole. The two tendencies appear to have equal weight with both Whitehead and the Thomists, but the Thomists pursue the ontological line more rigorously than does the English thinker.

207

Humanism. In contrast to the materialists, who also occa-sionally deal with the world as a whole, the metaphysicians are humanists. Their systems pay considerable attention to the philosophy of man. Certainly they are not so radical as the existentialists in this respect because man does not form the cornerstone of their philosophy; yet the great human problems of history, of morality, and of religion have all been enriched by valuable contributions from their thought.

Contemporary metaphysics generally reflects all the fea-tures peculiar to our age; it is thinking directed toward con-crete and human being; therefore it deserves to be recognized as one of the age's typical forms of expression.

E. THE FRENCH PHILOSOPHIE DE L'ESPRIT. LOUIS LAVELLE

In the last quarter century a unique philosophy under the name *philosophie de l'esprit* has developed in France. It is as sharply opposed to the older idealistic idea of universality as it is to positivism, and it seeks to curb the overweening power of the state. It has three guiding principles: the recognition of the absolute, an accounting for the whole of human experience, and a readiness to embrace all those spiritual efforts which pro-mote the understanding of the human person. Though they differ in particular respects, all of these philosophers are united by a common twofold character, a kind of intuitionism and an explicit inclination toward a Neoplatonic mode of thought. They all express themselves in deliberate but very difficult language.

The leader of the *philosophie de l'esprit* along with René Le Senne is Louis Lavelle. Lavelle's system is on so grand a scale that we cannot give even an adequate summary of it. He has been described as an existentialist, an idealist, and even as an "essentialistic existentialist". He may in fact be said to stand at the frontier between existentialist philosophy and the philosophy of being. He regards himself as a metaphysician and has published among other things a book on being, *De l'être* (1927) and an *Introduction à l'ontologie* (1947). In what follows we select from among his many doctrines a few which seem to be basic and also comparatively clear.

According to Lavelle there can be no metaphysics of the object. It is concerned entirely with the science of inward spirit (*de l'intimité spirituelle*). Lavelle believes that one finds the idea of being in such an inwardness and by a species of ontological proof he undertakes to show that this idea comprises a reality. Being reveals itself as the one and the univocal (*univoque*), but at the same time it is infinite and above all pure act, God. Whatever exists, exists through participation in a pure, infinite act. With this concept Lavelle seeks to overcome pantheism and to establish the transcendence of God. His metaphysics develops into an ethic of overcoming nature, of the achievement of selfhood and love. But we cannot pursue these ideas in detail, nor his subtle analyses of existence (in the "existentialist" sense), the object, the phenomenon, value, and time.

F. SAMUEL ALEXANDER

Alexander came from Australia and taught at Manchester. In his *Space, Time and Deity* (1920) he developed a great system of naturalistic and evolutionistic pantheism. Philosophy, that is to say, metaphysics, is for him the science of being as such and of its essential attributes. Space-time is the basic *stuff* of the universe. It is the totality of *pure events* or space-time points. Space-time is determined by categories which inherently belong to it and therefore by attributes which characterize every existing thing. Borrowing from Plato and Kant, Alexander erects a most interesting system of these categories. Besides these there are *qualities* which arrange themselves suc-

209

cessively in various levels of being because of a basic creative *nisus*. This concept of development, called *emergent evolution*, is found also independent of Alexander in the philosopher and biologist C. Lloyd Morgan (1852-1936). For a long time it was the most discussed English philosophy. It is plainly opposed to Spencer's philosophy but is akin to Bergson's. According to Alexander we should accept the facts of such evolution with *natural piety*. Until now four levels of being have emerged, pure motion, matter, life, and mind. In respect to the preceding level the succeeding level always appears as *divinity*. The beings who will follow as the fifth level are called "angels" or "gods" by Alexander. God is the whole of the universe striving toward deity.

For Alexander the theory of knowledge is simply a part of metaphysics. He defends with remarkable acuity a radical realism. Not just sense data but things have being in themselves. Knowledge is a relation, everywhere present, of togetherness, whereby the knowing being becomes aware of things which are together. Not only knowledge but also memory, anticipation, and imagination have transcendent objects. In memory, for example, these are independent objects which are distinguished by a real quality of *pastness*. A further interesting theory of Alexander's is his distinction between the *contemplation* of the object and the *enjoyment* of the subject, of its properties and acts.

Values are *tertiary qualities*. Whereas the primary and secondary qualities (e.g. colors) are unconditionally objective, values are said to have an objective basis only so far as there is a valuing subject at hand. They are in fact relations between such a subject and the object. There are three classes of values —the true, the good, and the beautiful. Religious values do not constitute a special class since religion is essentially the feeling of being involved in the cosmic progress toward deity.

For Paul Häberlin (b. 1878), the Basle philosopher, psychologist, and theorist of education, all metaphysics is an explication of the primordial fact, I am. For existence signifies first of all an encounter and in this the presence (*Dasein*) of what has being in itself is given. Being is one single substance, but it consists at the same time in a functional multiplicity of individuals which are its modes. The relationships between these individuals constitute the oneness of the one and only universe. Individuals are inherently active, therefore alive, and therefore there develops also a continuous, active process of change. Through this no new individuals arise, because, being simple and unanalyzable, they are eternal, but there do arise new subjective conditions. The reciprocal, simple determination of such conditions does not exclude the freedom of individuals, for every individual reacts in virtue of its previous subjective condition which arose in earlier free activity.

The world is infinite in space and time (and these are not two beings but two orders of being), yet it was created. Of course causality does not reach beyond the world to the ground of being but the world confronts us as an objective claim and the origin of this claim is God, the creator. God's nature is an utter mystery. The most faithful picture we are able to form of him is that of personality. God is neither in nor outside the world. He is "above" it for he is not the world but its creator.

Upon these metaphysical doctrines Häberlin has built a complete system of philosophy. We shall consider only a few of the propositions which concern axiology and the philosophy of man. According to Häberlin, a person is not identical with his body, for the soul also exists. This soul, an eternal individual, creates itself a body as one founds an organization. It governs the body in the manner of a "political" power. Its striving

Philosophy of Being

toward death is directed toward the creation of a new body. Whether it succeeds we do not as yet know. The soul is not identical with the mind (*Geist*). The mind is rather the volition of the soul to rise above vital interest to the objective. Häberlin defends objectivism in the domain of the theoretical as well as in that of values. A value judgment as such is always unconditionally true, but not the nature of the value so approved. The meaning of human existence lies in the effort of man to establish objective meaning for himself. We should add that for Häberlin true knowledge and true belief (*Glaube*) are identical. A belief which is dogmatically put forth as the true one is a false belief, a superstition (*Aberglaube*).

22. NICOLAI HARTMANN

A. CHARACTERISTICS

Nicolai Hartmann (1882-1950) is undoubtedly one of the most significant figures in contemporary philosophy and, along with Whitehead and Maritain, a pioneer of twentieth-century metaphysics. He is less interested than they are in building a system. His strength lies in his precise analyses and in his gift—rare among Germans—of presenting his ideas in a clear manner, yet having a profound insight into their implications. His works are, indeed, models of sober exactitude and scientific comprehensiveness.

Nicolai Hartmann comes from the Marburg school, and his early works still bear witness to the spirit of that idealistic movement. But in 1921 there appeared his first important book with a title calculated to shock all idealists, *Grundzüge einer Metaphysik der Erkenntnis*. Five years afterward he issued his *Ethik*. Later he devoted himself to working out a comprehensive ontology in three parts, the first laying the foundations for this science and entitled *Zur Grundlegung der Ontologie*

(1933), the other two, *Möglichkeit und Wirklichkeit* (1938), and *Der Aufbau der realen Welt* (1940), dealing with the structure of ontology. Besides these main works he has published many others, of which *Das Problem des geistigen Seins* (1933) is specially noteworthy in that it investigates and amplifies traditional doctrines upon individual spirit and Hegelian doctrines upon objective spirit. More important still is his *Die Philosophie des deutschen Idealismus* (1923-1929), especially for the second volume, which discusses Hegel.

Hartmann is strongly influenced by Aristotle, but though he always takes Aristotle's views into account, he does not adopt them en bloc. Phenomenology has made an impression upon him, and he also draws upon Kant and Hegel for his inspiration. Nineteenth-century thought, however, has scarcely any weight with him and he opposes positivism, subjectivism, mechanism, and materialism with a resoluteness equal to that of the life-philosophers and phenomenologists. He abandons the idealist position in favor of realistic doctrines and even replaces phenomenology both as to content and as to method by the philosophy of being, although he recognizes phenomenology to be useful within certain limits.

The most original developments in Hartmann's philosophy are his distinction between real and ideal being, his theory of "aporia," the unintelligible remainder in reality, and his doctrine of objective spirit. But these are only a few of the central notions of a philosophy which contains a host of truths forgotten since the time of Descartes and a wealth of insight with which Hartmann has stimulated the progress of philosophical thought, especially in ethics.

B. METAPHYSICS AND ONTOLOGY

In opposition to almost the whole of modern philosophy, Hartmann asserts the ontological nature of all fundamental

213

problems which philosophy attempts to solve. Even idealism or the most extreme subjectivism have, somehow or other, to explain at least the "illusion" of being, no matter how they try to avoid it; there is no form of theoretical thought which can refuse to be basically ontological, that is, does not propose questions about "being as such." It is obviously the essence of thought that one cannot think "nothing," one must think "something," and that "something" immediately raises the problem of being. Furthermore, the natural sciences are in no position to cut themselves off from a metaphysical background. Metaphysics is born of wonder at the fact of life, which cannot be explained either mechanically or teleologically. Psychology, the philosophy of history, logic, aesthetics, and above all epistemology and ethics, are faced with the same problems.

The older metaphysics had made two mistakes. First, it undertook to solve the insoluble. Metaphysics signifies the irrational, and the irrational is the unintelligible. But being has also an intelligible side. The persistence of numerous problems is proof of this, for example in the recurrent contradictions between freedom and determinism, immanence and transcendence, life and mechanism. We cannot hope for a solution of these problems, but with appropriate methods we can advance their elucidation and confine to smaller and smaller compass the unintelligible remainder.

Second, the older metaphysics made the mistake of erecting closed systems and of forcing reality into these molds. The time for such systems is past, says Hartmann. What has weight in the works of the great philosophers is not their systems but the problems which they work out. All systems celebrate triumphs in the empty breeze of speculation. A few principles are laid down and then one proceeds forward by deduction. But even if the unity of the world is to be considered as given we yet do not know what in fact is its ultimate principle. The method that is called for is precisely the opposite. The *philosophia prima* which is to be evolved can be a *philosophia ultima* for our cognitive capacities only because the *ratio cognoscendi* moves toward the *ratio essendi*.

In this critique of the older metaphysics we begin to see how Hartmann wishes the concepts, metaphysics and ontology, to be construed. In contrast to the classical usage of the term he does not regard metaphysics as a science but as a tissue of questions to which there are no answers. The intelligible aspect of being, on the other hand, falls into the domain of ontology.

Ontology in this sense is a science, but it is not identical with phenomenology which has great propaedeutic value but cannot constitute the whole of ontology. Phenomenology glides dangerously over the surface of problems, and on the basis of its very definition it does not reach beyond the external appearance of the real. It remains bound to mere matter of fact and cannot get beyond this.

Hartmann's magnificent and original investigations into the nature of problems as such have shown that even when an intelligible object is under discussion one always discovers it to be a mixture of the known and the unknown. The fact that problems may be distinguished from each other proves that something is known of the matter in hand, just as the fact of inquiring into it shows that it is not known. To state problems is the chief task of philosophy.

C. THE GIVENESS OF REAL BEING

The fundamental concepts of epistemology are being-in-itself and transcendence. That a being is "in-itself" means to say that it exists actually and not only for us; a transcendent act is one whose scope is not restricted to consciousness (thinking, imagining) but oversteps consciousness and unites itself

Philosophy of Being

to that which is independent of it and exists in itself. *Knowledge is a transcendent act;* yet it has this advantage over other transcendent acts, that it is purely receptive. The relationship of a subject to an object-in-itself is in this case completely one-sided and passive; it is true that there is a certain spontaneity in knowing but it is not an operation upon the object—it is fulfilled in the synthesis of images. The knowing relation is a relation between a real subject and an object-in-itself.

It is the contention of scepticism, criticism, and certain forms of idealism that there is no being-in-itself. These theories are not difficult to refute as they always play variations on three motifs. The first is the theorem of consciousness ("since the object exists in consciousness, it cannot exist in itself"); the second is the correlativistic prejudice ("there can be no being which is not the object of some subject"); the third rests upon the assumption that value and meaning in our world are only intelligible in the light of subjectivity. The reply to all these is that being-in-itself does not need to be proved, that it is given as the world itself is given, and that no theory can ignore it. The phenomenon of knowing is of such character that it surpasses its own phenomenal quality.

The analysis of knowledge, however, does not suffice to quell every doubt. For the fact of transcendence shows us no more than how a phenomenon offers us something over and above itself and enables us to decide upon the being or the nonbeing of its contents. Purely as a matter of principle the possibility remains that there is no being-in-itself in the object of knowledge; but what we call "knowledge" would clearly not be knowledge in that case. The theoretical force of such a doubt is small indeed for it must bear the burden of proof; still this does not quash the doubt.

The *emotionally transcendent* acts banish all doubts as to being-in-itself. One may distinguish emotionally receptive acts (to experience, to undergo, to suffer) in which we encounter unyielding reality; emotionally prospective acts (anticipation, readiness, curiosity, hope) in which we anticipate something real; and, finally, emotionally spontaneous acts (desiring, willing, doing, acting). The transcendence of these last acts consists in the tendency to elicit the real. It is a common characteristic of these acts that something "happens to" the subject in each case. The issue here is not about something "cognitive", and yet these acts prove that their objects are something-in-themselves far more surely than does knowledge. Even more vivid and direct is the perception of the being of other persons —so direct that even the most radical idealists do not venture to deny the existence of persons; this is because the emotional union between person and person is so immeasurably richer. For instance, we know another person's attitude toward us immediately, and this knowledge is quite obviously a fact although an obscure one.

Now the object of knowledge and the object of the emotionally transcendent acts are one and the same. Isolated knowledge is an abstraction and it is with the total context of life that we have to deal, working and living as we do within a cosmic context. The transcendence of phenomena in knowledge is uncertain in itself but is endowed with certainty through the emotional act's transcendence of phenomena which is embedded in the real structure of life. Thus one can reply to Descartes that the perception of an external reality is just as direct as that of one's inner self.

D. THE DIMENSIONS AND FORMS OF BEING

It is now clear that Hartmann's statement of fundamental problems and his theory of knowledge turn first of all on the issue of being qua being (*Seiendes als Seiendes*). His propositions about being and its properties may now be examined.

Here are encountered the comprehensive investigations of his main four-volume work of which only the most important ideas can be mentioned. The basic principle of Hartmann's doctrine of being is that being develops in two dimensions, namely (1) the four completely distinct spheres of being and (2) the levels of being (*Seinsstufen*) within these spheres.

In the spheres of being Hartmann distinguishes two primary ones, of real and of ideal being, which may also be designated as modes of being (*Seinsweisen*) and two secondary, the cognitive and the logical spheres. Real being must not be confused with actuality (*Wirklichkeit*) for there is both real possibility and ideal possibility, though this distinction is really part of modal analysis. As to the relation between the primary and secondary spheres, there is an intimate crossrelationship between the cognitive and the real modes of being, and between the logical and the ideal. Propositions about the latter are especially important, for Hartmann holds that ideal being is similar to real being in itself in that it can be known, and knowing is always by its very nature the grasp of what has being in itself. The most familiar types of ideal being are the realms of essences and values and of mathematical being. The first of these appears in reality as basic structure but without being exhausted in that context. There are entities in ideal being which do not become real, for example, spaces with more than three dimensions. On the other hand, there is real being which is not subject to the laws of ideal being; for example, the alogical, the value-negating, the real contradiction. All ideal being is general, and is either forms, conformity to law or relations. Compared with the real, the ideal is lesser being. We must reject Plato's view that it is something "higher, more sublime". Ideal being is not identical with the rational for in its domain there is also to be found the irrational, and this incidentally is a proof of its having independent being for the transintelligible is exempt from idealistic criticism.

Hartmann analyzes the other spheres in similar fashion. He then proceeds to specify the character of the second dimension of being, that of the strata or levels of being (*Seinsstufen*). In real being we find four levels, matter, life, consciousness, and spirit. Being known (*Erkenntnissein*), by a certain analogy to these, involves perception, intuition, knowledge, and comprehension (*Wahrnehmung, Anschauung, Erkenntnis, Wissen*). Logical being finally divides, as the tradition has it, into concept, judgment, and inference. These separate levels are determined through the categories, the principles of a given level. Hartmann distinguishes two kinds of categories: modal categories which are accorded a special investigation, and fundamental categories which can be arranged in opposing pairs. In contrast to Kant and Alexander, the latter are not arranged in a definite system but are only loosely strung together in a table of existential opposites (*Seinsgegensätze*). The twelve pairs involved here include form-matter, inner-outer, determination-dependence, quality-quantity.

Hartmann has devoted extensive study to the question of the categories in his comprehensive work *Der Aufbau der realen Welt: Grundriss der allgemeinen Kategorienlehre*, the third volume of his *Ontologie*. After thorough survey of earlier views his theory culminates in the formulation of many categorial laws. Some of the most important are these: the law of strength (the lower is the stronger), and its counterpart, the law of freedom (the higher level is autonomous, for in respect to the lower level it is the richer). While therefore every higher level is borne by a lower one, still their relations are not always the same. The organic, the level of life, is only an over-forming (*Überformung*) of the spatio-physical aspect of matter, while the levels of consciousness and spirit rise in a more independent process of over-building (*Überbauung*) above life; that is, in this case not all the lower categories re-appear.

The second great categorial group, the theory of the *modalities of being (Seinsmodi)* represents one of the most significant parts of Hartmann's metaphysics. What is notably original is that modal analysis leads to quite different results in the four spheres of being. Thus in each sphere there are distinguishable modalities of being. Of these, however, the laws which hold of real being are the most important. The modalities divide into the absolute modalities (reality and unreality) and the relative (possibility, impossibility, necessity). There is also a negative countermodality to necessity, namely contingency, of which the rule holds that absolute necessity is likewise absolute contingency. One should further emphasize Hartmann's theory of possibility according to which in real being only that is possible whose conditions are all real. Hence all that is possible is likewise real and necessary, and all that is negatively possible is likewise unreal and impossible. This does not mean of course that the modalities themselves are identical. Implication is not identity. The distinction between positive and negative possibility rests on the law of division of disjunctive possibility which is valid in real being though not in logical being.

In his ontology Hartmann has also addressed himself to the traditional distinction between essence and existence. These he calls "moments of being" (*Seinsmomente*): the "what" (*Sosein*) and the "that" (*Dasein*). It is noteworthy that these moments of being appear differently in both of the primary spheres of being. Thus the ideal "what" and "that" can be known *a priori*, but the real "that" only *a posteriori*. One cannot simply equate the "what" with the ideal and the "that" with real being. Actually there is no absolute difference between "what" and "that" in the existential relationships that obtain in the world for it is a question altogether of relative moments. The "that" of the leaf belongs to the "what" of the tree, and the "that" of the latter to the "what" of the forest. The distinction holds only for the whole of the universe and for particular beings.

E. SPIRITUAL BEING

From the neutral standpoint of being the spirit is for Hartmann simply another level of being, but this level is of such vast significance for man that he accords it exhaustive treatment. Here we learn that spiritual being (*das geistige Sein*) is entirely distinct from mental being (*das seelische Sein*) which is the level of conscious being and which even animals share. There is here a categorial novelty which can be understood only after detailed study of its essence. We can see, however, that the spirit constitutes a closed level of being articulated in three forms: personal, objective, and objectified spirit. The first two are the living forms of spirit. All spirit has existence, is real, individual, and temporal; its temporality is the same as that of this world (here he diverges from the Platonists and existentialists). But the spirit possesses its own categories and peculiarities; it is not only found in the process, it actually "is" process; there is no substance in it (as in natural processes), nor does it gradually develop itself (as life does); it must mark out its own identity by identifying itself with itself. Though nonspatial it is bound down to space (*raumgebunden*). It is located within the real world and even dependent upon it, but in the same way that a ruler is dependent upon the forces under his control.

Spiritual consciousness is a mark of the *individual spirit*, the unique, irreplaceable subject; such consciousness is ec-centric and thereby objective. However, the spirit is something more than just this; involved, as it is, in the actuality of the life context it acts as a pole for diversity within this context and is named "person." Personality is the categorial feature of the spiritual individual; like everything spiritual it is only susceptible of description, never of definition. Its first feature is that it spontaneously constitutes or fulfils its own self (*sich selbst vollziehen*); this leads Hartmann to speak of faithfulness in a manner that is reminiscent of Gabriel Marcel's doctrine. Another feature of the personal spirit is the transcendent quality of its acts; it faces a given situation just as much as an animal does. In the case of a person, however, the situation never forces him into unconditional surrender, but summons him to a transcendent act which he accomplishes through his consciousness of the object. The creature is a person when every element in its being prompts it to reach beyond its own life. By its very nature spirit is diffusive; it is ultimately free.

Objective spirit is more easily known than personal spirit. It is a fundamental characteristic of the spiritual life that its contents (intentional objects) can be detached from the person. Whenever a person objectifies something through expressing it, immediately it ceases to be his monopoly—it "travels" from person to person. This is the basic phenomenon of the objective spirit. All such contents (law, custom, language, belief, science, art) come within the content of the historical spirit, but their historical quality itself shows that they cannot be treated as content pure and simple, for they have life, they grow and decay—a particular mode of being. This is the sense in which we speak of "the spirit of Hellenism," "the spirit of a nation" etc; such a spirit is not identical either with individuals or with their aggregate nor is it the same as the community, though it never exists apart from a certain collectivity. In opposition to Hegel, Hartmann maintains that objective spirit is not a substance; it is the life of the spirit in its wholeness as it unfolds itself throughout human groups. Far from being a mere universal, it is unique, individual, historical, and autonomous— in brief, it is real and actual in the most emphatic sense.

Objective and personal spirit are related through alternately bearing and being borne by, each other; the individual flowers into objective spirit, and objective spirit lives in and through individuals. The objective spirit does not bequeath itself, it simply "hands itself on" continually (the law of tradition). None of its representatives exhausts its content, and for these reasons it exhibits an activity all of its own. What is remarkable about it is that no consciousness can ever be adequate to it, for it is neither a collective consciousness nor a collective person; no more is it an "unconscious" or a "superconscious" spirit. The consciousness of objective spirit is to be found in none of these but only in single persons; and, since it is always inadequately present in them, it is consequently an imperfect spirit. In the community it is represented through the vicarious consciousness of a *leading* individual.

Both objective and personal spirit objectify themselves to form *objectified spirit*. The latter presents extraordinarily difficult problems; whenever it appears it does so at two levels— the sensible and real structure being the first, acting as a support for the second, "spiritual content." How these two are united, how objectified spirit survives when separated from living spirit—these are some of the numerous problems dealt with by Hartmann in this part of his work, which also contains weighty reflections upon aesthetics, history, science, and other cultural matters.

F. ETHICS. FREEDOM OF THE WILL

Hartmann's profound work on ethics has had an enduring influence in Germany and the Anglo-Saxon countries. Unfortunately we must confine ourselves to a mere sketch of its main outlines. In the first part of this work Hartmann studies the structure of the ethical phenomenon. He takes over the basic doctrines of Max Scheler's ethics of value but fits them into a new system, develops them along lines already laid down, and introduces numerous changes. Thus he regards the existence of moral values as an independent domain and repudiates the doctrine of the collective person: the individual man alone is a person. This property renders man as a moral being axiologically autonomous. There is no teleological principle which might impose some kind of determinism from above. For if there were, man would be obliterated as a person and could not possibly be a moral being. In fact no one will ever be able to demonstrate a divine teleological providence beyond man's own.

In the second part of his work Hartmann erects the realm of ethical values in an elaborate system, the most complete and thorough-going yet seen. Here he sticks close to Aristotle, "the past master of ethical science," defending and deepening the Aristotelian doctrine of virtue, of the μεσότης. Virtue he says is only in the ontological sense a "middle" as against the axiological definition according to which, even in Aristotle, virtue is a supreme value, ἀκρότης. The μεσότης is not middling in value.

But in the last resort this ethic remains a resumption and extension of Aristotle's and Scheler's ideas, though elaborated in a very remarkable fashion. By contrast, in the third part of his great work Hartmann expounds a most original theory of *freedom* which swells into a magnificent synthesis through uniting the arguments from Aristotelianism, Thomism, Neo-Kantianism (Cohen) and, above all, Kant himself (purified of idealism). In company with Kant, Hartmann distinguishes negative freedom (indeterminacy) and positive freedom (self-determination). In regard to the causally determined world there cannot be negative freedom, there can be no indeterminism; but the problem of freedom lies beyond the conflict between determinism and indeterminism because determination by the laws of nature does not restrict freedom in the least—provided that causal determination is not conceived in a monistic fashion. Monism, however, as applied to the levels of being and to the laws of being has proved itself a false ontology. Freedom of the will in a world of several levels does not present an exceptional phenomenon; the law of autonomy finds its application in the relationship of all higher levels to the lower ones. The freedom of the will is not a subtraction from determination but an addition to it; it means that determination through causal laws is not eliminated at all, but is diverted by the intervention of a higher determination—freedom.

Meanwhile the freedom of the will involves also freedom in regard to the ethical principle (the values) itself. This is shown to be a negative freedom, because in contrast to the real world, which is thoroughly determined, ethical reality is not determined. The person determines himself so that by means of this determination he may then go on to determine the real world. Thus man appears as the point of contact for two heterogeneous forces—the real and the ideal worlds. It is through man alone, and through his freedom, that the values affect the real world.

But is the freedom of the will not an illusion? Hartmann establishes its reality by a procedure similar to that which he used to demonstrate that the object of knowledge exists in-itself; as in epistemology, the burden of proof rests with the sceptics. There is nothing in phenomena which could justify it; on the other hand, consciousness of guilt provides a sure indication that freedom is real.

The work concludes with references to a number of antin-

Philosophy of Being

omies between ethics and religion; the task of dealing with them is allotted to the philosophy of religion. But even such a philosophy is reduced to silence when it comes face to face with the enigma of irreducible irrationality.

23. ALFRED NORTH WHITEHEAD

A. CHARACTERISTICS. DEVELOPMENT

Alfred North Whitehead (1861-1947) is considered the outstanding philosopher of the Anglo-Saxon world in our time, and seems to be well deserving of such esteem. He is indeed an original thinker endowed with remarkable powers of mind. His career was an extremely unusual one for a philosopher. After completing his education at Cambridge, where he studied mathematics, he went on to teach geometry and mechanics for thirty years. At the age of fifty, in 1911, he was appointed reader in these subjects at University College, London; from 1914 until 1924 he was professor of applied mathematics at the Imperial College, London. He was already sixty-three when he became a professor of philosophy at Harvard in 1924 where he taught until 1937.

In his scientific publications three periods are clearly distinguishable. From 1898 onward he was producing works on mathematical logic, his crowning effort being the monumental *Principia Mathematica* (1910-1913) on which he collaborated with Russell. Later, physics became Whitehead's main interest and he published several important papers on the philosophy of physics. With the appearance of *Science and the Modern World* (1926) he finally established himself as a metaphysician. His major work *Process and Reality*, which is a complete system of thought, appeared in 1929.

Whitehead had an extraordinary versatile mind being a first-rate mathematician, one of the founders of modern mathematical logic, as well as the author of a philosophy of organism. Though a natural scientist by profession, he displayed a lively interest in history and revealed extensive acquaintance with that subject. His system was developed from physics, contained a wealth of biological ideas, and eventually came to concentrate on the philosophy of religion. This great logician has a style which occasionally echoes the language of the mystics. Catholicity of learning was united in his person to an equally catholic and sympathetic appreciation for the most diverse spiritual and artistic movements. Thoroughly positive in his modes of explanation, a tireless worker with a gift for detailed analysis, and a remarkable capacity for synthesis, Whitehead and his work constitute a model of the philosopher at his very best.

Whitehead's philosophical affiliations are not easily classified. Like Russell he is considered one of the English neorealists, because he employs their analytical method, and because he shares their high valuation of science and their realism. No other contemporary philosopher has worked up the results of the natural sciences into such a complete synthesis. He is also a Platonist, and he himself claims to be one in the strictest sense; but despite his assertion that European philosophy consists of footnotes to Plato, his Platonism is somewhat peculiar—according to him, for instance, the ideas possess no actuality but are pure possibilities. Numerous traces of Aristotelianism are also found in his works where his intellectualism is united with a far-reaching empiricism. In some respects (in his theory of prehension, for instance) he is akin to Leibniz, in others (substance) to Spinoza, while in his aesthetics he is indebted to Kant and to the Aristotelian tradition. Whitehead swears by dynamism and evolutionism just as firmly as Bergson, whose critical attitude toward scientism he also shares, although he insists that our approach to God must be a rational one.

227

Nevertheless it would be unjust to regard him as an eclectic, for the dominant feature of his system is its profound unity. His fundamental notions of creativity and prehension are entirely original, and he stretches them to their logical conclusion through applying them at every turn. Thus he seems to have been thoroughly modern in the sense that he was one of the leading and most modern of philosophers in an age wholly given over to twentieth-century physics, mathematics, biology, and philosophy; yet at the same time he maintained his metaphysical speculation on the timeless level at which Plato dealt with these problems.

The following is only a very summary account of Whitehead's system based mainly upon *Science and the Modern World*. His extraordinarily difficult main work can unfortunately not be discussed here.

B. PHILOSOPHY

Thought is abstract and we cannot think without abstractions. But abstractions are as dangerous as they are useful. They are often developed from inadequate foundations, as in modern natural science, for example, and can lead to intellectual intolerance, since one may overlook all those concrete elements which do not fit into an abstract scheme. Once abstractions are set up one tends to take them as dogmas and to regard them as realities. The fallacy of misplaced concreteness can condemn a civilization to sterility. Now the primordial task of philosophy is the critique of abstractions. The basic ideas assumed by scholars to be free of contradiction must be tested and comparisons made between the abstract schemata of the different sciences and between those of religion and the sciences. Philosophy also develops its own system relying upon more concrete intuitions than are used by the sciences. Philosophy appeals even to the testimony of poetry and religion.

Therefore it is not one among the sciences, but goes beyond all of them. It is indispensable, for without it man would develop synoptic theories without the sober guidance of understanding and reason. Thus philosophy may also be defined as striving for the complete rationalization of human experience.

Its methods, then, must be rational. Whitehead protests against the surrender of reason to brute fact which has occurred recently and hopes that the time is now ripe for a genuine rationalism. His demand for rational explanations is based on faith in reason which is the trust that the ultimate natures of things lie together in rational harmony. This faith cannot be justified either by induction or by deduction, but direct insight reveals to us a world governed by logical law and aesthetic harmony. It is this belief alone which makes science possible. We owe the spreading of this faith to the Greek dramatists, to classical and medieval thinkers. Yet he insists that this faith is not blind, since being itself is both rational and intelligible; the simple apprehension of being is sufficient to confirm it.

And yet, Whitehead is not a rationalist in the classical and narrow sense of the word. He considers contact with the concrete as the only fruitful procedure, and the ground of things must be sought always in the nature of determinate real beings because where there is no being there is no ground. Philosophy explains the abstract, not the concrete—it is experience alone which enables us to lay bare the truth. (Like Husserl, Whitehead does not restrict experience to perception.) Whitehead emphasizes his empiricism even more firmly by maintaining that metaphysics can only be descriptive.

He goes on to warn philosophers against employing the methods appropriate to the natural sciences; empirical generalizations do not provide the means for criticizing abstractions. To base metaphysics upon history would be just as ab-

Philosophy of Being

surd, because any interpretation of history presupposes metaphysics.

C. CRITICISM OF MATERIALISM

The fundamental doctrine of materialism, according to Whitehead, states that matter exists, or that there is matter and nothing else. Thus matter is conceived as anything that has the property of simple location in time and space. If this doctrine were true, time would be an accident of changeless matter; consequently an instant would have no duration. But it is plain that matter is a double abstraction—an entity is treated solely in its relationship to some other entity, and even within this relationship only its spatio-temporal factors are taken into consideration. This materialist schematization has achieved predominance and has powerfully affected scientific development since Galileo's time for various historical and technical reasons. And yet it is impossible to believe in it. Materialism inevitably leads one to deny the existence of secondary qualities, a clean contradiction of all experience; it leads just as inevitably to the equally false denial of human responsibility. Ultimately it destroys its own premise, that is, induction, because if matter simply consists of isolated fragments linked together through spatio-temporal relations alone, then there is no justification for inferring what will happen to one entity from what has happened to another. At the present day, materialism can no longer look to the natural sciences for support; the undulatory theory of light, the idea of atomicity (since its transference to biological fields), the doctrines of the conservation of energy and of evolution have all brought forth facts which point to the inadequacy of scientific materialism. Finally, the quantum theory has proved this philosophy to be quite untenable by demanding that "matter" itself should be conceived as organic. Nevertheless the chief argument against materialism remains philosophical—one can easily demonstrate that in its essence this doctrine attributes reality to a convenient and very fertile abstraction. Body, as Galileo and Descartes understood the term, does not exist; it is but an abstraction—the concept of body is a typical instance of the *fallacy of misplaced concreteness.*

D. THE THEORY OF ORGANIC MECHANISM

Every program for analyzing nature, if it is to be adequate, must give some account of the following notions—change, endurance, interfusion, value, organism, and eternal objects. A mountain both changes and endures; the things of nature are not isolated but interfused with each other; both the world and organisms exhibit value. Lastly there are those objects which, without enduring, are eternal, such as a particular color. Once a mountain has been worn away it is gone for good; if a replica were to arise it would be a new mountain. A color comes and goes, but it is the same color. Beyond all these categories—and, indeed, comprehending them all—we come to Whitehead's fundamental concept—the event. The world is not made up of things but of events, of what happens. A temporal section of an event ("a drop of experience") or an immediate act of immediate self-consciousness ("self-enjoyment") is an "occasion." Each event is a "prehension" and an organism. It is a prehension because it mirrors within itself the whole universe at once, as though knowing it blindly. It contains its own past within itself, it anticipates its future, and the present world of other events is represented in it by their effect on it. An event is thus the synthetic unity of the universe comprehended as oneness. On the other hand an event is an organism; its parts are not simply set together side by side but form a whole in which each member affects the whole and the whole acts as a determinant for each of its members. An electron, for ex-

231

ample, is profoundly altered through the fact that it enjoys membership in an atom and the atom likewise through belonging to a living tissue. Like Leibniz's monads every event is a mirror of the universe.

This is the best standpoint from which to coördinate the results of modern physics, of biology, and of the human sciences, and it reveals both the error of materialism and its extremely abstract character. In materialism, for example, space is an abstraction from events in their relationship of reciprocal interfusion, while time is an abstraction from the duration of successive events. Whitehead shares Bergson's ideas upon this subject, though he expressly repudiates the latter's anti-intellectualist attitude.

From the standpoint of organic mechanism the universe appears as a gigantic community in which everything influences everything else and no relations are purely external.

E. EPISTEMOLOGY

Whitehead agrees with *objectivism* in the sense that he believes that the world certainly includes acts of cognition but also contains something more. He adduces three reasons for this: our perceptive experience shows that we are situated within a world which extends far beyond us; history teaches that the past was in existence prior to ourselves; and human activity requires a transcendent world. This does not enable us to decide whether *realism* or *idealism* is correct. But Whitehead elects for the former, and he introduces his theory of prehension in reply to all idealist objections; the principle of immanence, according to which we only know what is "in" us, is invalid because it is derived from the materialist notion that things exist in isolation. Every event, in fact, transcends itself by means of prehension. Admittedly what we know *here* is something over *there*, but we do know it none the less. Nor is it surprising that error should arise in our knowledge or that we are influenced by subjective conditions because we know events so far as they form part of us.

This brief sketch of Whitehead's epistemology should be supplemented by at least some reference to his doctrine of induction and causality. Once the philosophy of organism is granted, induction is seen to be the transition from individual qualities toward a general characteristic shared by a community of occasions. Induction is not rational inference or the derivation of invariable laws but is a sort of divination. It discovers particular tokens of a community of occasions bounded in space and time. The problems of *causality* brings out the fact that our direct knowledge is twofold; we have direct knowledge of causality as well as of sense data (which Whitehead calls *presentational immediacy*). Traditional doctrines only acknowledge the latter and treat causality as either a hypothesis or an inference. Actually causal efficacy is directly apprehended and, far from being a conceptual superstructure, forms the basis of our knowledge by means of presentational immediacy.

F. PSYCHOLOGY

One of the greatest and most dangerous illusions of modern times has been the bifurcation of nature into matter and spirit. There is not the least doubt that spirit exists, for it is evident; but spirit should no more be regarded as a substance than should matter since, like the body, it is simply an array of events. Consciousness is a function. In this respect Whitehead follows the tenor of an essay of James's which he greatly admired entitled "Does Consciousness Exist?". Whitehead comes to the same functionalist conclusions as are expounded in that essay. Nevertheless, spirit should not be regarded as an epiphenomenon of matter; though it is certainly difficult to draw the

Philosophy of Being

line between them, one can say that every event is bipolar and that, consciousness is the event, seen from within. The occasions of mentality in bits of inorganic matter seem to be negligible, but they are obviously present in man and the higher animals. That there are occasions of mentality in which the concomitant material aspects are negligible (that is, that there are purely spiritual beings) is a thesis which the philosophy of organism cannot affirm. But neither can it reject it out of hand. One could maintain that the soul survives death or is immortal only on the evidence of certain special experiences, such as we encounter, for example, in religion.

G. METAPHYSICS

Whitehead does not distinguish between ontology and metaphysics; metaphysics is the description of the nature of things providing the presuppositions of all specialized investigation. The key to Whitehead's teaching upon this issue is his statement that the understanding of actuality requires a reference to ideality. If we analyse what is presented to us, it becomes plain that the actual is a flow of events, an eternal process in which there is neither substance nor anything that really endures. Whitehead embraces a radical dynamism, but he also recognizes that the appearance of any given event is a fact and calls for explanation—it forces us to assume the existence of several metaphysical factors which are not beings in the usual sense. In the first place there must be *eternal objects*, the possibilities of all those events which actually occur; they are the same as Plato's Ideas except that they must be conceived as purely objective potentialities. Secondly, the analysis reveals a blind creative urge (creativity) which seems to be both the efficient cause of the process and its matter; everything originates in the surge of this totally undetermined "substance" (in Spinoza's sense). Finally, since neither the eternal objects nor creativity are determinate and since they provide no explanation for concreteness, it becomes necessary to invoke a third factor which limits and determines beings in their process, and is actual, yet nontemporal. This *principle of limitation* or concretion is God. The way in which process fulfils itself is through the coöperation of the creative urge with the already existing event, and together they produce a new synthetic prehension. The latter has two sides—the resultant event produces a synthesis of eternal objects (which make their *ingression* into it positively or negatively); it also combines them with aspects of other real events. God determines what is to appear by imposing limitations and so makes determination possible— the result is the actual individual, the *superject*, the actual which is a value in itself because every concrete actuality is a value.

Thus every event in its own right forms a sort of synthesis of the universe by bringing together all aspects of the real world —all eternal things, the creative urge, and God. God therefore is immanent in the world. But an event always represents an addition to the world into which it enters; having its own individuality it creates a new actuality and a fresh value.

H. GOD

In Whitehead's opinion the method by which we come to knowledge of God must conform to several conditions. The way must be a rational one and cannot proceed from intuition alone since we do not possess any such intuition of God; nor can we rely upon St. Anselm's ontological argument. Aristotle's cosmological argument is also defective because it rests upon Aristotelian physics, which is archaic, and also because it makes God so utterly transcendent as to be useless for religious purposes. God's existence is to be assumed in order to explain phenomena because he fulfils the need for a *principle of con-*

235

cretion in two ways—without him neither the "how" nor the "what" of events would be comprehensible; if one denies God then one has also to deny that concrete events exist.

At first (1926) Whitehead thought that God's nature was not susceptible of any more precise definition than that given by Aristotle. In the following years, however, he worked out a complete theology based upon the distinction between two aspects of God—his primordial and his consequent nature. God's *primordial* nature reveals him as changeless and timeless; his actuality is complete and infinite; God is eternal but his eternity is a lifeless one. God in this way is merely an attribute of creativity and only comes to life through creation. All other qualities displayed by God are due to his *consequent* nature. God in his consequent nature is conscious and conceptual universal prehension; he is omniscient, and the ideal world is but an image of him. God coördinates all details of the world and adapts them to one another by means of this infinite contemplation. Nevertheless, God is limited by his consequent nature. He is constantly in process of becoming and is continually enriching himself through the prehension of new elements.

God is immanent in the world at the same time that he transcends it. He is immanent so far as he is present in every being. He is transcendent in the way every event transcends another event. Here Whitehead piles up contradictions and employs a language which is totally different from his normal one. It is the language of Neoplatonic mysticism. Only one further detail of his theology can be given here. Evil per se is something positive, according to Whitehead, but it leads to anarchy and degradation in the world. Since God is the principle of harmony, order, peace, and value, he cannot be the source of evil. From this Whitehead concludes that God is morally good and that he promotes qualitative progress. His goal receives its embodiment in the fragmentary ideals of the world in its current state. In this sense God is the guarantor of the world's value. He is battling continually against evil, the ideal companion of all who suffer and fight by his side.

24. THOMISM

A. CHARACTERISTICS AND REPRESENTATIVES

The Thomistic (also called "neo-Thomistic") school, which starts from the basic doctrines of Thomas of Aquinas (1224-1274), counts as one of the most important philosophical movements at the present day. The Catholic Church recommends Thomism (encyclical *Aeterni Patris*, 1879) and Thomists are in the main Catholics. Yet it is not the only philosophical movement within the Catholic world[9] and, on the other hand, it can claim several important adherents among non-Catholics (among them, for example, the American philosopher Mortimer Adler and the English philosopher E. L. Mascall). Little attention was paid to Thomism by circles outside the church until the First World War, but it has since become recognized as one of the most powerful factors at work in our age. Actually no other philosophical group seems to have so many thinkers in its ranks or so many centers of study at its disposal. It is sufficient to point out that the bibliographic or-

---

[9] The outstanding schools of contemporary Catholic philosophy may be listed as follows:
I. Augustinianism (intuitionist, actualist, and frequently pragmatist in tendency): Johannes Hessen, Peter Wust.
II. Neoscholasticism (intellectualist position). It consists of three schools—Scotism (Franciscan School); Suarezianism (P. Descors, L. Fuetscher); and Thomism. The latter may be subdivided in (a) a group which attempts to combine Thomism with modern nonscholastic currents (J. Maréchal, J. Geyser): (b) Molinism; (c) Thomism in the strict sense of the word, which is the most important both in the number of its thinkers and in the weight of its influence, although it is comparatively weakly represented in Germany.

237

gan of the school, the *Bulletin Thomiste*, gives notices and reviews of almost 500 works per year, and that no less than 25 specialist Thomist journals are published. Thomism has come to fruition in France and Belguim, but possesses centers of study and representatives in almost every country. Its outstanding centers include the Institut Supérieur de Philosophie at Louvain University founded by Désiré Mercier (1851-1926); the Catholic Institute at Paris; the Catholic University at Milan: the *Angelicum* at Rome; and the Swiss University of Freiburg. In recent years the school has also made progress in Anglo-Saxon countries, especially in the United States.

Here it is only possible to mention a very few of the vast number of thinkers who belong to this school. Of the older generation one should refer, after Mercier, to Ambroise Gardeil (1859-1931) and Joseph Gredt (1863-1940). The school's most systematic thinker is perhaps Réginald Garrigou-Lagrange (b. 1877), a pupil of Gardeil's; the most famous, however, is Jacques Maritain (b. 1882) who is regarded as the leading living Thomist; close to him comes, Antonin D. Sertillanges (1863-1948). Another French philosopher whose speciality has been the history of philosophy but who has won a hearing for a systematic works of his own is Étienne Gilson (b. 1884). Those of its representatives who write in German include Gallus M. Manser (1866-1950), Alexander Horvath (b. 1884), Joseph Mausbach (1861-1931), and the historian of medieval philosophy Martin Grabmann (1875-1949).

Modern Thomism is a school in the proper sense of the word; it has its own problems, its own method and a deposit of common doctrine acknowledged by all its representatives; in this respect it is similar to neopositivism, dialectical materialism, and Neo-Kantianism. At the same time various problems provoke quite strong differences of opinion within the school. Thomists not only apply themselves to all contemporary problems but also discuss a wealth of questions between themselves that are peculiar to their own school. In the congresses which they frequently hold, extended discussions usually take place. Recent congresses have discussed phenomenology (1932), the so-called Christian philosophy (1933), and the relations between philosophy and the natural sciences (1935). There were also sessions devoted to existentialism by the Roman Thomistic Academy in 1947.

B. BEING. ACT AND POTENCY

The metaphysics which constitutes the core of Thomistic philosophy is closely linked to ontology and takes being qua being as its object. The concept of being is not univocal but analogous, which means that the meaning of the word "being" when it is attributed to two different objects is different but proportionately identical. The most essential doctrine on the subject of being is that of act and potency, the key doctrine of the system which leads to all the rest. In other words, one distinguishes between actual being and potential being; the actual (whatever is in act, *actu*) in any given respect is that which *is* in that respect whereas the potential (in potency, *potentia*) is not yet in act but can become so; thus a child, for instance, has the power to become a mathematician and so is potentially a mathematician. Apart from God every being is made up of act and potency; their reciprocal relationship within concrete being is such that potency is the determinable ground whose determinant is act.

This teaching on act and potency receives its first important application in the theory of essence and existence. Every being apart from God consists of essence (*essentia*) and existence (*existentia*); existence is the act of the essence, which actualizes it, and though the two are certainly inseparable in concrete being, they nevertheless are really distinct.

239

Philosophy of Being

Another important application of the act-potency doctrine is made in the theory of categories. The fundamental category is substance, the being which alone enjoys intrinsic being; all other categories, the so-called "accidents" (*accidentia*), are determinations of substance, which means that they are related to substance as potency is related to act. Frequently the Thomistic teaching on substance has been misunderstood; this teaching does not conceive of substance as an inert subject of change but as a being-in-itself, a being in the fullest sense, as opposed to accidents, that is, mere determinations for which to be is to be-in-another-being.

In line with the act-potency doctrine is the Thomist theory of *becoming*. This is conceived as a transition from potency to act; as such it is an incomplete being and an impoverished reality. Consequently all becoming presupposes a substance in process of becoming, something fully in being. From this point of view Bergson's saying that there is more in becoming than in being seems to be self-contradictory. It is essential that this notion of becoming be sharply distinguished from that of activity, which is a metaphysical consequence from the actuality of being—the more being, the more activity. God as the fulness of being corresponds to the fulness of activity.

The doctrine of the four factors (*causae*) is also bound up with the act-potency doctrine but only a brief indication of it can be given here. The four factors are: matter (the stuff from which anything is made or proceeds); form (the determinant of matter); efficient cause; end. They constitute a definite ascending series in which the end acts as the highest cause. Every efficient cause, whether consciously or unconsciously, is essentially directed toward an end, whereas form can only be introduced into matter through an efficient cause.

All contingent beings are hierarchically ordered according to their actuality, that is, according to their fulness of being. The fundamental Thomist doctrine on this subject is hylomorphism (from the Greek ὕλη, matter, and μορφή, form), which states that every material being consists of matter, and of a form which determines this matter; matter is related to form as potency to act. If one analyzes any being from this point of view and mentally detaches its forms one after the other, one eventually arrives at prime matter (*materia prima*), the constituent of being which is completely stripped of all determination and which, as pure potentiality, balances on the brink of nonbeing. Prime matter is the principle of the multiplicity and divisibility in material things, whose unity is derived from form alone. Form permeates particular beings and it unites itself with matter in the closest bond between two really different elements which we encounter in the natural order. The lowest form of all is that of an inorganic body for it lacks organic unity and activity of its own; an inorganic body is the most passive being since it can only be actuated by another being. Life exhibits a greater unity and activity, because here organisms come into play which are endowed with their own purposeful activity, even though the purpose is frequently unconscious. No purely mechanical explanation of life is possible. This does not mean that one has to assume two different substances (material and vital) for plants and animals but rather that the life principle is a form, the supreme content, which determines the total being of any living thing. A still higher level of being is reached by animals; not only are they active, but their activity is directed toward a goal which they know; a sure sign that they enjoy greater fulness of being lies in the fact that they are more self-subsistent and possess a higher activity. Finally, surpassing material, vegetative, and animal forms, comes man with his spiritual soul, which comprehends perfection of all inferior forms within a higher and unique spiritual form; man also knows the goal of his activity and, what is more, he is free to choose it, thereby enjoying the greatest fulness of being to be found on earth.

D. SPIRIT

The highest degree of being is a privilege of spirit. Spirit is distinguished by its immateriality, which consists in its indivisibility and, above all, in its autonomy. It is not bounded by the order of space and time, for by penetrating material phenomena it comes to know immaterial intelligible essences and can will immaterial ends. These are its essential functions —to know and to will. Knowledge is either intuitive, known as "intellect" (*intellectus*) or else it is discursive, known as "reason" (*ratio*). Willing is a reaction similar to every other known reaction but belongs to the spiritual order, and therefore consists in reaction to spiritual knowledge; the will can direct itself toward immaterial essences, just as reason can know them. Because of its immateriality the will is open to infinity, therefore free from bondage to finite objects, and this means that it is able to behave freely toward them. It cannot be determined by any finite good; therefore it is not only free in the sense that it can choose spontaneously, but in the sense that, even when the conditions for a certain action have all been realized, it can act or not act.

Nevertheless the spirit in man is always intimately united with the whole psychophysical organism; the spiritual soul is the unique "form" of the human being. Man is akin to animals in his bodily construction and vital functions, and his essence even embraces vegetative and physicochemical functions. The spirit in him is obviously dependent upon the organism because he may be crippled by a slight disturbance of his nerve centers. This dependence, moreover, has many sides to it; on the cognitive side the senses and the imaginative faculty present objects for its spiritual knowledge, on the volitional side the instincts exert profound influence on the will. The fact that this dependence is objective and not subjective is of first-rate importance in the field of knowledge; it means that when a disturbance of the nerve centers directly (subjectively) affects the imaginative faculty and paralyzes it, the spirit is also paralyzed, because it no longer has an object to work on. On the other hand, there is no subjective dependence of the spirit upon the body; in spite of being the form of the body the spiritual soul rises above matter—it is also immortal because, being immaterial, it has no parts and cannot disintegrate at death.

E. KNOWLEDGE

Epistemology for most Thomists does not form the object of a separate discipline but is simply a compartment of metaphysics, as it is for Alexander and Hartmann. Epistemology is not the basis for a philosophy of being. The reverse is true—to know is to be another as other. The seeming obscurity of this statement is cleared up as soon as one recognizes the spiritual qualities of the soul. Since it is not material, it is not limited and, without ceasing to be what it is, it can "intentionally" become something other. This applies even to sensible knowledge so far as a certain immateriality is already present in such knowledge. Between sensible and spiritual knowledge, however, there exists a fundamental distinction, because the former only seizes upon the material and concrete, upon sensible accidents, and could never know either being as being or intelligible content of any sort. Spiritual knowledge, by contrast, is directed toward being; it alone has a direct grasp of the universal, which is the sole object that can be completely known. One should not infer from this that universals as such exist in the world; every real being is utterly individual and concrete, yet each has an intelligible essence. (Only that which is not a real being is irrational. Every being is a possible object of knowledge.) This essence exists concretely in the concrete, and is raised to universality through abstraction by the intellect; the intellect first of all removes its individual conditions and then compares it with other individuals in order to bestow universality upon it. In other words, intelligible content certainly does exist in things but the universal is an offspring of the spirit, a being produced by reason but founded in reality. Abstraction sets out from phantasms, the sensible representations supplied by the imagination. There is no *a priori* knowledge in Kant's sense. Once concepts have been formed, however, one only needs to analyze them in order to establish universal laws without having to refer back to sensible knowledge. Beginning from such laws one can think out new laws which result in genuine certainty, as the development of mathematics shows. This is because thinking elicits from the premises something which they did indeed contain, though only potentially. Thomistic epistemology is outspokenly realistic, and its realism is immediate and direct—the subject does not generate the object but simply produces its spiritual image, the so-called species. To know a thing does not mean to construct it, but to grasp it as it is in itself.

Thomism is also an intellectualist doctrine. We only acquire genuine knowledge of the truth through intellectual intuitions supported by discursive argumentation. Yet although this knowledge cannot be gained *a priori* and without experience, it must still be the result of a rational procedure. This position, however, does not imply a denial of experience and life, because spiritual knowledge is the highest form of experience and the perfection of life, the life of the spirit.

God's existence must be acknowledged. Since no irrational thing could possibly exist (because *ens et verum convertuntur*), one cannot admit the existence of empirically known being without acknowledging a creator. As a matter of fact the essence of every such being is really different from its existence, and one can never discover a sufficient ground for their union without recourse to a being in whom essence and existence are identical. Such a being has no limitation in its essence; therefore it must be infinite, pure act, the fullness of being and consequently of goodness, beauty, and every other value. Yet God should not be conceived as a created being infinitely magnified; he is a being in an analogous sense, in a sense different from that of the creature. Pantheistic theories are thus seen to be untenable because they proceed upon the assumption that it is impossible to have both an infinite God and a world at the same time. The Thomist argues against pantheism, that since God is the fullness of being, and since we describe being in terms of spirit, will, love, and knowledge, we must also conceive of God as a person, even if analogously.

God's relationship to the world may be described in the following manner: Firstly, as far as essence is concerned, every finite creature is a participation (*participatio*) in the essence of God, who must be thought of as the source and exemplar for all essence. Instead of the Platonic world of Ideas (which involves a contradiction according to the Thomists) we are presented here with God's real being. Secondly, the existence of every thing is equally a participation of his being. Thus created being, which is composed of act and potency, is a twofold participation in the infinite pure act (*actus purus*). But whereas God's being so strictly determines all *essence* that even God himself cannot alter essences, everything depends for its *exist-*

245

ence upon God's free will. Looked at from this point of view the whole of world history is interpreted as the realization of an eternal plan fully set out by God. Clearly, then, the world process is directed toward an end which can be none other than the one which even God himself pursues—and necessarily pursues—namely, God himself. Again, it is evident that *truth* in the logical, human sense is a derived truth since it is founded upon ontological truth, the conformity of created being to God's thought.

Philosophy knows God only as the first cause of the world and is unable to offer us any insight into his inner life. Revelation and faith alone render such knowledge possible, so far as it is possible at all. It is true, of course, that revelation cannot be introduced as a positive element into this philosophical system, because philosophy proceeds exclusively from natural experience and employs a purely rational method. On the other hand philosophy supplies no grounds for denying the possibility of revelation. Furthermore the content of revelation can never come into contradiction with philosophical and scientific doctrines, because both the world and revelation are the work of the same truthful and omniscient God. But for all that, philosophy can construct a theory of natural religion in complete independence of revelation; Thomism has always done so, especially in recent times.

G. ETHICS

There are two ways in which the human spirit may be related to being. Being, as the object of knowledge, forms the ground of truth and, as the good, provides the will with its object. The good is of three types—the unconditional good (*honestum*), the pleasant good (*delectabile*), and the useful good (*utile*), the third of these being but a function of the first. The Thomist *doctrine of values* is a doctrine of the good;

it is closely linked to Thomist teaching upon universals, since the values are themselves grounded in being and yet exist, as such, only in the evaluating subject. The major division within the province of value is between aesthetic value, where the attitude toward the good is contemplative, and practical value, involving a disposition toward action. The latter permits of division into two further provinces, that of technics, where the object of activity is an external one (*facere*), and that of morality where the agent is his own object (*agere*). According to the Thomists there are no religious values other than those which are at the same time moral values.

Thomistic ethics is an ethics of purpose. Through their persistent disagreement with the Kantian doctrine that ethics is based upon duty, and with the phenomenological conception in which the theory of value is the nucleus of ethics, the Thomists emphasize that ethics is essentially a doctrine about man's behavior and must therefore be derived from doctrine about his end. This end, which constitutes man's happiness, is conceived of as the uninterrupted and consummate activity of a perfect subject. And so the dynamic quality of Thomistic philosophy is illustrated in ethics as well. Since this uninterrupted activity is only possible if the subject is disciplined in all his faculties through persistent usage (*habitus*), this means that the virtues occupy a predominant position in the Thomistic system. Thomistic ethics are essentially characterological and educative; man is born with certain dispositions, but the effort to discipline himself is necessary before he can bring them to fulfilment. The virtues which he acquires in the course of this effort make him free in the deepest sense, though this is not the same as saying with Kant that the will should forcibly subject the feelings to moral laws; the ideal is much more to discipline man's whole psychological structure so that the man not only does good but can do good gladly and easily. The

247

chief virtue is prudence, which consists of the reason's being ready to pronounce a correct practical judgment upon concrete affairs—a further indication of Thomistic intellectualism. Nevertheless prudence can only operate as it should when the will is disposed toward justice in its widest connotation and when the feelings are brought under control through temperance and fortitude.

Thomism also allots a leading role to the *moral law*. Man's conduct is directly determined by his conscience, but the conscience itself is simply an expression of natural justice, that is, of the moral laws which are immanent in human nature (indwelling). Adultery, for example, is condemned by the moral law because man's (psychophysiological) nature demands that marriage should be indissoluble. The natural law receives both its application and its manifestation in positive law; it is actually an expression of the eternal law, of the divine plan which lies at the foundation of the world. Nevertheless this should not be interpreted to mean that Thomism regards God's will as the ultimate foundation of the moral order; God himself could never alter the fundamental laws of morality because they are rooted in his being, not in his will.

The *doctrine of society* also occupies a prominent place in Thomistic ethics. The individual man is the highest being in this world and all other beings are there to serve him. Society however, is no fiction, it is more than the aggregate of its members since its structure comprehends real relationships which could not be derived from man as an individual. Again, man is by nature a social creature and the common good is one of the motives for action within the order of virtue. Thus even the purely "personal" virtues, such as temperance, become obligatory through the demands of social justice, because man in himself represents a social value.

In all the other movements of contemporary philosophy we have noticed a limited fundamental idea which appears to narrow their outlook. Among the metaphysicians no such idea is to be found. The real reason for this is because they are philosophers of being who by very definition transcend all limited viewpoints and are able to work the partial institutions of other schools into their own systems. Consequently metaphysics today cannot simply be identified or contrasted with other philosophical movements—it towers over them just as philosophy towers over the special sciences.

This permits the metaphysicians to do justice to those eternal human concerns which are today more pressing than ever. Their philosophy is a philosophy of being in all its concreteness and is likewise a philosophy of the person. They do not reject any of the positive results established by the representatives of other movements; to take only one example, they allow the results of natural science to be genuine contributions to knowledge, yet they do the same with these as they do with all other facts—fit them into an organic context. Man is better understood here than in any of the other movements and is accorded the status to which his richness of being and the complexity of his problems entitle him. This personalism does not lead to the other spheres of reality being truncated, for there are no other systems so balanced, sober, and rational as those of the metaphysicians.

Their discussions go to the root of the most manifold problems. There can be no question of going into the details here, but as examples might be cited Whitehead's analysis of knowledge, the Thomist study of psychophysiological problems, Hartmann's exposition of freedom. Even their statement of these problems is sufficient to show how much wider is the

Philosophy of Being

range of their discussions in comparison with philosophers from other schools.

Of course each of the philosophical systems discussed has its own weaknesses. But in evaluating these systems one has always to bear in mind how much their achievements surpassed the capacity of late nineteenth-century philosophy, for they have produced an ontology and an organic conception of reality. An examination of contemporary metaphysics in the light of these two factors reveals Hartmann as the outstanding ontologist, but he refuses on principle to go in for metaphysical explanations (though he himself does not always remain true to this principle). At the other extreme is Alexander, whose striving after synthesis is frequently successful, but who has little to offer as an ontologist. Whitehead and the Thomists adopt an intermediate position by propounding both an ontology and a metaphysics. Yet Thomistic ontology is not inferior to Hartmann's, and it affords the basis for a more comprehensive and coherent conception of reality than is to be found in Hartmann.

Much more striking, however, than the differences between the tendencies within the philosophy of being, is the fundamental agreement which these differing conceptions exhibit. This is all the more remarkable in that these tendencies spring from such varied sources—Einstein's physics, the Marburg school, scholasticism. Running through most of their statements about the nature of knowledge and the hierarchical structure of the world, or about the spirit and its freedom, there is broad agreement among philosophers of being, and their systems are examples of all that is best in the achievements of contemporary philosophical study.

Our age still suffers from the unhealthy aftermath of previous thought which was hostile to metaphysics. But the fact that Europe now possesses a prominent group of genuine metaphysicians holds out hopes of a better future for the coming generations, a future in which man and his vital concerns will be better understood and more reverently cared for by a *rational* philosophy than at present.

Appendix

25. MATHEMATICAL LOGIC

A. SIGNIFICANCE AND GENERAL CHARACTERISTICS

Mathematical logic, known also as "symbolic logic" or "logistic," is for the most part now regarded as a special science and is often taught in university departments of natural science. Some philosophers regard it as a legitimate tool of philosophical analysis but the majority reject it. It nevertheless has considerable importance for contemporary philosophy not only because it is employed by many philosophers—for example, most English works on philosophy are unintelligible without it—but also because it has contributed materially to the development of various philosophical schools and systems (neopositivism, Whitehead, Russell, etc.) and has made it possible to formulate certain philosophical problems in a new way. However one may judge it in other respects, a certain knowledge of this discipline would seem to be indispensable if one is to understand a good deal of contemporary philosophy. For such reasons we shall here offer a sketch of certain fundamental concepts and methods as well as certain theses and problems of mathematical logic.

Let us begin by noting some misconceptions in order to show how mathematical logic should *not* be defined. Mathematical logic must not be identified with neopositivism. Its founders were Platonists—Frege, Whitehead, Russell (at the time *Principia Mathematica* was published), Łukasiewicz, Fraenkel, Scholz, and many others. Nowadays mathematical logic has adherents in almost all schools. Again, it is a mistake to define it as "symbolic". Of course it employs special symbols in a greater degree than did the classical logic but this is purely incidental and has very little to do with the essential character of mathematical logic. Finally, it is inaccurate to regard mathematical logic as an attempt to mathematize philosophy, or to reduce philosophy to mathematics. On the contrary, the very opposite, the reduction of mathematics to logic, was undertaken by Whitehead and Russell. What often leads to misunderstanding here is that mathematical logic uses symbols which have a similarity to those of mathematics. Thus mathematical logicians write "$x = y$" just as mathematicians do, but the symbol $=$ does not designate quantitative equality but identity, a nonmathematical relation.

The distinguishing characteristics of mathematical logic are its exclusion of psychological inquiries, the application of logic to logic itself, and formalism. First, logic excludes all phychological and epistemological considerations from its purvey. It is concerned with the analysis of the correctness (*Richtigkeit*) of purely formal logical laws such as the law of contradiction, the law of the hypothetical syllogism, and so on. Second, in mathematical logic one applies logic to logic itself in that one undertakes to deduce logical laws from the smallest possible number of principles (axioms and rules of inference) in the strictest way. Hence the interest of mathematical logicians is directed more toward the interconnection of logical laws, and one can discern a widespread tendency, which is basically an aesthetic one, to reduce to a minimum the number of principles, even at the cost of their simplicity. Third, mathematical logicians employ formalism. By this we understand the following method. The first step in the procedure is to choose certain symbols which have a definite meaning of their own. Attention is then immediately diverted from these meanings, and the rules of inference are so formulated that they apply only to the external typographical form of the symbols and not to their meanings. The whole deduction then proceeds in a "formalistic" manner, that is, it is a strict rule of mathematical

Appendix

logic that within the context of proof one must appeal to nothing but the forms of the symbols and the "formal" rules of inference which apply to such forms. It is only the finished system which is again interpreted as to content, but here the system itself must always be distinguished from its interpretations. For mathematical logicians this has the advantage that one can often give a system several interpretations and thus provide the foundations of several different disciplines in a single undertaking. Moreover, unless one adopts formalism it is impossible to proceed without error through the extremely abstract and complex sentences of mathematical logic.

B. BASIC CONCEPTS

We distinguish between constants and variables. Variables are letters in whose place one can put other formulae, that is, constants or complex formulae. If in a sentence (*Aussage, Satz*) a constant is replaced by a variable, the result is a "function," a schema for a sentence, which is neither true nor false. Thus, "x is a man" is a function and neither true nor false, whereas "Socrates is a man" is a true sentence. Again, functions can be transformed back into sentences, when one prefixes a quantifier to them. There are two kinds of quantifiers: universal quantifiers of the type "for all x . . ." [written "(x)"] and existential quantifiers, "there is at least one x such that . . ." [written "$(\exists x)$"]. The symbols are usually divided into so-called basic categories and functor categories. The basic categories are names (substantives) and sentences. The functors are symbols which require other symbols, that is, predicates in the widest sense of the term. For example, "sleeps," "and," "or," "loves," etc. That which is required by a functor is called an "argument." Thus, "John" is the argument of "sleeps" in "John sleeps." Functors are divided according to three principles of division. (1) First we have the division into sentence-forming, name-forming, and functor-forming functors. Thus, "sleeps" is sentence forming because "John sleeps" is a sentence, but "a good" is name forming because "a good child" is not a sentence but a name. (2) The second division of functors is into name-determining, sentence-determining, and functor-determining functors. Thus "it is not the case that" is a functor which determines a sentence, for example, "it is not the case that it is raining", while "sleeps" is a name-determining functor, as in "John sleeps." (3) Finally functors are divided according to the number of arguments which they determine, that is, into one-place, two-place, three-place, or, in general, n-place functors. While according to traditional logic predicates always determine only one subject, in logistic a predicate (functor) can determine several subjects (arguments). Thus, the sentence "John drinks beer" can be determined in such a way that "drinks" is a two-place functor and "John" and "beer" are its arguments. The word "gives" will count as a three-place functor, as in "John gives Peter a pipe".

In accordance with these principles, mathematical logic is divided into three main parts: (1) propositional logic or "theory of deduction", in which all functors are sentence-determining; (2) predicate and class logic, which deals with name-determining functors; and (3) the logic of relations which treats of the special properties of many-place functors.

C. PROPOSITIONAL LOGIC

Propositional logic deals only with sentences which are constructed by means of so-called truth functors. The latter are sentence-forming, sentence-determining, generally one- and two-place functors whose peculiarity consists in the fact that the truth value (also called more briefly, the "value", that is, either truth or falsity) of the sentence constructed by means

255

of them depends exclusively upon the truth value of their arguments and not upon their meaning. So, for example, negation is a truth functor, since the value of a negated true sentence is falsity and the value of a negated false sentence is truth, no matter what the sentence may be or what it may signify. The most widely employed functors are negation ("it is not the case that," written $\sim$ or as a bar above the symbol, $\bar{A}$), the logical sum ("either or both", written $\vee$), logical product ("and", written . or &), implication ("if . . . then", in the sense: either the antecedent is false or the consequent is true; or rather: "if p, then q" signifies "not p, or q"; this is written $\supset$ or $\rightarrow$), equivalence ("if and only if", written $\equiv$), and finally the Sheffer stroke functor ("not both", written |). The last-named functor is especially important because one can define all truth functors in terms of it.

By means of these functors we can combine sentential variables, that is, variables for which only sentences can be substituted. In this connection brackets or dots are employed. Thus, for example, "$p \vee q . \supset . q \vee p$" is to be read "if p or q, then q or p." Łukasiewicz has invented a notation which dispenses with brackets and dots and writes the functor directly in front of the arguments in question. There are at least two methods which make it possible for us to determine easily whether such a sentence is a law of logic or not, namely the so-called matrix method and the method of the normal form. Moreover, all sentences of the propositional calculus can be derived axiomatically from very few axioms, in fact from one single axiom, that of Nicod. Propositional logic is the most completely developed part of mathematical logic. It is regarded by the mathematical logicians as the simplest and most basic part of logic, which provides the framework, so to speak, of all other logical analysis and deduction.

The second part of mathematical logic falls into two divisions corresponding to the intensional and the extensional interpretation of formulae. According to the first interpretation which is fundamental, the sentence is analyzed into a sentence-forming, name-determining functor (commonly, φ, ψ, χ, etc.) and a name (commonly x, y, z as variables, and a, b, c as constants), so that the basic formula reads φx. Such formulae, when they contain variables, are called "matrices". They are combined by means of sentence-determining functors and transformed into sentences by means of quantifiers. In particular, the universal proposition "All φ is ψ" is interpreted by means of the so-called formal implication, "$(x) . \varphi x \supset \psi x$," and the particular proposition "There is a φ, which is ψ" by means of the formula "$(\exists x). \varphi x. \psi x$." This interpretation led to the rejection of many propositions of Aristotelian syllogistics. Yet while it did at first appear that these propositions would have to be regarded as false, later reflection has shown that it is only a matter of a different interpretation of the functors and that the Aristotelian logic, when taken in the sense of its founder, is correct.

Mathematical logic treats of two-place and many-place predicates as well as one-place predicates. Among these identity plays an especially important role. In line with the Leibnizian principle of the identity of indiscernibles identity is so defined that x and y are identical if, and only if, all properties of x are likewise properties of y, and conversely. From this definition various so-called extensionality theses can be deduced. These lead to many philosophical difficulties because in accordance with them two attributes which always occur in fact together must be identical. The concept of identity is also employed in the definition of so-called descriptions, for ex-

Appendix

ample, "the author of *Faust*." Russell formulated the theory of descriptions in order to avoid Meinong's assumption of the subsistence of round squares, for example, for on this interpretation "the round square does not exist" means exactly the same as "there is no object which is both a square and a circle." Existence is to be asserted only of descriptions. "The object which has the property φ exists" implies that there is one and only one such object, and if we attribute to it a further property, it must exist.

The logic of classes constitutes an extensional counterpart to the logic of predicates. A class (set, generally designated by α, β, γ, etc.) is always defined by a predicate. It is the set of all objects which possess a given property. Thus, for example, the class of human beings consists of all those objects to which humanity can be attributed. The most important basic concept of the logic of classes is that of membership "$x \varepsilon α$ (this is to be read "x is a member of $α$" or "x belongs to $α$"). There is also a null class, which has no elements. On the basis of the definition of classes and the theorems of the logic of predicates various definitions of the combinations of classes can be constructed, corresponding to those of sentences.

E. THE LOGIC OF RELATIONS

The logic of relations is in turn an extensional counterpart to the logic of two-place and many-place predicates just as the logic of classes is an extensional counterpart to the logic of one-place predicates. Since two-place relations (the only ones worked out so far) have many special properties, the logic of relations constitutes by far the longest chapter of mathematical logic. Here we can mention only a few basic concepts. Relations themselves are conceived of extensionally, as pairs of objects. Relations (like classes) are defined by a (two-place) predicate. Thus the relation of love is the set of pairs of persons who love each other. The symbol most commonly employed is xRy. Every relation has a converse: (Thus "greater than" is the converse of "less than"). Various relational descriptions are distinguished: individual (*the* husband of the Dutch queen), plural (*the* authors of the *Encyclopaedia Britannica*), double plural (the authors of Italian poems), and in general the so-called domain (written $D'R$, e.g. "authors"). Still more important are the concepts which are used for the purpose of compounding several relations such as the relative product (square of the half, brother of the mother, and the like) and the closely related relative power (father of the father is thus $father^2$). Another group of concepts is constituted by the properties of relations, for example, some are reflexive (that is, where xRx holds), others symmetrical (if xRy, then likewise yRx), still others transitive (if xRy and yRz, then xRz). The most important concept which serves for the construction of series is that of the ancestral relation (R or R^2 or R^3, etc.).

F. SEMIOTICS

Closely related to mathematical logic is so-called semiotics (Charles Morris) which is now commonly employed by mathematical logicians. Semiotics is the theory of symbols and falls into three parts, (1) logical syntax, the theory of the mutual relations of symbols, (2) logical semantics, the theory of the relations between the symbol and what the symbol stands for, and (3) logical pragmatics, the relations between the symbols, their meanings and the users of the symbols. The latter is still in its infancy but the two former, thanks especially to Alfred Tarski and Rudolf Carnap, are well-developed disciplines. The main idea of semiotics is that one must distinguish sharply between the symbol and what the symbol stands for. Thus, if one speaks about a word, the word must itself have a special

259

name. For example, if one speaks about the word "cat", one cannot do so in the same manner in which one speaks of a live cat. Likewise, one must distinguish sharply between the language *S* and metalanguage of *S*. The latter takes as its object the language *S* itself. Thus, there is a metamathematics (the theory of the language of mathematics) and a meta-logic (the theory of the language of logic).

It has been shown that a formalized, axiomatic system must always also contain metalogical elements. Such a system contains the following elements, (1) undefined symbols, (2) axioms, sentences assumed without proof, (3) formation rules, which determine which symbols or groups of symbols (formulae) have meaning in the system, (4) rules of inference, which permit new sentences to be deduced from the axioms. Now (3) and (4) are not logical but metalogical formulae since they concern the symbols of logic itself. Such sentences can again be formalized but in that case we must employ metametalogical sentences. Thus no system can ultimately be completely formalized.

On the basis of semiotics it has proved to be possible to develop exact methods with the aid of which it can be proved that a given system is consistent, that its axioms are independent (that they are not deducible from one another), and that it is complete (that every sentence which is not deducible from its axioms contradicts some sentence of the system). Similarly exact methods have been developed for axiomatization. In this connection the most important event was the discovery of Gödel's theorem. In 1930 Kurt Gödel showed that there are sentences in *Principia Mathematica* and in many other systems which are formally undecidable, that is, one cannot prove in the systems either that they are true or that they are false.

G. SOME SPECIAL PROBLEMS AND THEORIES

The concluding paragraphs take note of a few of the many problems of mathematical logic which have particular philosophical importance.

1) *Logic and Mathematics.*—Whitehead and Russell sought to deduce the whole of mathematics from pure logic. They and their supporters are accordingly denominated "logicists". Another school, the intuitionists, under the leadership of E. J. Brouwer, denies the possibility of such a reduction. They hold that logic is no more than a method which evolves along with mathematics and that the law of excluded middle does not always hold in mathematics. A third school, the formalists, led by David Hilbert (1862-1943), regards basic mathematical terms as undefined symbols and seeks only the development of systems which are unobjectionable and free of contradiction.

2) *The Theory of Types.*—In 1896 Burali-Forti discovered a contradiction in Cantor's set theory. In June, 1901 Russell succeeded in proving that the source of this was logical and not mathematical and that the logical system of Gottlob Frege, among others, contained contradictions. Nowadays we are acquainted with many such contradictions which are deducible from apparently evident premises. They are called "antinomies" or "paradoxes." The most celebrated of these is Russell's class antinomy. Suppose that all classes are either members of themselves or not members of themselves. Does this now hold also of the class of all classes that are not members of themselves? Every answer to this question leads to contradiction. In order to solve this antinomy, Russell and Whitehead constructed their theory of types by which objects are divided into various types or levels. Thus, in the sphere of classes, individuals are of type 1, classes of individuals are of type 2, classes of classes of individuals are of type 3. In general, if x

is an element of α, then α must be of a higher type than *x*. It later emerged that many antinomies (for example, the *Liar* or *Epimenides* of antiquity) are not logical but semantic antinomies which arise from a confusion of language with meta-language. The theory of types has been simplified in various ways but it has proved to be sound up to now. Despite many attempts no one has yet succeeded in constructing a system of mathematical logic free of contradiction without its aid.

3) *Multi-valued Logics.*—In 1920 Łukasiewicz, and a year later Emil Post independently, discovered that besides the "classical" mathematical logic which recognizes only two values (truth and falsity, symbolically, 1 and 0) other logics, in which more than two values are accepted, were not only possible but consistent and complete. Such logics, however, lack certain important theorems of the classical logic, for example, the principle of excluded middle is always missing. Such systems were rigorously developed by the axiomatic method and shown to be unobjectionable as formal systems. But whether these systems permit of any kind of interpretation which would allow us to regard them as *logical* systems is still a matter of dispute. A few mathematical logicians are hopeful of solving with their aid various problems of probability theory and of modal logic, while others maintain the contrary thesis, that they are not logical systems at all.

The newest developments of mathematical logic such as combinatorial logic or the so-called natural logics cannot be considered here. The discipline of logic is being ardently pursued and new ideas and systems are constantly turning up.

26. International Organizations

A. INTERNATIONAL CONGRESSES OF PHILOSOPHY

After 1900 international congresses of philosophy were to be held, in principle, every four years, The following congresses were actually held: First, Paris 1900; Second, Geneva 1904; Third, Heidelberg 1908; Fourth, Bologna 1911; Fifth, Naples 1924; Sixth, New York 1927; Seventh, Oxford 1930; Eighth, Prague 1934; Ninth, Paris 1937; (the Descartes Congress), Tenth, Amsterdam 1948; Eleventh, Brussels 1953. The lectures and often the debates of these congresses have been published. Until 1948 there was a standing committee for the organization of the congress. Since 1948 the International Federation of Philosophical Organizations has performed this duty.

Still other conferences under the name of international congresses for philosophy have taken place. But these are actually much more in the nature of private or national organizations. The only ones which are international in the strict sense are the congresses mentioned.

B. THE INTERNATIONAL INSTITUTE OF PHILOSOPHY

This institute was founded at the Ninth International Congress in 1937. Among its directors have been Léon Robin (1866-1947) Åke Petzäll, and Raymond Bayer. Since 1937 the institute issues the *Bibliographie de la Philosophie*, and since 1939 an annual critical bibliography divided into separate fields under the title *Philosophie*. From time to time discussions are held (Pontigny 1937, Amersfoort 1938, Lund 1947). It issues the *Bulletin Analytique de Philosophie* and is aiding the work on a *Corpus des Philosophes Français*. It also organizes many congresses and promotes coöperation among outstanding philosophers.

C. INTERNATIONAL FEDERATION OF PHILOSOPHICAL ORGANIZATIONS

This federation was founded on September 13, 1948. It unites almost 60 national and international organizations. The majority of these are European. The countries represented are Argentina, Australia, Belgium, Canada, Czechoslovakia, Denmark, Finland, France, Great Britain, Greece, Italy, Netherlands, Norway, Poland, Roumania, Sweden, Switzerland, United States, Uruguay, and Vatican City. Chile, Cuba, and Hungary are affiliated. Some eleven international federations are members of the federation.

Abbreviations

AP	*Archives de Philosophie*. Vals-près-Le Puy, Haute Loraine: 1923-.
BDP	*Blätter für deutsche Philosophie*. Berlin: 1923-.
BESP	Bochenski, I. M. *Bibliographische Einführungen in das Studium der Philosophie*. Berne: 1948-.
BT	*Bulletin Thomiste*. Paris: 1924-.
CBP	Muirhead, J. H. (ed.). *Contemporary British Philosophy*. 2 vols. London: 1924-1925.
DSPG	Schwarz, B. *Deutsche systematische Philosophie der Gegenwart nach ihren Gestalten*. 2 vols. 1931-1934.
DT	*Divus Thomas*. Freiburg, Switzerland: 1923-. (To be distinguished from *Divus Thomas* published in Piacenza, Italy: 1880-.)
E	*Erkenntnis*. Leipzig: 1930-1938.
EB	*Encyclopedia Britannica*.
GL	Gifford Lectures (Universities of Edinburgh, Glasgow, Aberdeen, and St. Andrews).
JP	*The Journal of Philosophy*. New York: 1904-.
JPPhF	*Jahrbuch für Philosophie und phänomenologische Forschung*. Halle: 1913-1930.
Kt.	*Kantstudien*. Berlin: 1897-1937.
LLP	Schilpp, P. A. The Library of Living Philosophers. New York: 1939-.
Metz	Metz, R. *Die philosophischen Strömungen der Gegenwart in Grossbritannien*. 2 vols. Leipzig: 1935 (English, 1938).
Mind	*Mind*. London: 1876-.
PAS	*Proceedings of the Aristotelian Society*. London: 1888-.
PGS	Schmidt, R. *Die Philosophie der Gegenwart in Selbstdarstellungen*. 7 vols. 1921-1929.
PJ	*Philosophisches Jahrbuch der Görresgesellschaft*. Fulda: 1888-.
PPhR	*Philosophy and Phenomenological Research*. Buffalo: 1940-.
PR	*The Philosophical Review*. Baltimore: 1892-.
PS	*Philosophy of Science*. Baltimore. 1934-.
PTFUS	Farber, M. *Philosophic Thought in France and the United States*. Buffalo: 1950.
RIP	*Revue Internationale de Philosophie*. Brussels: 1939-.
RMM	*Revue de Métaphysique et de Morale*. Paris: 1893-.
RNP	*Revue Néoscolastique de Philosophie*. Louvain: 1945. (Since 1946: *Revue Philosophique de Louvain*.)
RP	*Revue philosophique de France et de l'Etranger*. Paris: 1876-.
RT	*Revue Thomiste*. Paris: 1893-.

Abbreviations

SPA   *Sitzungsberichte der Preussischen Akademie der Wissenschaften.*
         1882–.
TCP   Runes, D. D. (ed.). *Twentieth Century Philosophy.* New York:
         1943.
Ue   Ueberweg, F. *Grundriss der Geschichte der Philosophie.* 12th ed.
         by T. K. Österreich. 1923-1928.
ZPF   *Zeitschrift für philosophische Forschung.* Meisenheim: 1946–.

Bibliography

The works of the philosophers who are the subjects of separate chapters are listed as completely as possible; sometimes important articles are added.

The works of the other philosophers are listed only if they were published after publication of Friedrich Überweg's *Grundriss der Geschichte der Philosophie*, Vol. IV (for Germany), 1923 and Vol. V (for other countries), 1928. Excepted from this rule are (a) the works of a few particularly important philosophers (e.g., William James) which are listed in their entirety and (b) the works of authors who published so much that only a selection could be listed.

The lists of works of the various authors and schools are followed by a limited list of the literature *about* them. Here, too, Überweg's *Grundriss* should be consulted for completeness.

The most important works are marked with an asterisk.

Most major works cited only in the original language or in German, are also available in English, particularly collections and the works of Lenin, Croce, Bergson, and the Thomists.

The beginning of the bibliography (General Bibliography) refers to sections 1 to 4 of chapter i, but excludes the bibliography for section 2 (The Crisis) which follows after 4; the other sections are listed in numerical order.

The bibliography was finished when the manuscript of the 2d German edition went to the printer, in 1950.

1, 3, 4. GENERAL BIBLIOGRAPHY

BIBLIOGRAPHY OF BIBLIOGRAPHY

Bochenski, I. M. and F. Monteleone. "Allgemeine philosophische Bibliographie," *BESP*, 1, 1948. De Raeymaeker L. *Einführung in die Philosophie* (German by E. Wetzel), 1949.

GUIDES

Ferro, C. *Guida storico-bibliografica allo studio di filosofia,* 1949. Lentz, J. *Vorschule der Weisheit,* 1941. De Raeymaeker, see above. Runes, D. C. (ed.) *Dictionary of Philosophy,* 1947.

RETROSPECTIVE BIBLIOGRAPHIES

* *Ue* IV, *Ue* V. Hoffmans, J. *La Philosophie et les philosophes,* 1920. *RNP,* 1910-1945. ZPF (supplement), 1941-1950.

CURRENT BIBLIOGRAPHIES

* *Bibliographie de la philosophie* (semiannually; ed. by Institut International de Philosophie), 1937–. *Bibliographie der Philosophie und Psychologie* (ed. by R. Dimpel), 1921-1931. *Literarische Berichte aus dem Gebiete der Philosophie* (ed. by A. Hoffmann), 1923–. *Philosophischer Literaturanzeiger,* 1949–. * "Répertoire bibliographique," *RNP,* 1934–. Reports in the following journals: *JP, Kt., L., Mind, Philosophic Abstracts, RMM, RNP, Revue des sciences philosophiques et théologiques, Sophia.*

COLLECTIONS OF AUTOBIOGRAPHIES

CBP. DSPG. PGS. Philosophes et savants français du XXᵉ siècle, 1926: I, Philosophie générale et métaphysique (ed. by J. Baruzzi); II, Philosophie de la science (ed. by R. Poirier); III, Le Problème moral (ed. by J. Baruzzi). *TCP.* For U. S. see below, sec. 12; for Italy see sec. 8.

GENERAL LITERATURE

Bréhier, E. *Histoire de la philosophie,* 1943-1944. Garcia Bacca, J. D. *Nueve grandes filosofos contemporaneos y sus temas,* 2 vols., Caracas: 1947. Heinemann, F. **Neue Wege der Philosophie,* 1929. Hübscher, A. *Philosophen der Gegenwart,* 1949. Laird, J. **Recent Philosophy,* 1936. Meyer, H. *Geschichte der abendländischen Weltanschauung,* Vol. V., 1947.

Sciacca, M. F. *La filosofia oggi*, 1945. Sertillanges, A. D. *Le Christianisme et les philosophies*, Vol. II, 1941. Wahl, J. "Philosophie," in *50 années de découvertes* (ed. by A. and A. Lejard), 1950.

BRITISH PHILOSOPHY

Aster E. *Geschichte der englischen Philosophie*, 1927. Metz, R. *Die philosophischen Strömungen der Gegenwart in Grossbritannien*, 1935 (English by J. H. Muirhead, 1938).

GERMAN PHILOSOPHY

Aster, E. *Die Philosophie der Gegenwart*, 1935. Brock, A. *An Introduction to Contemporary German Philosophy*, 1935. Gurvitch, G. *Les Tendences actuelles de la philosophie allemande*, 1930. Hessen J. *Die philosophischen Strömungen der Gegenwart*, 2d ed. 1940. Messer, A. *Die Philosophie der Gegenwart in Deutschland*, 8th ed. 1934.

FRENCH PHILOSOPHY

Benrubi, I. *Philosophische Strömungen der Gegenwart in Frankreich*, 1928; *Les Sources et les courants de la philosophie contemporaine en France*, 2 vols., 1933. Etcheverry, A. *L'Idéalisme français contemporain*, 1934. Farber, M. (ed.) *Philosophical Thought in France and the United States*, 1950. Hess, G. *Französische Philosophie der Gegenwart*, 1933. Lavelle, L. *Le moi et son destin*, 1936; *La Philosophie française entre les deux guerres*, 1942. Parodi, R. *La Philosophie contemporaine en France*, 2d ed. 1926. *PTFUS*. Wahl, J. *Französische Philosophie. Ein Abriss* (German by B. Beer), 1948.

2. THE CRISIS

BIBLIOGRAPHY

Bavink, B. *Ergebnisse und Probleme der Naturwissenschaften*, 9th ed. 1949.

269

WORKS OF THE PHYSICISTS

Eddington, A. S. *The Nature of the Physical World* (GL), 1928; *New Pathways of Science*, 1934; *The Philosophy of Physical Science*, 1938, new ed. 1949.

Einstein, A. *Mein Weltbild*. See also *The Philosophy of Albert Einstein*, LLP, 6, 1949.

Heisenberg, W. *Wandlungen in den Grundlagen der Naturwissenschaft*, 1935, 7th ed. 1947.

Jeans, J. *The Mysterious Universe*, 1930; *Physics and Philosophy*, 1942.

Jordan, P. *Die Physik des XX. Jahrhunderts*, 3d ed. 1938; *Die Physik und das Geheimnis des Lebens*, 1941.

Planck, M. *Das Weltbild der neuen Physik*, 4th ed. 1930; *Wege zur physikalischen Erkenntnis*, 1933, 3d ed. 1944.

CRISIS OF MATHEMATICS

See below, secs. 5, 6, 25.

PHILOSOPHICAL LITERATURE

Bavink, B. *Die Naturwissenschaften auf dem Wege zur Religion*, new ed. 1942; *Ergebnisse und Probleme der Naturwissenschaften*, 1914, 9th ed. 1949.

Dennert E. (ed.). *Die Natur, das Wunder Gottes*, 1938.

Dingler, H. *Der Zusammenbruch der Wissenschaften und das Primat der Philosophie*, 1926, 2d. ed. 1931.

Feibleman, J. *The Revival of Realism*, 1947.

Heiss, R. *Der Gang des Geistes*, 1948.

Hessen, J. *Die Geistesströmungen der Gegenwart*, 1937.

Jansen, B. *Aufstiege zur Metaphysik*, 1933.

Joad, C. E. M. *Guide to Modern Thought*, 1933, 4th ed. 1942.

Kerler, D. *Die auferstandene Metaphysik*, 1921.

Wenzl, A. *Metaphysik der Physik von heute*, 1935; *Die geistigen Strömungen unseres Jahrhunderts*, 1948.

Whitehead, A. N. *Science and the Modern World*, 1926.

Wust, P. *Die Auferstehung der Metaphysik*, 1920.

See also below, secs. 5, 11-13, 21, 24.

3, 4. [For bibliography see p. 267].

5. BERTRAND RUSSELL

General Literature on British Neorealism

Deuel, L. *Der erkenntnistheoretische Realismus in der Philosophie der Gegenwart* (Zurich: Dissertation, 1947). Feibleman, J. *The Revival of Realism*, 1947. Kremer, R. *Le Néoréalism américain*, 1920. Lovejoy, A. O. *The Revolt against Dualism*, 1930. Marc-Wogau, K. *Die Theorie der Sinnesdaten* (Uppsala Univ.: Arsskrift, 1945). Wahl, J. *Les Philosophies pluralistes d'Angleterre et d'Amérique*, 1920. *RIP*, 1, 1949.

G. E. Moore

WORKS

Principia Ethica, 1903, 2d ed. 1922; *"The Refutation of Idealism," Mind*, 1903; *Ethics*, 1912; *Philosophical Studies*, 1922 (contains "The Refutation"); "A Defence of Common Sense," *CBP* II; "Proof of an External World," *Proceedings, British Academy*, 1939.

FESTSCHRIFT

The Philosophy of G. E. Moore, LLP, 4, 1942.

C. D. Broad

WORKS

Perception, Physics, and Reality, 1914; *Scientific Thought*, 1923; "Critical and Speculative Philosophy," *CBP*, I; *The Mind and Its Place in Nature*, 1925, 2d ed. 1929; *Five Types of Ethical Theory*, 1930; *Examination of McTaggart's Philosophy*, 2 vols., 1933-1938.

Bertrand Russell

BIBLIOGRAPHY

Dennonn, L. E. In Festschrift, see below.

271

Bibliography

Bibliography

WORKS

German Social Democracy, 1896; *An Essay on the Foundations of Geometry*, 1897; *A Critical Exposition of the Philosophy of Leibniz*, 1900, 2d ed. 1937; *The Principles of Mathematics* I, 1903; 2d ed. 1937; *Philosophical Essays*, 1910; *Principia Mathematica* (with A. N. Whitehead): I, 1910; II, 1912; III, 1913; 2d ed.: I, 1925; II and III, 1927; *The Problems of Philosophy*, 1912; *Our Knowledge of the External World as a Field for Scientific Method in Philosophy*, 1914; *Principles of Social Reconstruction*, 1916; *Justice in War-Time*, 1916; *War the Offspring of Fear*, 1916; *Roads to Freedom: Socialism, Anarchism and Syndicalism*, 1918; *Mysticism and Logic and other Essays*, 1918; *The Philosophy of Logical Atomism*, 1918-1919, new ed. 1949; *Introduction to Mathematical Philosophy*, 1919, 2d ed. 1920; *The Practice and Theory of Bolshevism*, 1920, 2d ed. 1949; *The Analysis of Mind*, 1921; *The Problem of China*, 1922; *The Prospects of Industrial Civilization* (with Dora Russell), 1923; *The ABC of Atoms*, 1923; *Icarus or the Future of Science*, 1924; "Logical Atomism," CBP I; *ABC of Relativity*, 1925; *What I Believe*, 1925; *On Education*, 1926; *The Analysis of Matter*, 1927; *An Outline of Philosophy*, 1929, new ed. 1948; *Sceptical Essays*, 1928; *Marriage and Morals*, 1929; *The Conquest of Happiness*, 1930; *The Scientific Outlook*, 1931; *Education and Social Order*, 1932; *Freedom versus Organization 1814-1914*, 1934; *In Praise of Idleness*, 1935; *Which Way to Peace?*, 1936; *The Amberley Papers*, 1937; *Power: A New Social Analysis*, 1938; *An Inquiry into Meaning and Truth*, 1940; *A History of Western Philosophy*, 1946; *Physics and Experience*, 1946; *Philosophy and Politics*, 1947; *Human Knowledge, Its Scope and Limits*, 1948; *Authority and the Individual*, 1949; *Unpopular Essays*, 1950.

AUTOBIOGRAPHIES

"My Mental Development," in Festschrift, below; CBP I.

272

FESTSCHRIFT

The Philosophy of Bertrand Russell, LLP, 5, 1945.

LITERATURE

Kraus, O. *Wege und Abwege der Philosophie*, 1934. Marc-Wogau, K. *Die Theorie der Sinnesdaten* (Uppsala: Univ. Arsskrift, 1945). Metz. Schilpp, P. A. (ed.). *The Philosophy of Bertrand Russell*, 1944. Weberg, A. *Bertrand Russell's Empiricism*, 1937. Weitz, M. "The Method of Analysis in the Philosophy of Bertrand Russell" (Michigan: Dissertation, 1943).

6. NEOPOSITIVISM

BIBLIOGRAPHY

Dürr, K. "Der logische Positivismus," *BESP*, 11, 1948. *RIP*, 11, 1950.

GENERAL LITERATURE

Carnap, R. *Die Aufgabe der Wissenschaftslogik*, 1934. Feigl, H. "Logical Empiricism," *TCP*. Frank, Ph. *Modern Science and its Philosophy*, 1949. Kaufmann, F. in *PTFUS*. Kraft, V. *Der Wiener Kreis*, 1950. Mises, R. *Kleines Lehrbuch des Positivismus*, 1939. Morris, C. W. *Logical Positivism, Pragmatism and Scientific Empiricism*, 1937. *Neurath, O. and R. Carnap and H. Hann. *Wissenschaftliche Weltauffassung. Der Wiener Kreis*, 1929. Pap, A. *Elements of Analytic Philosophy*, 1949 (on the analytical school in general; bibliography). *RIP*, 11, 1950.

SELECTIONS

Feigl, H. and W. Sellars. *Readings in Philosophical Analysis*, 1949. Black M. (ed.), *Philosophical Analysis*, 1950.

SELECTED WORKS

Ayer, A. J. "Demonstration of the Impossibility of Metaphysics," *Mind*, 1934; "Verification and Experience," *PAS*, 1937;

273

Bibliography

Language Truth and Logic, 1938, 2d ed. 1946; *The Foundations of Empirical Knowledge*, 1940.

Carnap R. *Der Raum*, 1922; "Über die Aufgabe der Physik," *Kt.*, 1923; *Physikalische Begriffsbildung*, 1926; *Der logische Aufbau der Welt*, 1928; *Scheinprobleme in der Philosophie*. *Das Fremdpsychische und der Realismusstreit*, 1928; *Abriss der Logik*, 1929; *Logische Syntax der Sprache*, 1934 (English 1937); *Die Aufgabe der Wissenschaftslogik*, 1934; *Philosophy and Logical Syntax*, 1935; *Le Problème logique de la science*, 1935; *"Testability and Meaning," Philosophy of Science*, 1936; "Foundations of Logic and Mathematics," *International Encyclopedia of Unified Science*, 1939; *Introduction to Semantics*, 1942; *Formalization of Logic*, 1943; "On Inductive Logic," *Philosophy of Science*, 1945; "Modalities and Quantification," *Journal of Symbolic Logic*, 1946; *Meaning and Necessity: A Study in Semantics and Modal Logic*, 1947; *The Logical Foundations of Probability*, 1950.

Dubislav, W. *Die Definition*, 3d ed. 1930; *Die Philosophie der Mathematik in der Gegenwart*, 1932; *Naturphilosophie*, 1933.

Franck, Ph. *Das Kausalgesetz und seine Grenzen*, 1932; *Between Philosophy and Physics*, 1941; *Modern Science and its Philosophy*, 1950.

Reichenbach, H. *Axiomatik der relativistischen Raum-Zeitlehre*, 1920; *Ziele und Wege der heutigen Naturphilosophie*, 1931; "Wahrscheinlichkeitslogik," *SPA*, 1932; *Wahrscheinlichkeitslehre*, 1935; *Experience and Prediction*, 1938; *From Copernicus to Einstein*, 1942; *Philosophic Foundations of Quantum Mechanics*, 1944.

Ryle, G. *The Concept of Mind*, 1949.

Schlick, M. *Lebensweisheit*, 1908; *Raum und Zeit in der gegenwärtigen Physik*, 1917; *Allgemeine Erkenntnislehre*, 1918, 2d ed. 1925; "Erleben, Erkenntnis, Metaphysik," *Kt.*, 1926; *Fragen der Ethik*, 1930; *Les Énoncés scientifiques et la réalité du monde extérieur*, 1934; *Gesammelte Aufsätze* (ed. by Fr. Waismann), 1938; *Grundzüge der Naturphilosophie* (ed. by W. Hollitscher and J. Rauscher), 1948.

Wittgenstein, L. *"Logisch-philosophische Abhandlung," *Annalen der Naturphilosophie*, 1921, 2d ed. under the title "Tractatus Logico-Philosophicus" (German and English), 1922.
See also essays of these philosophers in *Erkenntnis*.

JOURNALS AND COLLECTIONS

Erkenntnis, Leipzig, 1930-1938; *International Encyclopaedia of Unified Science*, Chicago, 1938; *Journal of Unified Science*, The Hague, 1939 (continuation of *Erkenntnis*); *Analysis*, Oxford, 1933–; *Actes du Congrès international de philosophie scientifique* (1935), 1936.
Important sources are also *Journal of Philosophy, Mind, Philosophical Review, Philosophy of Science, Proceedings of the Aristotelian Society, Revue de synthèse, Theoria.*

CRITICAL LITERATURE

Farrell, B. A. "An Appraisal of Therapeutic Positivism," *Mind*, 1946. Feys, R. and A. *De positivistische Geestehounding*, 1949. Ingarden, R. "Der logische Versuch einer Neugestaltung der Philosophie," *Actes du 8ᵉ Congrès international de philosophie, Prague*, 1936; "L'Essai logistique d'une refonte de la philosophie," *RP*, 1936. Molitor, A. "Zur neupositivistischen Philosophie der Mathematik," *PJ*, 1940-1941. Petzäll, A. *Logistischer Positivismus*, 1931; *Zum Methodenproblem der Erkenntnisforschung*, 1935. Weinberg, J. R. *An Examination of Logical Positivism*, 1936. Werkmeister, C. "Sieben Sätze des logistischen Positivismus," *PJ*, 1942.

7. DIALECTICAL MATERIALISM

BIBLIOGRAPHIES

Seewann, F. L. Bibliographical references in Friedrich Engels, *Der Denker*, 1945. Bochenski, I. M. *Der sowjetrussische dia-*

Bibliography

lektische Materialismus, 1950 (Russian literature). See also current journals.

CLASSICAL WORKS (*See Also Ue* IV)

Marx, K. and F. Engels. *Historisch-kritische Gesamtausgabe* (ed. by D. Rjazanow and V. Adoratsky), 1927–. Marx K. *Der historische Materialismus. Die Frühschriften* (ed. by S. Landshut and J. P. Mayer), 2 vols., 1932. Engels Fr. (new editions): *Herrn Eugen Dührings Umwälzung der Wissenschaft*, 1934; *Ludwig Feuerbach und der Ausgang der klassischen Philosophie*, 1927; *Dialektik der Natur*, Marx-Engels-Archiv, 1927.

Lenin V. *Sämtliche Werke*, 30 vols. (Moscow: 1932 ff.); *Ausgewählte Werke*, 12 vols., 1932–; *Ausgewählte Werke*, 2 vols., 1946; *Materialismus und Empiriokritizismus*, 1908 (see *Sämtliche Werke*, vol. 13). Stalin, J. *"Über dialektischen und historischen Materialismus"* in *Geschichte der Kommunistischen Partei der Sowjetunion* (Berlin: 1947).

SELECTED WORKS

Adoratsky, V. *Dialectical Materialism*, 1936. Bucharin, N. and E. Preobrazensky. *Das ABC des Kommunismus*, 1921. Cornforth, M. *Science versus Idealism*, 1947. Haldane, J. B. S. *The Marxist Philosophy and the Sciences*, 1938. Lukacs, G. *Existentialisme ou marxisme?* 1948. Prenant, M. *Biologie et marxisme*, 1948. Rosental, M. and P. Judin. *Handbook of Philosophy*, 1949 (transl. by H. Selsam; most important semiofficial text). Shirokov, M. (ed.) *A Textbook of Marxist Philosophy* (Leningrad Institute of Philosophy; transl. by A. C. Moseley), 1937. Somerville, J. "Dialectical Materialism," *TCP; Soviet Philosophy*, 1946. *Die Wissenschaft im Lichte des Marxismus*, 1937.

DIALECTICAL-MATERIALIST JOURNALS

Unter dem Banner des Marxismus, 1927-1933; *Marx-Engels-Archiv*, Frankfurt, 1926–. See articles in *La Pensée; Blick*

*nach Osten (Eastern Review, Coup d'oeil à l'Est); Brücke;
The American Review of Soviet Russia; Soviet Russia Today;
Connaissance de l'URSS.*

CRITICAL LITERATURE

Berdiajev, N. *Wahrheit und Lüge des Kommunismus*, 1934;
Les Sources et le sens du communisme russe, 1938. Bochenski,
I. M. *Der sovietrussische dialektische Materialismus*, 1950.
Desroches, H. C. *Signification du marxisme*, 1949. Etcheverry,
A. et al. "La Philosophie du communism," *AP*, 1939. Gurian
W. *Der Bolschewismus*, 1931, 2d ed. 1932 (English 1932).
Hubatka, C. "Die materialistische Geschichtsauffassung"
(Gregorianum, Rome: Dissertation, 1942). Masaryk, Th. *Die
philosophischen und soziologischen Grundlagen des Marxis-
mus*, 1899. Monnerot, J. *Sociologie du communisme*, 1949.
Pastore, A. *La filosofia di Lenin*, 1946. Sombart, W. *Der pro-
letarische Sozialismus*, 2 vols., 1924. Walter, E. J. "Kritik der
Dialektik," *Rote Revue*, 1937; "Warum Kritik der Dialektik?"
ibid., 1938; "Der Begründer der Dialektik im Marxismus,"
Dialectica, 1947; "Die Dialektik in den Naturwissenschaften
nach dem Anti-Dühring," *ibid.*, 1948. Wetter, G. A. *Il
materialismo dialettico sovietico*, 1948.

JOURNALS

Soviet Studies, Oxford (much philosophical material); *The Russian Review*, New York; *PPhR; Synthese*, Amsterdam; *The
Current Digest of the Russian Press*, Washington.

8. BENEDETTO CROCE

Italian Philosophy

BIBLIOGRAPHY

A complete bibliography of Italian philosophy (for 1900-1949)
by E. Castelli and M. F. Sciacca was scheduled to be published by 1952. [By 1953, three volumes (A to T) were published by the Istituto di studi filosofici under the title *Bibliografia filosofica italiana dal 1900 al 1950.*—Translator.]

Bibliography

WORKS

Sciacca, M. F. "Italienische Philosophie der Gegenwart," *BESP*, 7, 1948; *Il secolo XX*, 1947. Mehlis, G. *Italienische Philosophie der Gegenwart*, 1932. *Filosofi italiani contemporanei* (autobiographies, ed. by M. F. Sciacca), 1944.

Benedetto Croce

BIBLIOGRAPHY

Castellano, G. *Benedetto Croce*. 2d ed. 1924; *L'opera filosofica, storica e letteraria di Benedetto Croce*, 1947 (to 1941).

WORKS

[Note: Croce's numerous works on the history of literature and art are not listed here.]
Materialismo storico ed economia marxistica, 1900; *Filosofia dello spirito:* *I, Estetica come scienza dell'espressione a linguistica generale, 1902; *II, Logica come scienza del concetto puro, 1905; *III, Filosofia della Pratica, economica ed etica, 1909; IV, Teoria e storia della storiografia, 1917; *Saggi filosofici*, 1910 ff. (8 vols.); *Saggio sul Hegel*, 1907; *Problemi di estetica e contributi alla storia dell'estetica italiana*, 1910, 2d ed. 1924; *La filosofia di G. B. Vico*, 1911, 2d ed. 1922; **Breviario di estetica*, 1913; *Cultura e vita morale*, 1914; *Contributo alle critica di me stesso*, 1918; *Primi Saggi*, 1919; *Pagine sparce* (ed. by G. Castellano), 1919; *Goethe*, 1919; *Nuovi saggi di estetica*, 1920; *Frammenti di etica*, 1922; *Elementi di politica*, 1925; *Aspetti morali vita politica* 1928; *La critica a storie dell'arte figurativa*, 1934; *Piccoli saggi di filosofia politica*, 1934; *Ultimi saggi*, 1935; La poesia, 1936; *La storia come pensiero e come azione*, 1938; *Il carattere della filosofia moderna*, 1941; *Storia dell'estetica per saggi*, 1942; *Aesthetica in nuce*, 1946; *Filosofia e storiografia*, 1949; *My Philosophy* (ed. by R. Klibansky), 1949.

AUTOBIOGRAPHY

PGS, IV

JOURNAL

La Critica, 1903–.

LITERATURE

Calogero, G. and D. Petrini. *Studi Crociani*, 1930. Carr, W. *The Philosophy of Benedetto Croce*, 1917. Castellango, G. *Benedetto Croce*, 1924, 2d ed. 1936 (bibliography). Chiocchetti, E. *La filosofia di Benedetto Croce*, 3d ed. 1924. Fano G. *La filosofia del Croce*, 1946. Fraenkel, A. M. *Die Philosophie Croces*, 1929. Lombardi, A. *La filosofia di Benedetto Croce*, 1946; *L'opera filosofica, storica e letteraria di Benedetto Croce* (bibliography).

9. Léon Brunschvicg

WORKS

Spinoza, sa philosophie, 1894, 3d enlarged edition under the title *Spinoza et ses contemporains*, 1923; *Qua ratione Aristoteles metaphysicam vim syllogismo inesse demonstraverit* (Paris: Dissertation, 1897); *La Modalité du jugement* (Paris: Dissertation, 1897), 2d ed. 1934; *Introduction à la vie de l'esprit*, 1900, 5th ed. 1932; *L'Idéalisme contemporain*, 1905, 5th ed. 1921; *Les Étapes de la philosophie mathématique*, 1912, 2d ed. 1929; *Nature et liberté*, 1921; *L'Expérience humaine et la causalité physique*, 1922; *La Génie de Pascal*, 1924; *Le Progrès de la conscience dans la philosophie orientale*, 2 vols., 1927; *De la connaissance de soi*, 1931; *Les Âges de l'intelligence*, 1934, 2d ed. 1937; *La Physique du XXᵉ siècle et la philosophie*, 1937; *Pascal*, 1932, 2d ed. 1937; *Descartes*, 1937, *L'Actualité des problèmes platoniciens*, 1937; *Rôle du pythagorisme dans l'évolution des idées*, 1937; *La Raison et la religion*, 1939; *Descartes et Pascal, lecteurs de Montaigne*, 1942; *Héritage de mots, héritage d'idées*, 1945; *L'Esprit européen*, 1947. See also various articles in *RMM* and in the proceedings of the fifth, eighth, and ninth International Congress of Philosophy.

279

Bibliography

FESTSCHRIFT

RMM, 1945.

LITERATURE

Deschoux, M. *La Philosophie de Leon Brunschvicg,* 1949.
Etcheverry, A. *L'Idéalisme français contemporain,* 1934. Car-
bonara, C. "Leon Brunschvicg," *L.,* 1929-1930. Gardeil, H. D.
Les Étapes de la philosophie idéaliste, 1935. Grebier, J. "La
Philosophie de Leon Brunschvicg," *L.,* 1925. Vernaux, R.
"L'Idéalisme de Leon Brunschvicg," *Revue de Philosophie,*
1934.

10. NEO-KANTIANISM

General

SELECTIONS

Hermann, K. *Einführung in die neukantische Philosophie. Mit
ausgewählten Lesestücken,* 1927.

LITERATURE (*See Also Ue* IV)

Chojnacki, P. *Die Ethik Kants und die Ethik des Sozialismus;
Ein Mittlungsversuch der Marburger Schule* (Freiburg,
Switzerland: Dissertation: 1924). Gurvitch, G. *Les Tendances
actuelles de le philosophie allemande,* 1930. Goedeke, P.
Wahrheit und Wert (discusses the Baden School. Munich:
Dissertation, 1928). Graupe, H. *Die Stellung der Religion im
systematischen Denken der Marburger Schule* (Berlin: Dis-
sertation, 1930). Hessen, J. *Die Religionsphilosophie des
Neukantianismus,* 2d ed. 1924. Keller, E. *Das Problem des
Irrationalen im wertphilosophischen Idealismus der Gegen-
wart,* 1931. Liebert, A. *Die Krise des Idealismus,* 1936.
Myrho, F. (ed.) *Eine Sammlung von Beiträgen aus der Welt
des Neukantianismus,* 1926. Schütze, W. *Die Idee der sozialen
Gerechtigkeit im neukantianischen und christlich-sozialen
Schrifttum in der zweiten Hälfte des 19. Jahrhunderts*
(Leipzig: Dissertation, 1938). Sternberg, K. *Neukantische*

Aufgaben, 1931. Wilmsen, A. *Zur Kritik des logischen Transzendentalismus*, 1935. Yura, T. *Geisteswissenschaft und Willensgesetz. Kritische Untersuchungen der Methodenlehre der Geisteswissenschaft in der Badischen, Marburger und Dilthey-Schule* (Hamburg: Dissertation, 1938).

JOURNALS

Archiv für systematische Philosophie, 1894-1931. *Idealismus*, 1934. *Kt.*, till 1933. L.

Philosophy of Value

LITERATURE

Messer, A. *Deutsche Wertphilosophie der Gegenwart*, 1926; *Wertphilosophie der Gegenwart*, 1930.
Reding, M. *Metaphysik der sittlichen Werte*, 1950 (bibliography). Solomonidis, D. *Esquisse d'une axiologie* (Geneva: Dissertation, 1946). Störring, G. *Die moderne ethische Wertphilosophie*, 1935. Wittmann, M. *Die moderne Wertethik*, 1940.

Paul Natorp

WORKS (*See Also Ue* IV)

Der Deutsche und sein Staat, 1924; *Vorlesungen über praktische Philosophie*, 1925.

FESTSCHRIFT

Zum 70. Geburtstag, 1924.

LITERATURE

Fichtner, A. *Transzendentalphilosophie und Lebensphilosophie in der Begründung von Natorps Pädagogik* (Leipzig: Dissertation, 1933). Graefe, J. *Das Problem des menschlichen Seins in der Philosophie Paul Natorps* (Würzburg: Dissertation, 1933). Gschwind, H. *Die philosophischen Grundlagen von Natorps Sozialpädagogik*, 1920.

281

Bibliography

Heinrich Rickert

BIBLIOGRAPHY

Faust, A. *Heinrich Rickert*, 1927. Ramming, G., see below.

WORKS (*See Also Ue* IV)

Kant als Philosoph der modernen Literatur, 1924; **Die Logik des Prädikats und das Problem der Ontologie*, 1930; *Die Heidelberger Tradition in der deutschen Philosophie*, 1931; *Über idealistische Politik als Wissenschaft*, 1931; *Goethes Faust*, 1932; *Grundprobleme der philosophischen Methodologie, Ontologie, Anthropologie*, 1934; "Kennen und Erkennen," *Kt.*, 1934; *Unmittelbarkeit der Sinndeutung*, 1939.

AUTOBIOGRAPHIES

DSPG, II; *PGS*, VII.

FESTSCHRIFTEN

Logos, 1923 and 1933

LITERATURE

Bauch, B. *BDP*, 1936 (obituary). Dirksen, A. *Individualität als Kategorie*, n.d. Faust, A. *Heinrich Rickert und seine Stellung innerhalb der Philosophie der Gegenwart*, 1927; "Heinrich Rickert," *Kt.*, 1936 (obituary). Fischer, J. "Die Philosophie der Werte bei Wilhelm Windelband und Heinrich Rickert," in *Festschrift Baeumler*, 1913. Ramming, G. *Heinrich Rickert und Karl Jaspers*, 1948. Schlunke, O. *Heinrich Rickerts Lehre vom Bewusstsein*, 1912. Schirren, W. *Rickerts Stellung zum Problem der Realität*, 1923. Spranger, E. "Rickerts System," *L.*, 1924.

Ernst Cassirer

BIBLIOGRAPHY

See Festschriften

SELECTED WORKS *(See Also Ue* IV)

Das Erkenntnisproblem in der Philosophie und Wissenschaft der neueren Zeit, 3 vols., 1906-1920, 3d ed. 1922-1923, English 1950; **Substanzbegriff und Funktionsbegriff,* 1910; *Kants Leben und Lehre,* 1918; **Philosophie der symbolischen Formen,* 3 vols.: I, Die Sprache; II, Das mythische Denken; III, Phänomenologie der Erkenntnis, 1929 (English summary: *An Essay on Man,* 1944); "Zur Theorie des Begriffes," *Kt.,* 1928; *Descartes,* 1939; *Zur Logik der Naturwissenschaften* (Göteborg Univ: Arsskrift, 1942); *The Myth of the State,* 1947.

FESTSCHRIFTEN

Klibansky, R. and H. J. Patton (eds.). *Philosophy and History. Essays Presented to Ernst Cassirer,* 1936 (bibliography). *The Philosophy of Ernst Cassirer,* LLP, 6, 1949.

LITERATURE

Heymans, G. "Zur Cassirer'schen Reform der Begriffslehre," *Kt.,* 1928. Pos, H. J., "Recollections of Ernst Cassirer" in LLP, 6, 1949 (obituary).

Arthur Liebert

WORKS *(See Also Ue* IV)

Ethik, 1924; *Geist und Welt der Dialektik,* 1929; *Erkenntnistheorie,* 2 vols., 1932; *Philosophie des Unterrichts,* 1935; *Die Krise des Idealismus,* 1936; *Der Liberalismus,* 1938; *Der universale Humanismus,* 1946.

JOURNAL

Philosophia, Belgrade, 1936-1940.

OBITUARY AND BIBLIOGRAPHY

Kropp, G. "Arthur Liebert," ZPF, 1948.

283

Bruno Bauch

WORKS (*See Also Ue* IV)

Anfangsgründe der Philosophie, 1920, 2d ed. 1932; **Wahrheit, Wert und Wirklichkeit,* 1932; "Das transzendentale Subject," *L.,* 1923-1924; *Der Geist von Potsdam und der Geist von Weimar,* 1926; *Die Idee,* 1926; *Philosophie des Lebens und Philosophie der Werte,* 1927; *Goethe und die Philosophie,* 1928; *Kultur und Nation,* 1929; *Die erzieherische Bedeutung der Kulturgüter,* 1930; "Wert und Zweck," *BDP,* 1934; **Grundzüge der Ethik,* 1935.

AUTOBIOGRAPHIES

PGS, II; *DSPG,* I.

LITERATURE

Keller, E. *Die Philosophie Bruno Bauchs als Ausdruck germanisher Geisteshaltung,* 1935.
Kuntze, F. "Wahrheit, Wert und Wirklichkeit," *Kt.,* 1928.
Rohner, A. *DT,* 1926 (review of "Wahrheit, Wert und Wirklichkeit").

11. HENRI BERGSON

BIBLIOGRAPHY

A Contribution to a Bibliography of Henry Bergson (Columbia University, New York: 1913). *RIP,* 10, 1949.

WORKS

La Spécialité, 1882; *Extraits de Lucrèce,* 1884; *Essai sur les données immédiates de la conscience* (Paris: Dissertation, 1889); *Quid Aristoteles de loco senserit* (Paris: Dissertation, 1889); **Matière et mémoire. Essay sur les relations du corps à l'esprit,* 1896; *Le Rire. Essai sur la signification du comique,* 1900; "Introduction à la métaphysique," *RMM,* 1903. **L'Évolution créatrice,* 1907; "L'Intuition philosophique," *RMM,* 1911; *Le Matérialisme actuel,* 1913; *La Signification* *de la guerre*, 1914; *La Philosophie française*, 1915; *L'Énergie spirituelle. Essais et conférences*, 1920; *Réflexions sur le temps, l'espace et la vie*, 1920; *Durée et simultanéité. A propos de la théorie d'Einstein*, 1922; **Les Deux Sources de la morale et de la religion*, 1932; *La Pensée et le mouvant*, 1934. See also letter to A. D. Sertillanges (*Vie intellectuelle*, 1937) and to J. de Tonquedec (*Dieu dans l'Évolution créatrice*, 1912).

SELECTIONS

Gillouin, R. *Choix de textes*, 1928.

FESTSCHRIFTEN

Béguin, A. and P. Thévenaz (eds.). *Essais et témoignages inédits*, 1941. Valery, P. et al. *Etudes bergsoniennes*, 1942. *RIP*, 10, 1949.

LITERATURE

Chevalier, J. Bergson, 1926, 21st ed. 1941. Cresson, A. *Henri Bergson, sa vie et son œuvre*, 1941. Husson, L. *l'Intellectualisme de Bergson: Genèse et développement de la notion bergsonienne d'intuition*, 1947. Ingarden, R. *"Intuition und Intellekt bei Henri Bergson," *JPPhF*, 1922. Jankelevitch, V. *Henri Bergson*, 1931. Jurevics, P. *Henri Bergson, Eine Einführung in seine Philosophie*, 1949. Keller, A. *Eine Philosophie des Lebens*, 1914. Kroner, R. *Henri Bergson*, 1910. Le Roy, E. *Une philosophie nouvelle, Henri Bergson*, 1912; "Bergson et le Bergsonism," *AP*, 1947. Lewkowitz, J. *Die Philosophie Henri Bergsons*, 1914. Maritain, J. *La philosophie bergsonienne*, 1914, 2d ed. (revised) 1930; *De Bergson à S. Thomas d'Aquin*, 1914. Meckauer, W. *Der Intuitionismus und seine Elemente bei Henri Bergson*, 1917. Ott, E: *Henri Bergson, der Philosoph der modernen Religion*, 1914. Penido, M. **La Méthode intuitive de Henri Bergson* (Freiburg, Switzerland: Dissertation, 1918); *Dieu dans le Bergsonisme*,

Bibliography

1934. Rickert, H. *Die Philosophie des Lebens,* 1920, 2d ed.
1922. De Tonquedec, J. *Dieu dans l'Évolution créatrice,* 1912.

12. PRAGMATISM AND BERGSONISM
American Philosophy

BIBLIOGRAPHY

Winn, R. "Amerikanische Philosophie," *BESP,* 2, 1948.

LITERATURE

Adams, G. P. and W. P. Montague (eds.). *Contemporary American Philosophy, Personal Statements,* 1930. Anderson, P. R. and M. H. Fisch. *Philosophy in America from the Puritans to James,* 1939 (bibliography). *PTFUS.* Harlow, V. E. *A Bibliography and Genetic Study of American Realism,* 1931. Kremer, R. *Le Néoréalisme américain,* 1920. Müller, G. E. *Amerikanische Philosophie,* 1936. Schneider, H. W. *A History of American Philosophy,* 1946. Wahlt, J. *Les Philosophies pluralistes d'Angleterre et d'Amérique,* 1920 (English, 1924). Townsend, H. G., *Philosophical Ideas in the United States,* 1934.

General

BIBLIOGRAPHY

Leroux, E. *Bibliographie méthodique du pragmatisme américain, anglais et italien,* 1923.

LITERATURE

Baumgarten, E. *Der Pragmatismus: R. W. Emerson, W. James, J. Dewey,* 1938. Dewey, J. "The Development of American Pragmatisme," *TCP.* Jacoby, G. *Der Pragmatismus,* 1909. Leroux, E.
Le Pragmatisme américain et anglais, 1923. Pratt, J. B. *Pragmatism,* 1908. Schinz, A. *Antipragmatism,* 1909. Walker, J. *Theories of Knowledge,* 1910, 2d ed. 1934.

William James

BIBLIOGRAPHY

Perry, R. W. *A List of the Published Writings of Williams James*, 1920 (more than 300 titles).

WORKS

The Principles of Psychology, 1890; *A Text Book of Psychology. Briefer Course*, 1892; *The Will to Believe*, 1897; *Human Immortality*, 1898, 2d ed. 1899; *Talks to Teachers on Psychology and to Students on Some of Life's Ideals*, 1899; *The Varieties of Religious Experience* (GL), 1902; *Pragmatism, A New Name for Some Old Ways of Thinking*, 1907; *A Pluralistic Universe*, 1909; *The Meaning of Truth*, 1909; *Some Problems of Philosophy, A Beginning to an Introduction to Philosophy*, 1911; *Memories and Studies*, 1911; *Essays in Radical Empiricism*, 1912 (includes "Does Consciousness Exist?"); *Collected Essays and Review* (ed. by R. B. Perry), 1920; *Letters of William James* (ed. by his son Henry James), 1920; Durendeaud, E. (ed.). *Études et réflexions d'un psychiste*, 1924.

FESTSCHRIFT

In Commemoration of William James, 1842-1942, 1942.

LITERATURE

Bergson, H. "Sur le pragmatisme de William James," *La Pensée et le mouvant*, 1934. Boutroux, E. *William James*, 1911 (English, 1912); Knox, H. W. *The Philosophy of William James*, 1914. Flournoy, T. *La Philosophie de William James*, 1912. Maire, G. *William James et le pragmatisme religieux*, 1933 (bibliography). Perry, R. W. *The Thought and Character of William James*, 2 vols., 1937. Reverdin, H. *La Notion d'expérience d'après William James*, 1913. Stumpf, C. "William James nach seinen Briefen," *Kt.*, 1927. Turner. J. *Examination of William James's Philosophy*, 1919. Wahl, J.

287

*"William James d'après ses lettres," *Vers le concret*, 1932. Znamierowski, C. *Der Wahrheitsbegriff im Pragmatismus* (Basel: Dissertation, 1912).

F. C. S. Schiller

WORKS

Riddles of a Sphynx, by a Troglodyte, 1891, 2d ed. 1894, 3d ed. 1910; "Axioms as Postulates," *Personal Idealism* (ed. by H. Sturt) 1902; *Humanism*, 1903, 2d ed. 1912; *Studies in Humanism*, 1907, 2d ed. 1912; *Plato or Protagoras?*, 1908; *Formal Logic*, 1912, 2d ed. 1931; *Problems of Belief*, 1924; *Tantalus or the Future of Man*, 1924; *Eugenics and Politics*, 1926; *Social Decay and Eugenical Reform*, 1932; *Must Philosophers Disagree? Essays in Popular Philosophy*, 1934; *Our Human Truths*, 1939.

AUTOBIOGRAPHY

CBP, I.

LITERATURE

Johnston, M. *Truth According to Professor Schiller* (Freiburg, Switzerland: Dissertation, 1934). Walker, J. See above, under General. White, S. S. *A Comparison between the Philosophy of Ferdinand C. S. Schiller and John Dewey* (Chicago: Dissertation, 1939).

John Dewey

BIBLIOGRAPHY

Thomas, M. H. and H. W. Schneider. *Bibliography of John Dewey, 1882-1933*, 2d ed. 1939.

SELECTED WORKS

The School and Society, 1899; *Studies in Logical Theory*, 1903; *Ethics* (with J. H. Tufts), 1908; *The Influence of Darwin on Philosophy and Other Essays*, 1910; *Essays in Experimental Logic*, 1916; *Democracy and Education*, 1916; *Crea-*

tive Intelligence, 1917; **Human Nature and Conduct*, 1920; **Experience and Nature*, 1925; **The Quest for Certainty* (GL), 1929; *Art and Experience*, 1934; *Philosophy and Civilization*, 1939; **Logic, the Theory of Inquiry*, 1938; "Theory of Valuation," *Encyclopedia of Unified Science*, I, 1939; *Freedom and Culture*, 1940; *Problems of Men*, 1946; *Knowing and the Known* (with A. F. Bentley), 1950.

SELECTIONS

Ratner, J. *Education Today*, 1940; *Intelligence Today*, 1940.

FESTSCHRIFT

The Philosophy of John Dewey, LLP, 1, 1939.

LITERATURE

Feldmann, W. *John Dewey*, 1934. Hook, S. *John Dewey*, 1939; "The Place of John Dewey in Modern Thought," *PTFUS*; *John Dewey. The Philosophy of Science and Freedom, 1950.* Leander, F. *John Dewey*, 1939. Ratner, J. (ed.). *The Philosophy of John Dewey*, 1928.

Edouard Le Roy

WORKS (*See Also Ue* V)

L'Exigence de l'idéalisme et le fait de l'évolution, 1927; **Le Problème de Dieu*, 1929; **La Pensée intuitive*, 2 vols., 1929-1930; *Les Origines humaines et l'évolution de l'intelligence*, 1931; *Introduction à l'étude du problème religieux*, 1944.

LITERATURE

Balthasar, N. "Le Problème de Dieu d'après M. Edouard Le Roy," *RNP*, 1931. Rast, M. "Der Gottesbegriff in der Religionsphilosophie von Edouard Le Roy," *Zeitschrift für katholische Theologie*, 1934.

Maurice Blondel

See 21, below (Philosophy of Being).

The Dialectical School

SELECTED WORKS

Bachelard, G. *La Formation de l'esprit scientifique*, 1938; *La Philosophie du non*, 1940; *Le Rationalisme appliqué*, 1949. Gonseth, F. *Les Mathématiques et la réalité*, 1936; *Qu'est-ce que la logique?*, 1937; *La Philosophie mathématique*, 1939; (ed.) *Les Entretiens de Zurich* (1938), 1941; (ed. in collaboration with H. S. Gagnebin) *Déterminisme et libre arbitre*, 1941, 2d ed. 1947; *La Géométrie et le problème de l'espace*, 4 brochures, 1945-1949. Hainard, R. *Nature et mécanisme*, 1946. König, H. *Der Begriff der Helligkeit*, 1947.

JOURNAL

Dialectica, Zürich, 1947–.

13. HISTORICISM AND GERMAN LIFE-PHILOSOPHY

Friedrich Nietzsche

BIBILOGRAPHY

Oehler, R. *Nietzsche-Register*, 1926 (incomplete).

COLLECTIONS

Gesammelte Werke, ed. by A. Baeumler (India-paper edition 6 vols., pocket edition 12 vols.), 1930–. *Historisch-kritische Gesamtausgabe*, München, 1933–.

LITERATURE

Andler, C. *Les Précurseurs de Nietzsche*, 1920; *La Jeunesse de Nietzsche*, 1921; *Le Pessimisme esthétique de Nietzsche*, 1921; *Nietzsche et le transformisme intellectualiste*, 1922; *La Maturité de Nietzsche*, 1928; *La Dernière Philosophie de Nietzsche*, 1930. Bertram, E. *Nietzsche, Versuch einer Mythologie*, 1918, 2d ed. 1920. Brin, S. G. *Kollektivistisches in der Philosophie Nietzsches* (Basel: Dissertation, 1948). Copleston, F. *Nietzsche, Philosopher of Culture*, 1942. Emmerich, E. *Wahrheit und Wahrhaftigkeit in der Philosophie Nietzsches* (Bonn: Dissertation, 1933). Flake, O. *Nietzsche,* 1946. Hildebrandt, K. *Gesundheit und Krankheit in Nietzsches Leben und Werk,* 1926. Jaspers, K. *Nietzsche,* 1936; *Nietzsche und das Christentum,* 1946. Klein, O. *Das Apollinische und Dionysische bei Nietzsche und Schelling,* 1935. Klages, L. *Die psychologischen Errungenschaften Nietzsches,* 1926, 2d ed. 1930. Pfeil, H. **Nietzsche und die Religion,* 1948. Reyburn, H. A. *Nietzsche, A Story of a Human Philosopher,* 1948; **Friedrich Nietzsche,* 1946. Schlegel, W. *Nietzsches Geschichtsauffassung,* 1937. Steiff, U. *Friedrich Nietzsches Philosophie des Triebes,* 1940. Vetter, A. *Nietzsche,* 1926. Wolf, P. *Nietzsche und das christliche Ethos,* 1940.

Wilhelm Dilthey

BIBLIOGRAPHY

Zeeck, H. *Arch. für Geschichte der Philosophie,* 1911.

WORKS

Gesammelte Schriften, 12 vols., 1913–; *Briefwechsel zwischen Dilthey und dem Grafen Paul Yorck v. Wartenburg, 1877-1897,* 1923; *Der junge Dilthey, Lebensbild in Briefen und Tagebüchern* (ed. by Clara [Dilthey] Misch), 1933.

LITERATURE

Bischoff, D. *Wilhelm Diltheys geschichtliche Lebensphilosophie,* 1935. Bollnow, O. F. **Dilthey, Einführung in seine Philosophie,* 1936. Dempf, A. "Wilhelm Dilthey," *BDP,* 1933. Glock, K. T. *Wilhelm Diltheys Grundlegung einer wissenschaftlichen Lebensphilosophie,* 1939. Groethuysen, B. *Introduction à la pensée allemande depuis Nietzsche,* 1926; *Idée et pensée, Réflexions sur le journal de Dilthey,* 1934. Hodges, H. A. *Dilthey, An Introduction,* 1944. Flory, P. M. *The Principle of Teleology in the Philosophy of Wilhelm Dilthey* (Cornell University: Dissertation, 1934). Landsgrebe, L. *Wilhelm Diltheys Theorie der Geisteswissenschaften,* 1928. Meinecke, F. *Die Entstehung des Historismus*, 2d ed., 1946. Misch G. *Introduction to Vol. V of Gesammelte Schriften*, 1924; *Vom Lebens- und Gedankenkreis Wilhelm Diltheys*, 1947; *Lebensphilosophie und Phänomenologie*, 1930, 2d ed. 1931.

Rudolf Eucken

LITERATURE (*See Also Ue* IV)

Becher, E. *Rudolf Eucken und seine Philosophie*, 1927. Kalweit, P. *Euckens religionsphilosophische Leistung*, 1927. Schack, H. *Denker und Deuter*, 1938.

Oswald Spengler

WORKS

Heraklitische Studien, 1905; *Der Untergang des Abendlandes*, 2 vols., 1918-1922, 2d ed. 1923-1924; *Preussentum und Sozialismus*, 1920; *Der Staat*, 1924; *Der Mensch und die Technik*, 1931; *Reden und Aufsätze*, 1937.

LITERATURE

Bacskai, B. *Verfall und Aufstieg der Kulturen*, 1943. Haering, T. L. *Die Struktur der Weltgeschichte*, 1921. Spiess, E. Various essays, *DT*, 1922-1923. Schröter, M. *Metaphysik des Untergangs*, 1948. *L.* (special issue), 1921.

Arnold J. Toynbee

SELECTED WORKS

A Study of History, 6 vols., 1934-1939 [now 10 vols.—Translator]; *A Study of History*, abridgment by D. C. Somervell, 1947; *Civilization on Trial*, 1948.

R. G. Collingwood

SELECTED WORKS

An Essay on Philosophical Method, 1934; *The Historical Imagination*, 1935; *An Essay on Metaphysics*, 1940; *The New*

Leviathan, 1941; *Idea of Nature*, 1945; *The Idea of History*, 1946.

Hermann Keyserling

SELECTED WORKS (*See Also Ue* IV)

Menschen als Sinnbilder, 1926; *Die neuenstehende Welt*, 1926; *Wiedergeburt*, 1927; *Das Spektrum Europas*, 1928; *La Vie intime*, 1933; *La Révolution mondiale et la responsibilité de l'esprit*, 1934; *Sur l'art de la vie*, 1936; *Das Buch vom persönlichen Leben*, 1936; *De la souffrance à la plénitude*, 1938; *Betrachtungen der Stille und Besinnlichkeit*, 1941; *Das Buch vom Ursprung*, 1947.

PUBLICATIONS OF THE SCHOOL OF WISDOM

Der Leuchter (annual; ed. by Hermann Keyserling), 1919–. *Der Weg der Vollendung*, 1920–.

LITERATURE

Adolph, H. *Die Philosophie des Grafen Keyserling*, 1927. Röhr, R. *Keyserlings magische Geschichtsphilosophie*, 1939. Vollrath, W. *Graf Keyserling und seine Schule*, 1923.

Ludwig Klages

BIBLIOGRAPHY

Deussen, J., see below; also Festchrift.

SELECTED WORKS

Stefan George, 1902; *Prinzipien der Charakterologie*, 1910, 4th ed. under the title *Die Grundlagen der Charakterkunde*, 1928, 7th and 8th ed. 1936; *Handschrift und Charakter*, 1916, 19th and 20th ed. 1941; *Geist und Seele*, 1917; *Mensch und Erde*, 1920, 7th ed. 1937; *Vom Wesen des Bewusstseins*, 1921, 3d ed. 1933; *Vom kosmogonischen Eros*, 1922, 4th ed. 1941; *Die psychologischen Errungenschaften Nietzsches*, 1926; *Der Geist als Widersacher der Seele:* I, Leben und Denkvermögen, 1929, 2d ed. 1937; II, Die Lehre vom Willen,

293

1929, 2d ed. 1939; III, Die Wirklichkeit der Bilder; *Goethe als Seelenforscher*, 1932, 2d ed. 1940; *Vom Wesen des Rhythmus*, 1933; *Der Mensch und das Leben*, 1937, 2d ed. 1940. *Ursprünge der Seelenforschung*, 1942.

AUTOBIOGRAPHY

DSPG, II.

SELECTIONS

Kern, H. (ed.). *Vom Sinn des Lebens, Worte des Wissens*, 1940.

FESTSCHRIFT

Prinzhorn, H. (ed.). *Die Wissenschaft am Scheidewege von Leben and Geist, Ludwig Klages zum 60. Geburtstag.*

LITERATURE

Bense, M. *Anti-Klages*, 1937. Deussen, J. *Klages Kritik des Geistes*, 1934 (bibliography). Kliefoth, M. *Erleben und Erkennen*, 1938. Lersch, Th. "Ludwig Klages," *BDP*, 1928; "Eine Philosophie des Lebens," *BDP*, 1931. Ninck, M. "Zur Philosophie Ludwig Klages'," *Kt.*, 1931. Prinzhorn, H. *Charakterkunde der Gegenwart*, 1931. Schaber, G. *Die Theorie des Willens in der Psychologie von Ludwig Klages*, 1939. Walter, G. "Ludwig Klages und sein Kampf gegen den Geist," *Philosophischer Anzeiger*, 1928. Witte, W. *Die Metaphysik Ludwig Klages'*, 1939.

14. EDMUND HUSSERL
Franz Brentano

BIBLIOGRAPHY

Kraus, O. *Franz Brentano*, 1919. Seiterich, E., see below.

COLLECTED WORKS

Kastil A. and O. Kraus (eds.) *Gesammelte philosophische Werke*, 1922–. (Not completed at time of writing.)

294

WORKS (*See Also Ue* IV)

Die Lehre Jesu und ihre bleibende Bedeutung, 1922; **Psychologie vom empirischen Standpunkt,* 3 vols., 1924-1928; *Versuch über die Erkenntnis,* 1925; *Über die Zukunft der Philosophie,* 1929; *Vom Dasein Gottes,* 1929; **Wahrheit und Evidenz,* 1930; *Kategorienlehre,* 1933.

FESTSCHRIFTEN

Monatshefte für pädagogische Reform, 1918. Fürth, R. (ed.) *Naturwissenschaft und Metaphysik,* 2 vols., 1938.

LITERATURE

Brück, M. *Ueber das Verhältnis Edmund Husserls zu Franz Brentano* (Bonn: Dissertation, 1953). Hauber, V. *Wahrheit und Evidenz bei Franz Brentano* (Tübingen: Dissertation, 1936). Katkov, G. "Bewusstsein, Gegenstand, Sachverhalt" (*Encyclopedia Britannica* essay), *Archiv für die gesamte Psychologie,* 1930. Kraus, O. **Franz Brentano, Zur Kenntnis seines Lebens und seiner Lehre,* 1919. Margolius, H. *Die Ethik Franz Brentanos,* 1929. Most, O. *Die Ethik Franz Brentanos und ihre geschichtlichen Grundlagen,* 1931. Rogge, E. *Das Kausalprinzip bei Franz Brentano,* 1935. Seiterich, E. *Die Gottesbeweise bei Franz Brentano* (Freiburg i. B.: Dissertation, 1936). Utitz, E. "Franz Brentano," *Kt.,* 1918. Werner, A. *Die psychologisch-erkenntnistheoretischen Grundlagen der Metaphysik Franz Brentanos,* 1931. Kastil, A. *Die Philosophie Franz Brentanos* [1951].

Alexius Meinong

LITERATURE (*See Also Ue* IV)

Martinak, E. *Meinong als Mensch und Lehrer,* 1925

WORKS

See *Ue* IV.

Carl Stumpf

WORKS (*See Also Ue* IV)

Gefühl und Gefühlsempfindung, 1928; **Erkenntnislehre*, 2 vols., 1939-1940.

LITERATURE

Hartmann, N. *SPA*, 1937 (memorial speech).

Edmund Husserl

BIBLIOGRAPHY

Patocka, J. *RIP*, 2, 1939.

WORKS

Ueber den Begriff der Zahl, 1887; *Philosophie der Arithmetik*, I, 1891; *Psychologische Studien zur elementaren Logik*, 1894; *Der Folgerungskalkül und die Inhaltslogik*, 1891; **Logische Untersuchungen*, 2 vols., 1900-1901, 2d revised ed. (3 vols.) 1913-1921; "Philosophie als strenge Wissenschaft," *L.*, 1910-1911; "Ideen zu einer reinen Phänomenologie und phäno-menologischen Philosophie," *JPPhF*, 1913, 3d ed. 1928; *Vorlesungen zur Phänomenologie des inneren Zeitbewusstseins* (ed. by Martin Heidegger), 1928; "Phänomenology," *Encyclopedia Britannica*, 14th ed. 1929; ***"Formale und trans-zendentale Logik," *JPPhF*, 1929; "Nachwort zu meinen 'Ideen'," *JPPhF*, 1930; *Méditations cartésiennes* (transl. into French by G. Pfeiffer and E. Lévinas), 1932; "Die Krisis der europäischen Wissenschaften und die transzendentale Phäno-menologie," *Philosophia* (Belgrade), 1936; *Erfahrung und Urteil* (ed. by L. Landgrebe, Prague), 1939; "Die Frage nach dem Ursprung der Geometrie als intentional-historisches Problem," *RIP*, 2, 1939 (ed. by E. Fink); "Entwurf einer 'Vorrede' zu den 'Logischen Untersuchungen'," *Tijdschrift voor Philosophie*, 1939 (ed. by E. Fink); "Grundlegende Untersuchungen zum phänomenologischen Ursprung der Räumlichkeit der Natur," *Philosophical Essays*, 1940 (see below, Festschrifts); "Notizen zur Raumkonstitution," *PPhR*, 1940-1941; "Phänomenologie und Anthropologie," *ibid.*, 1941-1942; "Die Welt der lebendigen Gegenwart und die Konstitution der ausserleiblichen Umwelt," *ibid.*, 1945-1946.

POSTHUMOUS WORKS

Husserliana (The Hague), 1950: I, Cartesianische Meditationen und Pariser Vorträge (ed. by S. Strasser); II, Die Idee der Phänomenologie. Fünf Vorlesungen (ed. by W. Biemel); III, Ideen zu einer reinen Phänomenologie und phänomenologischen Philosophie. Additional volumes in preparation.

About Husserl's literary estate, see Van Breda, H. L. "Les Archives de Husserl à Louvain," *RNP*, 1945.

FESTSCHRIFTEN

"Festschrift Edmund Husserl," *JPPhF* (special volume), 1929. Farber M. (ed.) *Philosophical Essays in Memory of Edmund Husserl*, 1940.

LITERATURE

Becker, O. "Die Philosophie Edmund Husserls," *Kt.*, 1930. Berger, G. *Le Cogito dans la philosophie de Husserl* (Paris: Dissertation, 1941). Ehrlich, W. *Kant und Husserl*, 1923. Farber, M. **The Foundation of Phenomenology*, 1943. Fink, E. "Die phänomenologische Philosophie Husserls in der gegenwärtigen Krisis," *Kt.*, 1933 (with a foreword by Husserl in which he says "There is no sentence in this work to which I do not completely subscribe"). Kraft, J. *Von Husserl zu Heidegger*, 1932. Lévinas, E. **La Théorie de l'intuition dans la phénoménologie de Husserl*, 1930. Osborn, A. D. *The Philosophy of Edmund Husserl in its Development* (Columbia University: Dissertation, 1934). "La Phénoménologie," *Journées d'études de la Société Thomiste*, I, 1932. Reyer, W. *Einführung in die Phänomenologie*, 1926. Rovighi, G. V. *La filosofia di Edmund Husserl*, 1939. Welch, E. P. *The Philosophy of Husserl*, 1941.

JOURNALS

Jahrbuch für Philosophie und phänomenologische Forschung,
Halle, 1913-1930 (11 vols.). *PPhR,* 1940–.

15. MAX SCHELER

BIBLIOGRAPHY

Kraenzlin, G. *Max Schelers phänomenologische Philosophie,
mit einer monographischen Bibliographie,* 1934.

WORKS

Beiträge zur Feststellung der Beziehungen zwischen den logischen und ethischen Prinzipien (Jena: Dissertation, 1899);
Die transzendentale und die psychologische Methode, 1900,
2d ed. 1922; *Über Ressentiment und moralisches Werturteil,*
1912; *"Der Formalismus in der Ethik und die materielle
Wertethik. Neuer Versuch der Grundlegung eines ethischen
Personalismus,"* JPPhF, 1913-1916, 2d ed. 1921, 3d ed. 1927.
*Zur Phänomenologie und Theorie der Sympathiegefühle und
von Liebe und Hass,* 1913, 2d ed. under the title *Wesen und
Formen der Sympathie,* 1923, new ed. 1948; *Der Genius des
Krieges und der deutsche Krieg,* 1915; *Abhandlungen und
Aufsätze,* 2 vols., 1915, 2d ed. under the title *Vom Umsturz
der Werte,* 1919; *Krieg und Aufbau,* 1916; *Die Ursachen des
Deutschenhasses,* 1917; *Vom Ewigen im Menschen,* 1921;
Schriften zur Soziologie und Weltanschauungslehre: I,
Moralia, 1923; II, Nation und Weltanschauung, 1923; III-1,
Konfessionen, 1924; III-2, Arbeits- und Bevölkerungsprobleme, 1924; "Probleme einer Soziologie des Wissens," in
Versuche einer Soziologie des Wissens (ed. by Max Scheler),
1924, 2d ed. under the title *Die Wissensformen und die Gesellschaft,* 1926; "Idealismus-Realismus," *Philosophischer Anzeiger,* 1927; *Die Stellung des Menschen im Kosmos,* 1928,
new ed. 1947; *Philosophische Weltanschauung,* 1929; *Mensch
und Geschichte,* 1929; *Die Idee des Friedens und des Pazifismus,* 1931; *Schriften aus dem Nachlass,* I, 1933.

298

Altmann, A. *Die Grundlagen der Wertethik,* 1931. Bachus, A. *Einzelmensch, Familie und Staat in der Philosophie Schelers* (Bonn: Dissertation, 1936). Daniels, D. *Die Gemeinschaft bei Max Scheler und Thomas von Aquin* (Freiburg, Switzerland: Dissertation, 1925). Eklund, H. **Evangelisches und Katholisches in Max Schelers Ethik* (Uppsala Univ.: Arsskrift, 1932). Geyser, J. *Max Schelers Phänomenologie der Religion nach ihren wesentlichen Lehren,* 1924. Heber, J. *Das Problem der Gotteserkenntnis in der Religionsphilosophie Max Schelers,* 1931. Hugelmann, H. *Schelers Persönlichkeitsidee* (Leipzig: Dissertation, 1927). Kerler H. **Max Scheler und die impersonalistische Lebensanschauung,* 1917. Kreppel, F. *Die Religionsphilosophie Max Schelers* (Erlangen: Dissertation, 1926). Lennerz, P. *Schelers Konformitätssystem und die Lehre der katholischen Kirche,* 1924. Pöll, W. *Wesen und Wesenserkenntnis* (Munich: Dissertation, 1936). Przywara, E. *Religionsbegründung. Max Scheler-J. H. Newman,* 1923. Rohner, A. *"Thomas von Aquin und Max Scheler," *DT,* 1923-1926. "Symposium on the Significance of Max Scheler for Philosophy and Social Science," *JPPhR,* 1942. Wilhelm, S. *Das Bild des Menschen in der Philosophie Max Schelers* (Dresden: Dissertation, 1937). See also above, sec. 10, under Philosophy of Value.

16. THE GENERAL CHARACTER OF EXISTENTIALIST PHILOSOPHY

General

[Note: The extensive Italian literature of existentialism is listed here only by way of exception. On this see Belezza, V. A. "Bibliografia dell'esistenzialismo italiano," *Archivio di filosofia,* Rome: 1946.]

BIBLIOGRAPHY

RIP, 9, 1949.

299

WORKS

Andersen, W. *Der Existenzbegriff und das existentielle Denken in der neueren Philosophie und Theologie,* 1940. Arendt, H. "La Philosophie de l'existence," *Deucalion,* 1947. Bollnow, O. F. **Existenzphilosophie,* 3d ed., 1949. Brunner, A. "Ursprung und Grundzüge der Existenzphilosophie," *Scholastik* (Eupen, Belgium), 1938. Camus, A. *et al. De l'Existence,* 1945. Cayre, F., De Corte, M., Descoos, P., *et al.* "L'Existentialisme," *Revue de philosophie* (1946), 1947. Fabro, C. *Introduzione all'esistenzialismo,* 1942. Heinemann, F. *Neue Wege der Philosophie,* 1929. Jolivet, R. **Les Doctrines existentialistes de Kierkegaard à Jean-Paul Sartre,* 1948. Ortegat, P. *Intuition et religion. Le Problème existentialiste,* 1947. Pfeiffer, J. *Existenzphilosophie, eine Einführung in Heidegger und Jaspers,* 1933, new ed. 1949. Przywara, E. *Christliche Existenz,* 1934. Wahl, J. *Existence humaine et transcendance,* 1944; *Petite histoire de "l'existentialisme,"* 1947 (English, 1949); Werner, M. *Der religiöse Gehalt der Existenzphilosophie,* 1943.

Søren Kierkegaard

BIBLIOGRAPHY

Jolivet, R. "Kierkegaard," *BESP,* 4, 1948.

WORKS

Works of Kierkegaard (transl. by W. Lowrie, D. F. and L. M. Swenson, *et al.*), 1945–.

LITERATURE

Bohlin, T. *S. Kierkegaard,* 1923, 2d ed. 1927. Dempf, A. *Kants Folgen,* 1935. Fischer, F. C. *Die Nullpunktexistenz, dargestellt an der Lebensform Kants,* 1933. Jolivet, R. *Introduction à Kant,* 1946. Künzli, A. *Die Angst des modernen Menschen* (Zürich: Dissertation, 1947). Löwith, K. *Kant und Nietzsche,* 1933. Ruttenbeck, W. **S. Kierkegaard, der christliche Denker*

und sein Werk, 1929. Wahl, J. **Etudes Kierkegaardiennes,*
1938.

Nikolai Berdyaev

SELECTED WORKS

Das Schicksal der Menschen in unserer Zeit, 1935; *Cinq méditations sur l'existence,* 1936; *Essai de métaphysique eschatolo-
gique,* 1946; *Dialectique existentielle du divin et de l'humain,*
1947.

Maurice Merleau-Ponty

WORKS

La Structure du comportement, 1942; **Phénoménologie de la
perception,* 1945; *Humanisme et terreur,* 1947; *Sens et nonsense,* 1948.

Simone de Beauvior

PHILOSOPHICAL WORKS

L'Existentialisme et la sagesse des nations, 1948; *Pour une morale
de l'ambiguïté,* 1947 (English, 1948); *Le Deuxième Sexe,*
1949, 2 vols.

17. MARTIN HEIDEGGER

BIBLIOGRAPHY

De Waelhens, A., see below. Meiler R., see below.

WORKS

Die Lehre vom Urteil im Psychologismus (Freiburg i. B.: Dissertation 1914); *Die Kategorien- und Bedeutungslehre des
Duns Scotus,* 1916; "Der Zeitbegriff in der Geschichtswissen-
schaft," *Zeitschrift für Philosophie und philosophische
Kritik,* 1916; *"Sein und Zeit, I," *JPPhF,* 1927; also separately,
1929, 6th ed. 1949; *Kant und das Problem der Metaphysik,*
1929, 2d ed. 1951; "Vom Wesen des Grundes," *JPPhF* (Festschrift Husserl), 1929, 3d ed. 1949; *Was ist Metaphysik?,*
1929, 5th ed. 1949; *Die Selbstbehauptung der deutschen Uni-*

Bibliography

versität, 1933; "Platons Lehre von der Wahrheit," *Jahrbuch für geistige Überlieferung*, 1942, 2d ed. with an annex entitled "Brief über den 'Humanismus'," 1947; *Vom Wesen der Wahrheit*, 1943, 2d ed. 1949; *Holzwege*, 1950; *Erläuterungen zu Hölderlins Dichtung*, 1937-1944, 2d ed. 1951.

FESTSCHRIFTEN

Martin Heideggers Einfluss auf die Wissenschaften, 1944. *Anteile, Martin Heidegger zum 60. Geburtstag*, 1950.

LITERATURE

Beck, M. "Kritik der Schelling-Jaspers-Heidegger'schen Ontologie," *Philosophische Hefte*, 1934. Delp, A. *Tragische Existenz. Zur Philosophie Martin Heideggers*, 1935. Delpgaauw, B. "Heidegger en Sartre," *Tijdschrift voor Philosophie*, 1948. Droege, T. "Die Existenzphilosophie Martin Heideggers," *DT*, 1938. Dryoff, A. "Glossen zu Heideggers Sein und Zeit," in *Philosophia Perennis*, II, 1930. Fischer, A. *Die Existenzphilosophie Martin Heideggers*, 1935. Hoberg, C. A. *Das Dasein im Menschen* (Munich: Dissertation, 1937). Kraft, J. *Von Husserl zu Heidegger*, 1932. Lévinas, E. "Martin Heidegger et l'ontologie," *RP*, 1932; *En découvrant l'existence avec Husserl et Heidegger*, 1949. Meiler, R. *Heideggers Existenzphilosophie im Aufriss*, 1945. Misch, G. *Lebensphilosophie und Phänomenologie*, 1930, 2d ed. 1931. Müller, M. *Existenzphilosophie im geistigen Leben der Gegenwart*, 1949. Schott, E. *Die Endlichkeit des Daseins nach Martin Heidegger*, 1930. Sternberger, A. *Der verstandene Tod*, 1934. De Waehlens, A. *La Philosophie de Martin Heidegger*, 1945. De Waehlens A. and W. Biemel. Introduction to Heidegger's French edition of *Vom Wesen der Wahrheit* (*De l'essence de la vérité*), 1948.

18. JEAN-PAUL SARTRE

BIBLIOGRAPHY

Jolivet, R. "Französische Existenzphilosophie," *BESP*, 9, 1948.

PHILOSOPHICAL WORKS

L'Imagination, 1938; *Esquisse d'une théorie de l'émotion*, 1939; *L'Imaginaire*, 1940; *L'Être et le Néant*, 1943; *L'Existentialisme est un humanisme*, 1946 (English, 1948); *Réflexions sur la question juive*, 1946; *Descartes* (edited and introduced by Sartre), 1946.

JOURNAL

Les Temps modernes, 1945–.

LITERATURE

Beigbeder, M. *L'Homme Sartre*, 1947. Campbell, R. *Jean-Paul Sartre ou une littérature philosophique*, 1945. Haefliger, O. *Wider den Existentialismus*, 1949. Jeanson, F. *Le Problème moral et la pensée de Sartre* (introduction by Sartre), 1947. Paissac, H. *Le Dieu de Sartre*, 1950. Varet, G. *L'Ontologie de Sartre*, 1948. De Waelhens, A. "Heidegger et Sartre," *Deucalion*, 1946. Wahl, J. "La Liberté chez Sartre," *ibid.*; "Essai sur le néant d'un problème," *ibid.*

19. GABRIEL MARCEL

BIBLIOGRAPHY

Jolivet, R. "Französische Existenzphilosophie," *BESP*, 9, 1948.

PHILOSOPHICAL WORKS

"Les Conditions dialectiques d'une philosophie de l'intuition," *RMM*, 1912; *Existence et objectivité*, 1914; *Journal métaphysique* (1913-1923), 1927, new ed. 1935; "Positions et approches concrètes du mystère ontologique," in *Le Monde cassé*, 1933, and separately, 1949; *Être et avoir*, 1935 (English, 1949); *Du refus à l'invocation*, 1940; *Homo viator*, 1944; *La Métaphysique de Royce*, 1945; "Regard en arrière" in the Festschrift (see below); *The Philosophy of Existence*, 1949; *The Mystery of Being* (GL), I, 1950.

303

Bibliography

FESTSCHRIFT

Existentialisme chrétien: Gabriel Marcel présenté par E. Gilson, 1947 (bibliography).

LITERATURE

De Corte M. *La Philosophie de Gabriel Marcel,* 1937. Introduction to *Positions et approches* (by Marcel), 1949. Delhorme, J. "La Philosophie de Gabriel Marcel," *RT,* 1938; Ricoeur, P. *Gabriel Marcel et Karl Jaspers,* 1947. Wahl, J. "Le Journal métaphysique de Gabriel Marcel" in *Vers le concret,* 1932.

Martin Buber

WORKS

Daniel, 1913; *Ich und Du,* 1923; *Zwiesprache,* 1929; *Die Frage an den Einzelnen,* 1936; *Dialogisches Leben,* 1947; *Hasidism,* 1948.

LITERATURE

Kohn, H. *Martin Buber,* 1930. Maringer, S. *Martin Bubers Metaphysik der Dialogik* (Zürich: Dissertation, 1936). Smith, S. G. *The Thought of Martin Buber,* 1949.

20. KARL JASPERS

WORKS

Allgemeine Psychopathologie, 1913, 4th revised ed. 1946; **Psychologie der Weltanschauungen,* 1919, 3d ed. 1925; *Strindberg und van Gogh,* 1922, 2d ed. 1926; *Die Idee der Universität,* 1923; *Die geistige Situation der Zeit,* 1931, new ed. 1948 (English, 1933); *Max Weber, Deutsches Wesen im politischen Denken, im Forschen und Philosophieren,* 1932; **Philosophie:* I, Philosophische Weltorientierung; II, Existenzerhellung; Metaphysik, 1932, 2d ed. (Vol. I) 1948; *Vernunft und Existenz,* 1935; *Nietzsche, Einführung in das Verständnis des Philosophierens,* 1936, 2d ed. 1947; *Existenzphilosophie,* 1938; *Descartes und die Philosophie,* 1937; *La* *mia filosofia* (Italian by R. De Rosa), 1946; *Die Idee der Universität*, 1946 (a second work; not identical with the earlier work of like name, published in 1923); *Die Schuldfrage*, 1946; *Nietzsche und das Christentum*, 1946; *Philosophische Logik:* I, Von der Wahrheit, 1947; *Der philosophische Glaube*, 1948 (English, 1949); *Vom Wesen und Ziel der Geschichte*, 1949; *Einführung in die Philosophie*, 1949.

LITERATURE

Feith, R. E. *Psychologismus und Transzendentalismus bei Karl Jaspers*, 1945. Dufrenne, M. and P. Ricoeur. **Karl Jaspers et la philosophie de l'existence*, 1947 (foreword by Jaspers). Gehlen, A. "Jaspers' Philosophie," *BDP*, 1932. Hersch, J. *L'Illusion philosophique* (Geneva: Dissertation, 1936). Marcel, G. *Du refus à l'invocation*, 1940. Pareyson, R. *La filosofia dell'esistenza di Carlo Jaspers*, 1940. Ramming, G. *Heinrich Rickert und Karl Jaspers*, 1948. Ricoeur, P. *Gabriel Marcel et Karl Jaspers*, 1948. De Tonquedec, J. *Une philosophie existentielle: L'Existence d'après Karl Jaspers*, 1945. Welte, B. *Der philosophische Glaube bei Karl Jaspers*, 1949 (symposium). See also Bollnow and Pfeiffer, above, sec. 16, under General.

21. Metaphysics

General

WORKS

Kerler, D. H. *Die auferstandene Metaphysik*, 1921. Lehmann, G. *Die Ontologie der Gegenwart in ihren Grundgestalten*, 1933. Menzer, P. *Deutsche Metaphysik der Gegenwart*, 1931. Metz. Wust, P. *Die Auferstehung der Metaphysik*, 1920. *RIP*, 5, 1939 (bibliography).

Hans Driesch

BIBLIOGRAPHY

Heinichen, O. *Drieschs Philosophie*, 1924.

Bibliography

WORKS (*See Also Ue* IV)

Metaphysik, 1924; *Relativitätstheorie und Philosophie,* 1924; *Grundprobleme der Psychologie,* 1926; *Metaphysik der Natur,* 1927; *Die sittliche Tat,* 1927; *Der Mensch und die Welt,* 1928; *Philosophische Forschungswege, Ratschläge und Warnungen,* 1930; *Parapsychologie,* 1932; *Die Überwindung des Materialismus,* 1935; *Die Maschine und der Organismus,* 1935; *Alltagsrätsel des Seelenlebens,* 1938; *Selbstbesinnung und Selbsterkenntnis,* 1940; *Biologische Probleme höherer Ordnung,* 1941.

AUTOBIOGRAPHIES

PGS, I. *DSPG,* I.

FESTSCHRIFTEN

Schneider H. and W. Schingnitz (eds.) *Wissen und Leben,* 1927. Schingnitz, W. (ed.) *Ordnung und Wirklichkeit,* 1927. *Archiv für Entwicklungsmechanik der Organismen,* 2 vols., 1927.

LITERATURE

Gehlen, A. *Zur Theorie des Setzens und des setzenhaften Wissens bei Driesch,* 1927. Heinichen, O. See above, bibliography. Heuss, E. *Rationale Biologie und ihre Selbstkritik,* 1938. Oakeley, H. D. "On Professor Driesch's Attempt to Combine a Philosophy of Life and a Philosophy of Knowledge," *PAS,* 1921. Ungerer, E. "Drieschs Philosophie des Organischen," *BDP,* 1941.

Heinrich Maier

WORKS (*See Also Ue* IV)

"Alois Riehl," *Kt.,* 1926; *Philosophie der Wirklichkeit,* 3 vols., 1926-1935; "Die mechanische Naturbetrachtung und die 'vitalistische' Kausalität," *SPA,* 1928. "Die Anfänge der Philosophie des deutschen Idealismus," *SPA,* 1930.

LITERATURE

Hartmann, N. "Heinrich Maiers Beitrag zum Problem der Kategorien," *SPA*, 1938. (Obituary), *BDP*, 1934. Spranger, E. "Gedächtnisrede auf Heinrich Maier," *SPA*, 1934.

Othmar Spann

SELECTED WORKS

Der wahre Staat, 1921, 4th ed. 1938; *Tote und lebendige Wissenschaft*, 1921, 4th ed. 1935; *Kategorienlehre*, 1924, 2d ed. 1939; *Der Schöpfungsgang des Geistes. Die Wiederherstellung des Idealismus auf allen Gebieten der Philosophie*, 1928; *Gesellschaftsphilosophie*, 1928; *Geschichtsphilosophie*, 1932; *Philosophenspiegel. Die Hauptlehren der Philosophie begrifflich dargestellt*, 1933; *Kämpfende Wissenschaft*, 1934; *Erkenne dich selbst!*, 1935; *Naturphilosophie*, 1937; *Religionsphilosophie*, 1947; *Othmar Spann. Das philosophische Gesamtwerk im Auszug* (ed. by H. Riehl), 1950.

LITERATURE

Dunkmann, K. *Der Kampf um Othmar Spann*, 1928. Räber, Hans. *Othmar Spanns Philosophie des Universalismus*, 1937. Räber, Ludwig. (Review of *Kategorienlehre*), *DT*, 1940. Wrangel, G. *Das universalistische System von Othmar Spann* (Freiburg i. B.: Dissertation, 1929).

William Ralph Inge

SELECTED WORKS

Faith and Knowledge, 1904; *Truth and Falsehood in Religion*, 1906; *The Philosophy of Plotinus*, 2 vols. (GL), 1918, 3d ed. 1929; *Outspoken Essays*, 2 vols., 1919-1922; "Philosophy and Religion," *CBP*, I; *God and the Astronomers*, 1933.

John Laird

WORKS

Problems of the Self, 1917; *A Study in Realism*, 1924; "How Our Minds May Go Beyond Themselves In Their Knowing,"

307

CBP, I; *Our Minds and Our Bodies*, 1925; *A Study in Moral Theory*, 1926; *Modern Problems in Philosophy*, 1928; *The Idea of Value*, 1929; *Knowledge, Belief and Opinion*, 1931; *Morals and Western Religions*, 1931; *Hume's Philosophy of Human Nature*, 1932; *Hobbes*, 1934; *An Inquiry Into Moral Notions*, 1935; *Recent Philosophy*, 1936; **Theism and Cosmogology* (GL), 1940; *Mind and Deity (GL), 1941.

A. E. Taylor

SELECTED WORKS

The Problem of Conduct, 1901; *Elements of Metaphysics*, 1903, 9th ed. 1930; "The Freedom of Man," CBP, II; *The Problem of Evil*, 1929; **The Faith of a Moralist* (GL), 2 vols., 1930, 2d ed. (1 vol.) 1937; *Philosophical Studies*, 1934; *The Christian Hope of Immortality*, 1938; *Does God Exist?*, 1945. Also a large selection of books and essays on the history of philosophy.

OBITUARY

Porteous, A. J. D. *Mind*, 1946

Maurice Blondel

SELECTED WORKS

**L'Action* (Paris: Dissertation, 1893), new ed. 1950 (cited as "first *Action*"); *Histoire et Dogme*, 1904; *Une énigme historique: le "vinculum substantiale d'après Leibniz et l'ébauche d'un réalisme supérieur*," 1930; *Le Problème de la philosophie catholique*, 1932; *La Pensée, 2 vols., 1934-1935; *Pour la philosophie intégrale*, 1934; *L'Être et les êtres*, 1935; *L'Action*, 2 vols., 1936-1937 (cited as "second *Action*"; not a second edition of the first *Action*); *Lutte pour la civilisation et philosophie de la paix*, 1939; *La Philosophie et l'esprit chrétien*, 2 vols., 1944-1946; *Exigences philosophiques du christianisme*, 1950.

FESTSCHRIFT

Archambault, P. (ed.) *Hommage à Maurice Blondel*, 1946.

LITERATURE

Archambault, P. *Vers un réalisme integral. L'Œuvre philosophique de Maurice Blondel*, 1928; *Initiation à la philosophie blondelienne*, 1941. D'Hypernon, T. *Le Blondélisme*, 1933. Dumery, H. *La Philosophie de l'action*, 1949. Lefèvre, F. *L'Itinéraire philosophique de Maurice Blondel*, 1928. Romeyer, B. *La Philosophie religieuse de Maurice Blondel*, 1943.

Günther Jacoby

WORKS

Herders und Kants Ästhetik, 1907; *Der Pragmatismus*, 1909; *Herder als Faust*, 1911; *Allgemeine Ontologie der Wirklichkeit*, 2 vols., 1925-1932; "Geist" in *Pädagogisches Lexikon* (ed. by H. Schwarz), 1929; "Neue Ontologie," *Geistige Arbeit*, 1935; "Die Welt als Vorstellung und die Welt als Wille ontologisch betrachtet," *Gedächtnisschrift für Arthur Schopenhauer*, 1938.

LITERATURE

Günther, E. *Die ontologischen Grundlagen der neueren Erkenntnislehre*, 1933. Freitag-Löringhoff, B. *Die ontologischen Grundlagen der Mathematik*, 1937.

René Le Senne

WORKS

Introduction à la philosophie, 1925, 2d ed. 1939; *Le Mensonge et le caractère* (Paris: Dissertation, 1930); *Le Devoir* (Paris: Dissertation, 1930); *La Description de la conscience, obstacle et valeur*, 1934; *Traité de morale générale*, 1942; *Traité de caractérologie*, 1945; *Le Devoir*, 1950.

LITERATURE

Delasalle, J. "La Philosophie de M. René Le Senne," *RNP*, 1936.

309

Bibliography

Louis Lavelle

BIBLIOGRAPHY

Delfgaauw, see below.

WORKS

La Dialectique du monde sensible (Paris: Dissertation, 1921); *La Perception visuelle de la profondeur* (Paris: Dissertation, 1921); *De l'Être*, 1927, 2d ed. (revised) 1947; *La Conscience de soi*, 1933; *La Présence totale*, 1934; *Le Moi et son destin*, 1936; *De l'Acte*, 1937; *L'Erreur de Narcisse*, 1939. *Le Mal et la souffrance*, 1940; *La Parole et l'écriture*, 1942, 2d ed. 1947; *La Philosophie française entre les deux guerres*, 1942; *Du temps et de l'éternité*, 1945; *Introduction à l'ontologie*, 1947; *Les Puissances du moi*, 1948.

LITERATURE

Delfgaauw, B. M. I. *Het spiritualistisch existentialisme van Louis Lavelle* (University of Amsterdam: Dissertation, 1947). Grasso, G. *Louis Lavelle* (Brescia: n.d.). Nobile O. M. *La filosofia di Louis Lavelle*, 1943. Truc, G. *De Jean-Paul Satre à Louis Lavelle*, 1946. De Waelhens, A. "Une philosophie de la participation. L'actualisme de M. Louis Lavelle," *RNP*, 1939.

Samuel Alexander

BIBLIOGRAPHY

Philosophical and Literary Pieces, see below.

WORKS

Moral Order and Progress, 1889, 3d ed. 1899; Locke, 1908; *Space, Time and Deity*, 1920, 2d ed. 1927; *Beauty and Other Forms of Value*, 1933; *Philosophical and Literary Pieces* (ed. by J. Laird), 1939.

LITERATURE

Devaux, Ph. *Le Système* d'Alexander, 1929. Van Hall, G. *The*

Theory of Knowledge of Alexander (Rome, Gregorianum: Dissertation, 1936). Konvitz, M. R. *The Nature of Value; The Philosophy of Samuel Alexander,* 1946. Laird J. "Memoir" in *Philosophical and Literary Pieces,* 1939. McCarthy, J. W. *The Naturalism of Samuel Alexander,* 1948 (bibliography). Metz. Stout, G. H. "Samuel Alexander," *Mind,* 1940. "The Philosophy of Samuel Alexander, *Mind,* 1940.

C. Lloyd Morgan

WORKS

Animal Life and Intelligence, 1890; *Introduction to Comparative Psychology,* 1894; *Psychology for Teachers,* 1895; *Habit and Instinct,* 1896; *The Interpretation of Nature,* 1905; *Animal Behaviour,* 1908; *Instinct and Experience,* 1912; *Herbert Spencer's Philosophy of Science,* 1913; **Emergent Evolution* (GL), 1923; **Life, Mind and Spirit* (GL), 1926; *Mind at the Crossways,* 1929; *The Animal Mind,* 1930; *The Emergence of Novelty,* 1933.

Paul Häberlin

BIBLIOGRAPHY

Kamm, P. in *Kleine Schriften,* see below, Festschrift.

SELECTED WORKS

Wissenschaft und Philosophie, 2 vols., 1910-1912; *Die Grundfragen der Philosophie,* 1914; *Der Leib und die Seele,* 1923; *Das Geheimnis der Wirklichkeit,* 1927; *Allgemeine Ästhetik,* 1929; *Das Wunderbare,* 1930, 5th ed. 1940; *Das Wesen der Philosophie,* 1934; *Wider den Ungeist,* 1936; **Naturphilosophische Betrachtungen,* 2 vols., 1939-1940; *Der Mensch. Eine philosophische Anthropologie,* 1941; *Ethik im Grundriss,* 1946. *Logik im Grundriss,* 1947; *Handbüchlein der Philosophie,* 1949.

FESTSCHRIFT

Paul Häberlin, Kleine Schriften (ed. by P. Kamm), 1948.

22. NICOLAI HARTMANN

WORKS

Platos Logik des Seins, 1909; *Des Proklus Diadochus philosophische Anfangsgründe der Mathematik,* 1909; "Zur Methode der Philosophiegeschichte," *Kt.,* 1910; "Systembildung und Idealismus" in *Philosophische Arbeiten,* 1912; *Philosophische Grundfragen der Biologie,* 1912; "Die Frage der Beweisbarkeit des Kausalgesetzes," *Kt.,* 1919; **Grundzüge einer Metaphysik der Erkenntnis,* 1921, 4th ed. 1949; *Aristoteles und Hegel, Beiträge zur Philosophie des deutschen Idealismus,* 1923, 2d ed. 1933; "Diesseits von Idealismus und Realismus," *Kt.,* 1924; **Ethik,* 1926, 3d ed. 1949; *Die Philosophie des deutschen Idealismus:* I, Fichte, Schelling und die Romantik, 1923; II, Hegel, 1929; *Zum Problem der Realitätsgegebenheit,* 1931; **Das Problem des geistigen Seins,* 1933, 2d ed. 1949; "Der philosophische Gedanke und seine Geschichte, *SPA,* 1936; **Zur Grundlegung der Ontologie,* 1935, 3d ed. 1949; **Möglichkeit und Wirklichkeit,* 1938, 2d ed. 1949; **Der Aufbau der realen Welt,* 1940, 2d ed. 1949; "Neue Wege der Ontologie" in *Systematische Philosophie* (ed. by Nicolai Hartmann), separately published in 1949; *Philosophie der Natur,* 1950.

AUTOBIOGRAPHY

DSPG, I.

LITERATURE

Cohn, J. "Zu Nicolai Hartmanns Wertethik," *L.,* 1926. Endres, J. "Zur Teleologieauffassung Nicolai Hartmanns, *PJ,* 1942; "Der Schichtegedanke bei Nicolai Hartmann," *DT,* 1947. Guggenberger, A. *Der menschliche Geist und das Sein. Eine Begegnung mit Nicolai Hartmann,* 1942. Hirning, H. *Nicolai Hartmanns Lehre vom objektiven Geist und seine These von der Voraussetzungslosigkeit der Philosophie* (Tübingen: Dissertation, 1937). Konrad, A. *Irrationalismus und Subjektivis-*

mus, 1939. Kuhaupt, H. *Das Problem des erkenntnistheoretischen Realismus in Nicolai Hartmanns Metaphysik der Erkenntnis* (Münster: Dissertation, 1938). Lehmann, G. "Das Problem der Realitätsgegebenheit," *BDP*, 1932. Münzhuber, J. "Nicolai Hartmanns Ontologie und die philosophische Systematik," *BDP*, 1939. Seelbach, A. *Nicolai Hartmanns Kantkritik*, 1933.

See also above, sec. 10, under Philosophy of Value.

23. ALFRED NORTH WHITEHEAD

BIBLIOGRAPHY

The Philosophy of Alfred North Whitehead, LLP, 3, 1941. Cesselin, F., see below.

WORKS

[Note: Purely mathematical works are not listed here.]

A Treatise of Universal Algebra, with Applications, 1898 (includes "The Algebra of Logic"); "Memoir on the Algebra of Logic," *American Journal of Mathematics*, 1902; "On Cardinal Numbers," *ibid*. (with Bertrand Russell); "On Mathematical Concepts of the Material World," *Philosophical Transactions of the Royal Society*, 1906; "Mathematics," *EB*, 11th ed., 1911; *Principia Mathematica* (with Bertrand Russell), 3 vols., 1910-1913, 2d ed. 1925-1927; "Space, Time, and Relativity," *PAS*, 1916; "La Théorie relationiste de l'espace," *RMM*, 1916; "The Organisation of Thought," *PAS*, 1917; *An Enquiry Concerning the Principles of Natural Knowledge*, 1919; "Time, Space, Material: Are They the Ultimate Data of Science?" *PAS*, supplement, 1919; *The Concept of Nature*, 1920, 2d ed. 1926; "The Idealistic Interpretation of Einsteins Theory," *PAS*, 1922; "The Philosophical Aspects of the Principle of Relativity," *PAS*, 1922; *The Principle of Relativity with its Applications to Physical Science*, 1922; "Uniformity and Contingency," *PAS*, 1923; "The Principle of Simultaneity," *PAS*, supplement, 1923; *Science*

313

and the Modern World, 1926, new ed., 1946; *Religion in the Making,* 1926; *Symbolism, Its Meaning and Effect,* 1928; **Process and Reality* (GL), 1929, 2d ed. 1950; *The Aims of Education and Other Essays,* 1929; *The Function of Reason,* 1929; "The Nature of Mathematics," *EB,* 14th ed., 1929; **Adventures of Ideas,* 1933, new ed. 1947; *Nature and Life,* 1934; *The Modes of Thought,* 1938; "The Mathematics and the Good" in *The Philosophy of Alfred North Whitehead,* LLP, 3, 1941 (see Festschriften, below); *Essays in Science and Philosophie,* 1947 (with autobiography).

FESTSCHRIFTEN

Philosophical Essays for Alfred North Whitehead . . . , 1936.
The Philosophy of Alfred North Whitehead, LLP, 3, 1941.

LITERATURE

Alexander, S. "Qualities," *EB,* 14th ed., 1929. Bera, M.-A. *Alfred North Whitehead. Un philosophe de l'expérience,* 1948. Blyth, J. W. *Whitehead's Theory of Knowledge* (Brown University: Dissertation, 1936); "On Mr. Hartshorne's Understanding of Whitehead's Philosophy," *Philosophical Review,* 1937. Cesselin, F. *La Philosophie organique de Whitehead,* 1950. Das, R. *The Philosophy of Whitehead,* 1938. Emmet, D. **Whitehead's Philosophy of Organism,* 1932. Foley, L. A. *A Critique of the Philosophy of Being of Alfred North Whitehead in the Light of Thomistic Philosophy* (Washington: Dissertation, 1946). Johnson, A. H. "The Psychology of Alfred North Whitehead," *Journal of General Psychology,* 1945. Hartshorne, Ch. *Philosophy and Psychology of Sensation,* 1934; "On Some Criticism of Whitehead's Philosophy," *Philosophical Review,* 1935; "The Interpretation of Whitehead," *ibid.,* 1939; "Das metaphysische System Whiteheads," *ZPF,* 1948. Lintz, E. J. *The Unity of the Universe According to Alfred North Whitehead* (Freiburg, Switzerland: Dissertation, 1939). Mascall, E. L. *He*

Who Is, 1943. Moxley, D. J. "The Conception of God in the Philosophy of Whitehead," *PAS*, 1934. Stallknecht, N. P. *Studies in Philosophy of Creation*, 1934. Stebbing, L. S. "Concerning Substance," *PAS*, 1930; "Is the 'Fallacy of Simple Location' a Fallacy?" *PAS*, supplement, 1927. Wahl, J. "La Philosophie spéculative" in *Vers le concret*, 1932. Wells, H. K. *Process and Unreality*, 1950. Wind, E. "Mathematik und Sinnesempfindung. Materialien zu einer Whitehead-Kritik," *L.*, 1932.

24. THOMISM

[Note: Under the headings "bibliography" to "journals" only works by Thomists in the strict sense of the word are listed. English, Latin, and Italian works are mostly omitted in this selected bibliography.]

BIBLIOGRAPHY

Wyser, P. "Thomas v. Aquin," *BESP*, 13-14, 1950; "Der Thomismus," *ibid.*, 15-16, 1951; Mandonnet, P. and J. Destrez. *Bibliographie Thomiste*, 1921 (12,219 titles; continued in *Bulletin Thomiste*, 1924, and in *DT*, 1926–. Bourke, V. J. *Thomistic Bibliography, 1920-1940*, 1945.
Bibliographies of Jacques Maritain: *The Thomist*, 1943; *RT*, 1949.

INTRODUCTIONS

Gilson, E. *Le Thomisme, 1920, 5th ed. 1945. Maritain, J. *Introduction générale à la philosophie*, 1921. (Many editions.) Sertillanges, A. D. *Les Grandes Thèses de la philosophie thomiste*, 1928. De Wulf, M. *Initiation à la philosophie thomiste*, 2d ed. 1949.

SYSTEMATIC WORKS

Gredt, J. *Elementa philosophiae aristotelico-thomisticae*, 2 vols., 1899, 7th ed. 1937 (German, 1935). Jolivet, R. *Traité*

315

de philosophie, 4 vols., 1939-1942, 3d ed. 1949–. Mercier, D. *et al. Cours de philosophie*, 11 vols., 1892–. (Many editions.)

THOMAS COMMENTATORS

S. Thomas d'Aquin, *Somme Théologique* (Éditions Revue des Jeunes), 1925–. (Detailed commentaries; Latin; French; so far 46 vols.) Complete unabridged German-Latin edition of *Summa Theologica*, translated by German and Austrian Dominicans and Benedictines, 1934–. (Thorough commentary; so far 13 vols.) Farrell, W. A. *Companion to the Summa*, 4 vols., 1941–.

SELECTED WORKS

Barbado, E. M. *Introduction à la psychologie expérimentale*, 1931.
Baur, L. *Metaphysik*, 1922, 3d ed. 1935.
Delos, J. T. *La Société internationale et les principes du droit public*, 1929.
Fabro, C. *La nozione metafisica di partecipazione secondo S. Tommaso d'Aquino*, 1929.
De Finance, J. *Être et agir dans la philosophie de S. Thomas*, 1945.
Forest, A. *La Réalité concrète et la dialectique*, 1931; *La Structure métaphysique du concret selon S. Thomas d'Aquin*, 1931; *Du consentement à l'être*, 1936.
Garin, P. *La Théorie de l'idée suivant l'école thomiste*, 2 vols., 1932.
Garrigou-Lagrange, R. *Le Sens commun*, 1909, 3d ed. 1932; *Dieu*, 1915, 5th ed. 1928; *Le Réalisme du principe de finalité*, 1932.
Geiger, L. B. *La Participation dans la philosophie de S. Thomas d'Aquin*, 1942.
Gilson, E. *L'Esprit de la philosophie médiévale* (GL), 1932, 2d ed. 1944; *Le Réalisme thomiste et la critique de la connaissance*, 1939; *L'Être et l'essence*, 1948.

Greenwood, T. *Les Fondements de la logique symbolique* (2 parts), 1938.

Horvath, A. *Die Metaphysik der Relationen* (Freiburg, Switzerland: Dissertation, 1914); *Das Eigentumsrecht nach dem hl. Thomas von Aquino,* 1929; *Der thomistische Gottesbegriff,* 1941.

Lachance, L. *L'Humanisme politique de S. Thomas,* 2 vols., 1939; *Le Concept de droit selon Aristote et S. Thomas,* 2d ed. 1946.

Legrand, J. *L'Univers et l'homme dans la philosophie de S. Thomas,* 1945.

Manser, G. M. *Das Wesen des Thomismus,* 1932, 3d ed. 1949; *Das Naturrecht in thomistischer Beleuchtung,* 1944.

Maritain, J. *Art et Scolastique,* 1919, 3d ed. 1935; *Réflexions sur l'intelligence,* 1924, 5th ed. 1939; *Distinguer pour unir ou les degrés du savoir,* 1932, 2d ed. 1946; *Sept leçons sur l'être,* 1934; *Science et sagesse,* 1935; *La Philosophie de la nature,* 1936; *Quatre essais sur l'esprit dans sa condition charnelle,* 1939.

Mausbach, J. *Dasein und Wesen Gottes,* 2 vols., 1929-1930.

Noël, L. *Le Réalisme immédiat,* 1938.

Nys, D. *La Notion de temps,* 1904, 3d ed. 1925; *La Notion de l'espace,* 1922, 2d ed. 1930.

Penido, M. *Le Rôle de l'analogie en théologie dogmat,* 1931 (important philosophical introduction).

Pieper, J. *Wahrheit der Dinge,* 1947; *Was heisst philosophieren?,* 1948.

Rabeau, G. *Species. Verbum,* 1938; *Le Jugement d'existence,* 1938.

De Raeymaeker, L. *Philosophie de l'être,* 1946, 2d ed. 1947.

Ramirez, J. "De analogia," *Ciencia Tomista,* 1921-1922 (new edition in preparation).

Reiser, B. *Formalphilosophie oder Logik,* 1920.

Richard, T. *Philosophie du raisonnement dans la science d'après S. Thomas d'Aquin,* 1919.

Le Rohellec, J. *Problèmes philosophiques,* 1933.

Bibliography

Roland-Gosselin, M. D. *Essai d'une étude critique de la connaissance,* 1932.
Sentroul, L. *Kant et Aristote,* 1910.
Schilling, O. *Staats- und Sozialethik des hl. Thomas von Aquino,* 2d ed. 1930.
Sertillanges, A. D. *La Philosophie de S. Thomas d'Aquin,* 2 vols., 1931, 2d ed. 1940.
Tischleder, P. *Ursprung und Träger der Staatsgewalt nach der Lehre des hl. Thomas von Aquino und seiner Schule,* 1923.
Tonquedec. J. *Les Principes de la philosophie thomiste. La Critique de la connaissance,* 1929.
Webert, J. *Essai de métaphysique thomiste,* 1927.
Welty, E. *Gemeinschaft und Einzelmensch,* 1935; *Von Sinn und Wert der menschlichen Arbeit,* 1946.
Wittmann, M. *Die Ethik des hl. Thomas von Aquino,* 1933.

SELECTED JOURNALS

Angelicum, Rome. *BT. Ciencia Tomista,* Salamanca. *DT,* Freiburg. *Divus Thomas,* Piacenza. *Doctor Communis,* Rome. *Dominican Studies,* Oxford. *The New Scholasticism,* Washington. *Revue de philosophie,* Paris. *Revue des sciences philosophiques et théologiques,* Paris. *RNP. RT. Rivista di filosofia neoscolastica,* Milan. *The Thomist,* Washington. *Tijdschrift voor philosophie,* Louvain.

DICTIONARIES, ENCYCLOPEDIAS

Brugger, W. *Philosophisches Wörterbuch,* 1948. *The Catholic Encyclopedia,* 1907-1914 and supplement, 1922. *Dictionnaire de Théologie catholique,* 1908–. Schütz, L. *Thomaslexikon,* 1881, 2d ed. 1885.

FESTSCHRIFTEN AND CONGRESS PROCEEDINGS

Acta I Congressus Thomistici Internationalis, 1925. *Acta II Congressus Thomistici Internationalis,* 1936. *Mélanges Thomistes,* Le Saulchoir, 1923, 2d ed. 1935. *Xenia Tomistica* (ed. by S. Szabo), 3 vols., 1925.

318

LITERATURE ON THE HISTORY OF THOMISM

Dezza, P. *Alle origini del neotomismo*, 1940. Heuss, A. *Neuscholastische Begründungsversuche für das Kausalprinzip* (Bonn: Dissertation, 1930). Przywara, E. "Die Problematik der Neuscholastik," *Kt.*, 1928 (unreliable). De Raeymaeker, L. *Introductio generalis ad philosophiam thomisticam*, 1931. Riet, G. *L'Épistémologie thomiste*, 1946. Viel, A. "Mouvement thomiste au XIXᵉ siecle," *RT*, 1909. De Wulf, M. "Le Mouvement thomiste," *RNP*, 1901.

CRITICAL LITERATURE

Descoqs, P. *Essai critique sur l'hylémorphisme*, 1924; *Institutiones metaphysicae generales*, 1925; "La Distinction d'essence et d'existence," *Archives de Philosophie*, 1929; *Thomism et Scolastique, à propos de M. Rougier*, 1927. Eucken, R. *Thomas von Aquino und Kant, ein Kampf zweier Welten*, 1901. Fütscher, L. *Die ersten Seins- und Denkprinzipien*, 1930; *Akt und Potenz, eine kritisch-systematische Auseinandersetzung mit dem neueren Thomismus*, 1933. Hessen, J. *Die Weltanschauung des Thomas von Aquino*, 1926. Mitterer, A. *Wandel des Weltbildes von Thomas auf heute*, 2 vols., 1935-1936. Rougier, L. *La Scolastique et le thomisme*, 1925. Santeler, J. *Der Platonismus in der Erkenntnislehre des hl. Thomas von Aquino*, 1939. Stufler, J. *Gott der erste Beweger aller Dinge*, 1936. Zybura, J. S. (ed.) *Present-Day Thinkers and the New Scholasticism*, 1926.

Other Neoscholastic Thinkers

SELECTED WORKS

Geyser, J. *Einige Hauptprobleme der Metaphysik*, 1923; *Auf dem Kampffelde der Logik*, 1926; *Das Prinzip vom zureichenden Grunde*, 1930; *Das Gesetz der Ursache*, 1933.
Marechal, J. *Le Point de départ de la métaphysique* (5 parts), [1922]-1947.

319

Przywara, E. *Religionsbegründung: Max Scheler-J. H. Newman*, 1923; *Kant heute*, 1930; *Analogia entis*, 1932.
Rintelen, F. J. *Philosophia perennis*, 2 vols., 1930 (Festschrift with bibliography).
Rousselot, P. *L'Intellectualisme de S. Thomas*, 2d ed. 1924.
De Vries, J. *Denken und Sein*, 1937.

SELECTIONS

Christliche Philosophie in Deutschland 1920-1945, 1949.

JOURNALS

Antonianum, Rome. *AP. Gregorianum*, Rome. *PJ. Scholastik*, Eupen (Belgium). *Wissenschaft und Weisheit*, Freiburg i. B.

25. MATHEMATICAL LOGIC

BIBLIOGRAPHY

Church, A. "A Bibliography of Symbolic Logic," *The Journal of Symbolic Logic*, 1936 (being continued in the same journal). Beth, E. W. "Symbolische Logik und Grundlegung der exakten Wissenschaften," *BESP*, 3, 1948.

INTRODUCTIONS

Bochenski, I. M. *Précis de logique mathématique*, 1949. Carnap, R. *Abriss der Logistik*, 1929. Hilbert, D. and W. Ackermann. *Grundzüge der theoretischen Logik*, 1928, 3d ed. 1947. Tarski A. *Einführung in die mathematische Logik und in die Methodologie der Mathematik*, 1937 (English, 1941).

SYSTEMATIC WORKS

Feys, R. *Logistiek*, I, 1944. Hilbert, D. and P. Bernays. *Grundlagen der Mathematik*, 2 vols., 1934-1939, 2d ed. (Ann Arbor) 1944. Quine, W. v. O. *Mathematical Logic*, 1940, 2d ed. 1947. Scholz, H. *Vorlesungen über die Grundzüge der mathematischen Logik*, 2 vols., 1948-1949. Whitehead, A. N. and B.

320

Russell. *Principia mathematica*, 3 vols., 1910-1913, 2d ed. 1925-1927.

LITERATURE ON THE HISTORY OF MATHEMATICAL LOGIC

Beth, E. W. *Geschiedenis der Logica*, 1944, 2d ed. 1947; *"Hundred Years of Symbolic Logic," *Dialectica*, 1947. Feys, R. *De ontwikkeling van het logisch denken*, 1949. Joergensen, J. *A Treatise of Formal Logic*, I, 1931. Scholz, H. *Geschichte der Logik*, 1931. See also under Festschriften of Russell and Whitehead, above.
For further literature see E. W. Beth, *BESP*, 3, 1948.

Index

[NOTE: An asterisk preceding the page number refers to the bibliography.]

325

Index